Psychology Crossword Challenger

By Lewis Morris

www.insiderswords.com/PsychX

ISBN-13:978-1718017818

Imagine using Crossword Puzzles to help you learn perform better on exams, master difficult topics, and get a leg up on a new subject. Our new series of crossword puzzle review books uses the "Insider's Language" of the subject to help you learn the vocabulary and terminology necessary to ace your courses and exams.

Are Crossword Puzzles really a useful tool for test review and studying?

ABSOLUTELY!!!

Solving a crossword puzzle helps you develop vocabulary, reasoning, spelling, and word attack skills. To be successful, you must be able to identify and manipulate the vocabulary words in the puzzle. This requires you to learn new vocabulary and key terms. It requires differentiating between similar words.

Completing a crossword requires spelling, which forces you to use dictionary skills. By fitting in words, you will be required to evaluate, weigh, and discriminate between many similar words.

As a test review tool, you will find that crossword puzzles will help you relax and enjoy your review time. They are especially effective in reducing test anxiety while teaching you essential terminology found on the test.

Compared to flashcards and other vocabulary review methods, crosswords require more active thinking and engagement.

If you are a visual learner, you will be attracted to puzzles because they work off a grid that is front and center. You can easily monitor your progress and identify your weaker areas.

If you are a kinesthetic learner, you will enjoy the fact that the puzzles require strategy and a step-by-step process for completion.

All types of learners report great satisfaction in completing a puzzle.

We recommend that you use this book before beginning a formal course of study or Test Review. It will help you master the key language and terminology of the subject and let you relax. Completing the puzzles gives you a leg up on the subject and will make your studying go smoother and with less frustration. Many of our readers report using our books before the semester starts so they go into the first class already understanding the key terminology of the course.

1. *Using the Across and Down clues, write the correct words in the numbered grid below.*

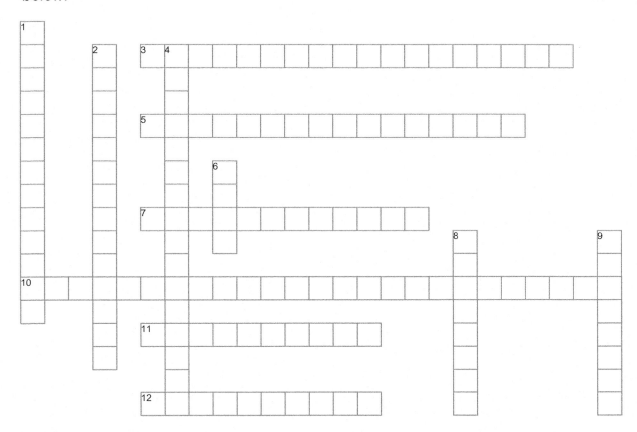

ACROSS

3. Framework for initial understanding formulated by children to explain their experiences of the world.

5. A disorder defined by a large discrepancy between individuals' measured IQ and their actual performance.

7. The scientific study of the brain and of the links between brain activity and behavior.

10. A behavioral therapy technique in which a client is taught to prevent the arousal of anxiety by confronting the feared stimulus while relaxed.

11. Drug that depresses or slows down the activity of the central nervous system.

12. A form of consciousness alteration designed to enhance self-knowledge and well-being by achieving a deep state of tranquility.

DOWN

3. Framework for initial understanding formulated by children to explain their experiences of the world.

5. A disorder defined by a large discrepancy between individuals' measured IQ and their actual performance.

7. The scientific study of the brain and of the links between brain activity and behavior.

10. A behavioral therapy technique in which a client is taught to prevent the arousal of anxiety by confronting the feared stimulus while relaxed.

11. Drug that depresses or slows down the activity of the central nervous system.

12. A form of consciousness alteration designed to enhance self-knowledge and well-being by achieving a deep state of tranquility.

A. Meditation
D. Structuralism
G. Depressant
J. Menarche

B. Learning disorder
E. Neuroscience
H. Foundational theory
K. Projective test

C. Object permanence
F. Systematic desensitization
I. Norm
L. Etiology

2. *Using the Across and Down clues, write the correct words in the numbered grid below.*

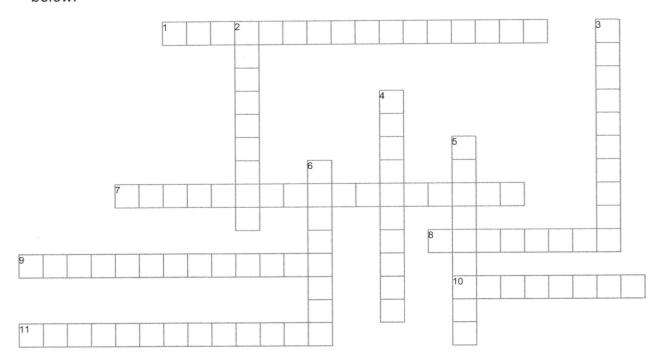

ACROSS

1. Process that does not require attention; it can often be performed along with other tasks without interference.

7. A disorder characterized by a flight from home or work accompanied by a loss of ability to recall the personal past.

8. According to Freud, a state in which a person remains attached to objects or activities more appropriate for an earlier stage of psychosexual development.

9. A schedule of reinforcement in which a reinforcer is delivered for the first response made after a fixed period.

10. Preprogrammed tendency that is essential to a species' survival.

11. A surgical procedure performed on brain tissue to alleviate a psychological disorder.

DOWN

1. Process that does not require attention; it can often be performed along with other tasks without interference.

7. A disorder characterized by a flight from home or work accompanied by a loss of ability to recall the personal past.

8. According to Freud, a state in which a person remains attached to objects or activities more appropriate for an earlier stage of psychosexual development.

9. A schedule of reinforcement in which a reinforcer is delivered for the first response made after a fixed period.

10. Preprogrammed tendency that is essential to a species' survival.

11. A surgical procedure performed on brain tissue to alleviate a psychological disorder.

A. Population   B. Fixed interval   C. Depressant   D. Fixation
E. Psychosurgery   F. Etiology   G. Obedience   H. Automatic process
I. Instinct   J. Dissociative fugue   K. Cognition

3. *Using the Across and Down clues, write the correct words in the numbered grid below.*

ACROSS

3. Is a previously neutral stimulus that comes to elicit a conditioned response.

7. A group in an experiment that is not exposed to a treatment or does not experience a manipulation of the independent variable.

9. The genetic structure an organism inherits from its parents.

10. A schedule of reinforcement in which a reinforcer is delivered for the first response made after a fixed period.

11. A form of thinking in which one draws a conclusion that is intended to follow logically from two or more statements or premises.

DOWN

3. Is a previously neutral stimulus that comes to elicit a conditioned response.

7. A group in an experiment that is not exposed to a treatment or does not experience a manipulation of the independent variable.

9. The genetic structure an organism inherits from its parents.

10. A schedule of reinforcement in which a reinforcer is delivered for the first response made after a fixed period.

11. A form of thinking in which one draws a conclusion that is intended to follow logically from two or more statements or premises.

A. Genotype
D. REM
G. Sleep apnea
J. Control group

B. Fixed interval
E. Cognitive
H. Scheme
K. Deductive reasoning

C. Conditioned stimulus
F. Fixed ratio
I. Self concept

4. *Using the Across and Down clues, write the correct words in the numbered grid below.*

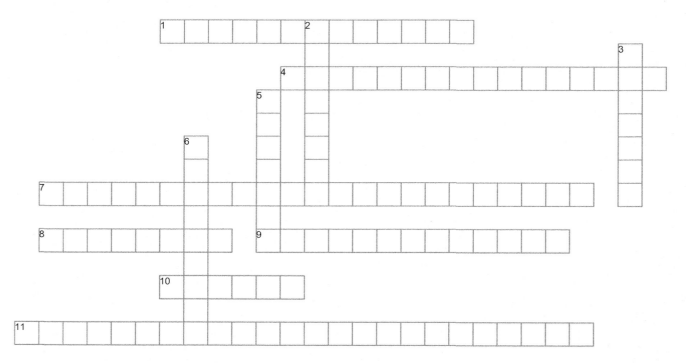

ACROSS

1. Seeks to clarify the typical communication patterns of the partners and then to improve the quality of their interaction.

4. A procedure by which participants have an equal likelihood of being assigned to any condition within an experiment.

7. A mood disorder characterized by intense feelings of depression over an extended time, without the manic high phase of bipolar depression

8. According to Freud, a state in which a person remains attached to objects or activities more appropriate for an earlier stage of psychosexual development.

9. The lifelong process whereby an individual's behavioral patterns, values, standards, skills, attitudes, and motives are shaped to conform to those regarded as desirable in a particular society.

10. The way in which words are strung together to form sentences.

11. In operant conditioning, a pattern of delivering and withholding reinforcement.

DOWN

1. Seeks to clarify the typical communication patterns of the partners and then to improve the quality of their interaction.

4. A procedure by which participants have an equal likelihood of being assigned to any condition within an experiment.

7. A mood disorder characterized by intense feelings of depression over an extended time, without the manic high phase of bipolar depression

8. According to Freud, a state in which a person remains attached to objects or activities more appropriate for an earlier stage of psychosexual development.

9. The lifelong process whereby an individual's behavioral patterns, values, standards, skills, attitudes, and motives are shaped to conform to those regarded as desirable in a particular society.

10. The way in which words are strung together to form sentences.

11. In operant conditioning, a pattern of delivering and withholding reinforcement.

A. Syntax
B. Fixation
C. Thalamus
D. Random assignment
E. Insight
F. Schedules of reinforcement
G. Socialization
H. Shyness
I. Major depressive disorder
J. Phenotype
K. Couple therapy

5. *Using the Across and Down clues, write the correct words in the numbered grid below.*

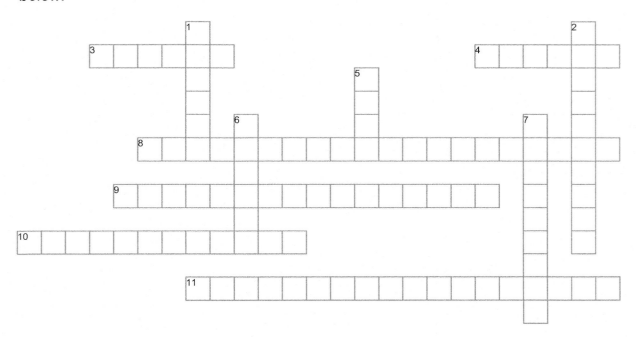

ACROSS

3. The body is sensitive to the source of pressure in the stomach, gastric pressure will cause a person to full while an inflated balloon will not.

4. An unlearned response elicited by specific stimuli that have biological relevance for an organism.

8. Type of therapy that assumes that a patient's problems have been caused by the psychological tension between unconscious impulses and the constraints of his or her life situation.

9. The receptors for this information are tiny hairs in fluid-filled sacs and canals in the inner ear.

10. Insulating material that surrounds axons and increases the speed of neural transmission.

11. Framework for initial understanding formulated by children to explain their experiences of the world.

DOWN

3. The body is sensitive to the source of pressure in the stomach, gastric pressure will cause a person to full while an inflated balloon will not.

4. An unlearned response elicited by specific stimuli that have biological relevance for an organism.

8. Type of therapy that assumes that a patient's problems have been caused by the psychological tension between unconscious impulses and the constraints of his or her life situation.

9. The receptors for this information are tiny hairs in fluid-filled sacs and canals in the inner ear.

10. Insulating material that surrounds axons and increases the speed of neural transmission.

11. Framework for initial understanding formulated by children to explain their experiences of the world.

A. Foundational theory
D. Brain stem
G. Hunger
J. Psychodynamic therapy

B. Reflex
E. Phobia
H. Memory
K. Myelin sheath

C. Perception
F. Vestibular system
I. Soma

6. *Using the Across and Down clues, write the correct words in the numbered grid below.*

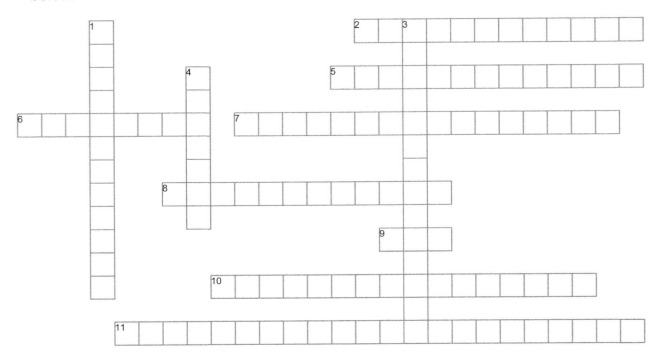

ACROSS

2. Founded the first formal experimental psychology laboratory in 1879 in Leipzig, Germany.

5. The field of psychology that specializes in mental testing.

6. The learned, relatively stable tendency to respond to people, concepts, and events in an evaluative way.

7. The systematic procedures and measurement instruments used by trained professionals to assess and individual's functioning, aptitudes, abilities, or mental states.

8. The global capacity to profit from experience and to go beyond given information about the environment.

9. The physical basis for the transmission of genetic information.

10. Consistent procedure for giving instructions, scoring responses, and holding all other variables constant except those being systematically varied.

11. Group effects that arise from individuals' desire to be correct and right and to understand how best to act in a given situation.

DOWN

2. Founded the first formal experimental psychology laboratory in 1879 in Leipzig, Germany.

5. The field of psychology that specializes in mental testing.

6. The learned, relatively stable tendency to respond to people, concepts, and events in an evaluative way.

7. The systematic procedures and measurement instruments used by trained professionals to assess and individual's functioning, aptitudes, abilities, or mental states.

8. The global capacity to profit from experience and to go beyond given information about the environment.

9. The physical basis for the transmission of genetic information.

10. Consistent procedure for giving instructions, scoring responses, and holding all other variables constant except those being systematically varied.

11. Group effects that arise from individuals' desire to be correct and right and to understand how best to act in a given situation.

A. Wilhelm Wundt   B. Operant   C. Formal assessment
D. DNA   E. Locus of control   F. William James
G. Attitude   H. Control procedure I. Informational influence
J. Intelligence   K. Psychometrics

7. *Using the Across and Down clues, write the correct words in the numbered grid below.*

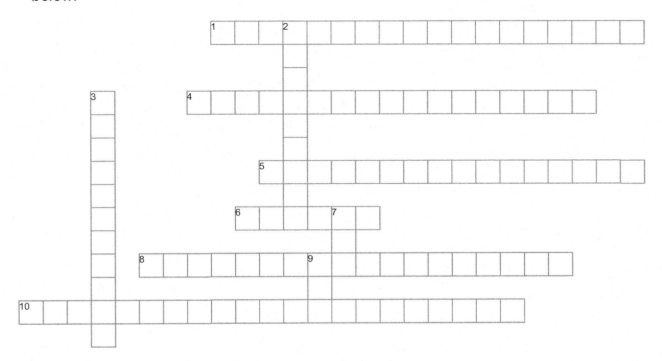

ACROSS

1. Attempts to establish general laws and generalizations, and seeks to obtain objective knowledge through scientific methods.

4. A biologically determined reinforcer, such as food and water.

5. The sense concerned with bodily position and movement of the body parts relative to one another.

6. The genetic information for an organism, stored in the DNA of its chromosomes.

8. A research design in which the same participants are observed repeatedly, sometimes over many years.

10. Is the response elicited by an unconditioned stimulus without prior training or learning.

DOWN

1. Attempts to establish general laws and generalizations, and seeks to obtain objective knowledge through scientific methods.

4. A biologically determined reinforcer, such as food and water.

5. The sense concerned with bodily position and movement of the body parts relative to one another.

6. The genetic information for an organism, stored in the DNA of its chromosomes.

8. A research design in which the same participants are observed repeatedly, sometimes over many years.

10. Is the response elicited by an unconditioned stimulus without prior training or learning.

A. Unconditioned response
D. Genome
G. MRI
J. Olfaction

B. Acquisition
E. Longitudinal design
H. Nomothetic research

C. Kinesthetic sense
F. Primary reinforcer
I. DID

8. *Using the Across and Down clues, write the correct words in the numbered grid below.*

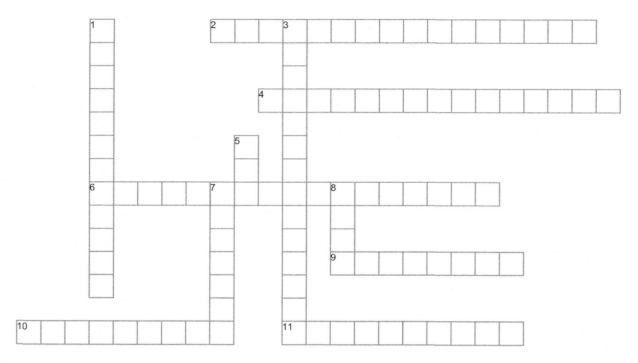

ACROSS

2. Belief about attributes and behaviors regarded as appropriate for males and females in a particular culture.

4. A mood disorder characterized by alternating periods of depression and mania.

6. A group in an experiment that is exposed to a treatment or experiences a manipulation of the independent variable.

9. False or irrational belief maintained despite clear evidence to the contrary.

10. Drug that causes arousal, increased activity, and euphoria.

11. The tendency of a decision-making group to filter out undesirable input so that a consensus may be reached, especially if it is in line with the leader's viewpoint.

DOWN

2. Belief about attributes and behaviors regarded as appropriate for males and females in a particular culture.

4. A mood disorder characterized by alternating periods of depression and mania.

6. A group in an experiment that is exposed to a treatment or experiences a manipulation of the independent variable.

9. False or irrational belief maintained despite clear evidence to the contrary.

10. Drug that causes arousal, increased activity, and euphoria.

11. The tendency of a decision-making group to filter out undesirable input so that a consensus may be reached, especially if it is in line with the leader's viewpoint.

A. Experimental group   B. ADHD   C. Groupthink   D. LTM
E. Stimulant   F. Bipolar disorder G. Delusion   H. Gender stereotype
I. Decision making   J. Insight   K. Iconic memory

9. *Using the Across and Down clues, write the correct words in the numbered grid below.*

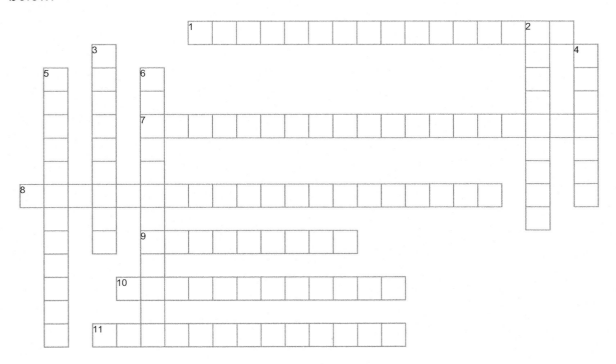

ACROSS

1. Sexual arousal is the motivational state of excitement and tension brought about by physiological and cognitive reactions to erotic stimuli.

7. The convergence of the expectations of a group of individuals into a common perspective as they talk and carry out activities together.

8. A statistical estimate of the degree of inheritance of a given trait or behavior, asses by the degree of similarity between individuals who vary in their extent of genetic similarity.

9. Missing information filled in on the basis of a sample of evidence or on the basis of prior beliefs and theories.

10. The region of the brain that regulates emotional behavior, basic motivational urges, and memory, as well as major physiological functions.

11. The field of psychology that specializes in mental testing.

DOWN

1. Sexual arousal is the motivational state of excitement and tension brought about by physiological and cognitive reactions to erotic stimuli.

7. The convergence of the expectations of a group of individuals into a common perspective as they talk and carry out activities together.

8. A statistical estimate of the degree of inheritance of a given trait or behavior, asses by the degree of similarity between individuals who vary in their extent of genetic similarity.

9. Missing information filled in on the basis of a sample of evidence or on the basis of prior beliefs and theories.

10. The region of the brain that regulates emotional behavior, basic motivational urges, and memory, as well as major physiological functions.

11. The field of psychology that specializes in mental testing.

A. Sexual motivation
E. Psychometrics
I. Generativity

B. Heritability estimate
F. Norm crystallization
J. Shyness

C. Manic episode
G. Limbic system
K. Obedience

D. Cognition
H. Inference

10. *Using the Across and Down clues, write the correct words in the numbered grid below.*

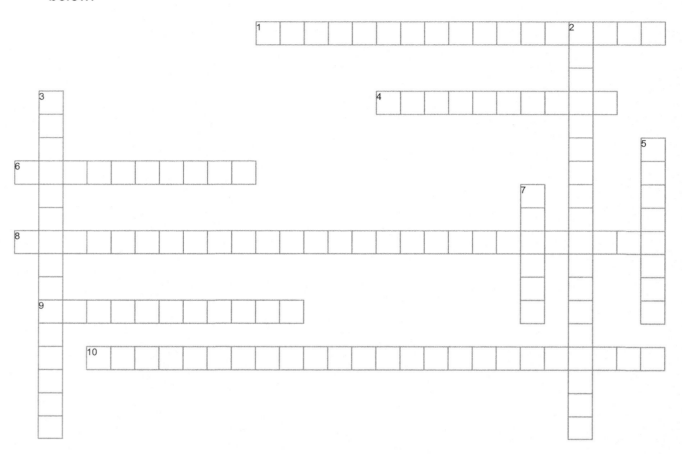

ACROSS

1. A concept in personality psychology referring to a person's constant striving to realize his or her potential and to develop inherent talents and capabilities.

4. The extent to which people believe that their behaviors situations will bring about rewards.

6. The tendency of a decision-making group to filter out undesirable input so that a consensus may be reached, especially if it is in line with the leader's viewpoint.

8. Research methodology that determines to what extent two variables, traits, or attributes are related.

9. Constancy or equilibrium of the internal conditions of the body.

10. A consistent relationship between a response and the changes in the environment that it produces.

DOWN

1. A concept in personality psychology referring to a person's constant striving to realize his or her potential and to develop inherent talents and capabilities.

4. The extent to which people believe that their behaviors situations will bring about rewards.

6. The tendency of a decision-making group to filter out undesirable input so that a consensus may be reached, especially if it is in line with the leader's viewpoint.

8. Research methodology that determines to what extent two variables, traits, or attributes are related.

9. Constancy or equilibrium of the internal conditions of the body.

10. A consistent relationship between a response and the changes in the environment that it produces.

A. Correlational research method
D. Reinforcement contingency
G. Aversion therapy
J. Validity

B. Sample
E. Self actualization
H. Groupthink

C. Homeostasis
F. Expectancy
I. Trichromatic theory

11. *Using the Across and Down clues, write the correct words in the numbered grid below.*

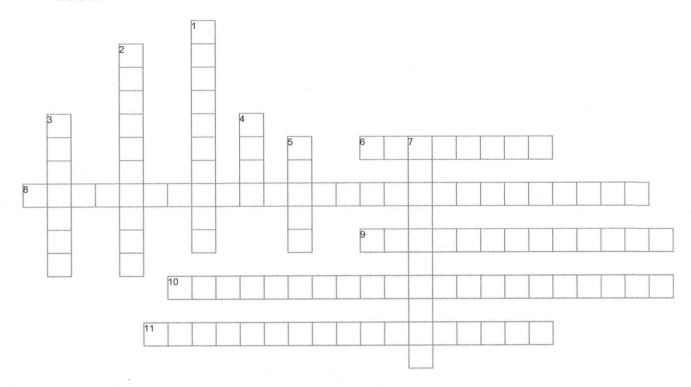

ACROSS

6. A psychological model that emphasizes an individual's phenomenal world and inherent capacity for making rational choices and developing to maximum potential.

8. An anxiety disorder in which an individual feels anxious and worried most of the time for at least six months when not threatened by any specific danger or object.

9. Different versions of a test used to assess test reliability; the change of forms reduces effects of direct practice, memory, or the desire of an individual to appear consistent on the same items.

10. A judgment based on the information readily available in memory.

11. The ways in which individual's social interactions and expectations change across the life span.

DOWN

6. A psychological model that emphasizes an individual's phenomenal world and inherent capacity for making rational choices and developing to maximum potential.

8. An anxiety disorder in which an individual feels anxious and worried most of the time for at least six months when not threatened by any specific danger or object.

9. Different versions of a test used to assess test reliability; the change of forms reduces effects of direct practice, memory, or the desire of an individual to appear consistent on the same items.

10. A judgment based on the information readily available in memory.

11. The ways in which individual's social interactions and expectations change across the life span.

A. Frame
D. Humanist
G. Availability heuristic
J. Generalized anxiety disorder

B. Social role
E. Maturation
H. Rule
K. Puberty

C. Parallel forms
F. Social development
I. Motivation

12. *Using the Across and Down clues, write the correct words in the numbered grid below.*

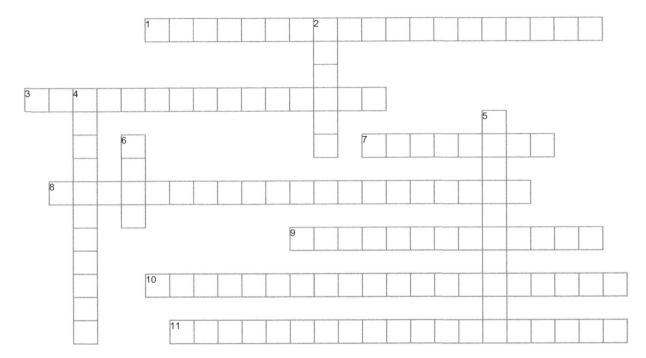

ACROSS

1. Is a response elicited by some previously neutral stimulus that occurs as a result of pairing the neutral stimulus with an unconditioned stimulus.

3. The systematic use of principles of learning to increase the frequency of desired behaviors and

7. A process based on experience that results in a relatively permanent change in behavior or behavioral potential.

8. A disorder characterized by unexplained physical complaints in several categories over many years.

9. A schedule of reinforcement in which a reinforcer is delivered for the first response made after a variable number of responses whose average is predetermined.

10. The hypothesis that the structure of the language and individual speaks has an impact on the way in which that individual thinks about the world.

11. The bodily changes, maturation, and growth that occur in an organism starting with conception and continuing across the life span.

DOWN

1. Is a response elicited by some previously neutral stimulus that occurs as a result of pairing the neutral stimulus with an unconditioned stimulus.

3. The systematic use of principles of learning to increase the frequency of desired behaviors and

7. A process based on experience that results in a relatively permanent change in behavior or behavioral potential.

8. A disorder characterized by unexplained physical complaints in several categories over many years.

9. A schedule of reinforcement in which a reinforcer is delivered for the first response made after a variable number of responses whose average is predetermined.

10. The hypothesis that the structure of the language and individual speaks has an impact on the way in which that individual thinks about the world.

11. The bodily changes, maturation, and growth that occur in an organism starting with conception and continuing across the life span.

A. Variable ratio
D. Opiate
G. Behavior therapy
J. Fear

B. Somatization disorder
E. Linguistic relativity
H. Fixed ratio
K. Learning

C. Physical development
F. Conditioned response
I. Homeostasis

13. *Using the Across and Down clues, write the correct words in the numbered grid below.*

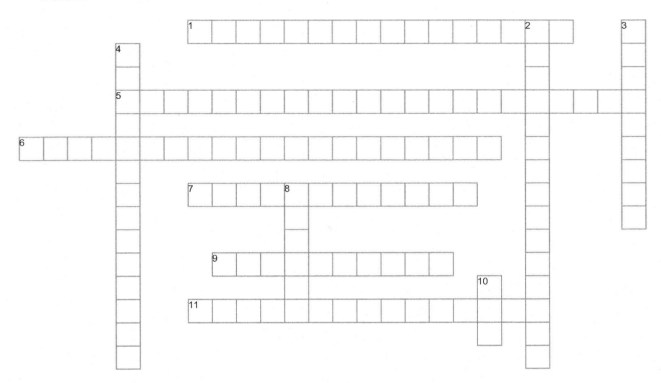

ACROSS

1. The receptors for this information are tiny hairs in fluid-filled sacs and canals in the inner ear.

5. The automatic extension of conditioned responding to similar stimuli that have never been paired with the unconditioned stimulus.

6. The study of the development of cognitive abilities across species and the continuity of abilities from nonhuman animals to humans.

7. A group in an experiment that is not exposed to a treatment or does not experience a manipulation of the independent variable.

9. People begin life with their mind as a blank tablet, and the mind acquires information through experiences with the world.

11. The process by which people select, interpret, and remember social information.

DOWN

1. The receptors for this information are tiny hairs in fluid-filled sacs and canals in the inner ear.

5. The automatic extension of conditioned responding to similar stimuli that have never been paired with the unconditioned stimulus.

6. The study of the development of cognitive abilities across species and the continuity of abilities from nonhuman animals to humans.

7. A group in an experiment that is not exposed to a treatment or does not experience a manipulation of the independent variable.

9. People begin life with their mind as a blank tablet, and the mind acquires information through experiences with the world.

11. The process by which people select, interpret, and remember social information.

A. Stimulus generalization
D. Control group
G. Distal stimulus
J. Social cognition
B. Phenotype
E. Comparative cognition
H. Empiricist
K. DID
C. Retina
F. Vestibular system
I. Edward Titchener

14. *Using the Across and Down clues, write the correct words in the numbered grid below.*

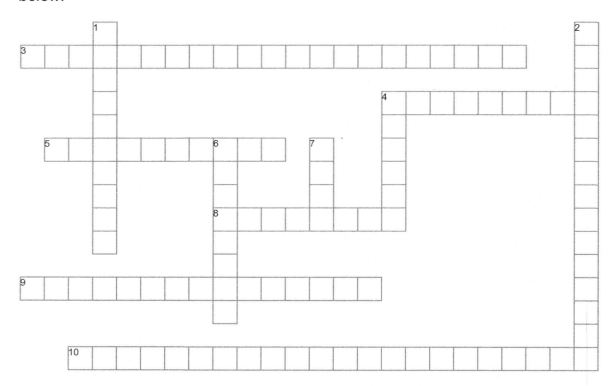

ACROSS

3. Statistical procedures that allow researchers to determine whether the results they obtain support their hypotheses or can be attributed to chance variation.

4. A learned attitude toward a target object, involving negative affect (dislike or fear), negative beliefs (stereotypes), that justify the attitude, and a behavioral intention to avoid, control, dominate, or eliminate the target object.

5. People begin life with their mind as a blank tablet, and the mind acquires information through experiences with the world.

8. The part of the limbic system that controls emotions, aggression, and the formation of emotional memory.

9. A behavioral technique in which clients are exposed to the objects or situations that cause them anxiety.

10. Research effort designed to describe what is characteristic of a specific age or developmental stage.

DOWN

3. Statistical procedures that allow researchers to determine whether the results they obtain support their hypotheses or can be attributed to chance variation.

4. A learned attitude toward a target object, involving negative affect (dislike or fear), negative beliefs (stereotypes), that justify the attitude, and a behavioral intention to avoid, control, dominate, or eliminate the target object.

5. People begin life with their mind as a blank tablet, and the mind acquires information through experiences with the world.

8. The part of the limbic system that controls emotions, aggression, and the formation of emotional memory.

9. A behavioral technique in which clients are exposed to the objects or situations that cause them anxiety.

10. Research effort designed to describe what is characteristic of a specific age or developmental stage.

A. Exposure therapy   B. Phobia   C. Insanity
D. Internalization   E. Perception   F. Inferential statistics
G. Prejudice   H. Normative investigation   I. PTSD
J. Empiricist   K. Amygdala

15. *Using the Across and Down clues, write the correct words in the numbered grid below.*

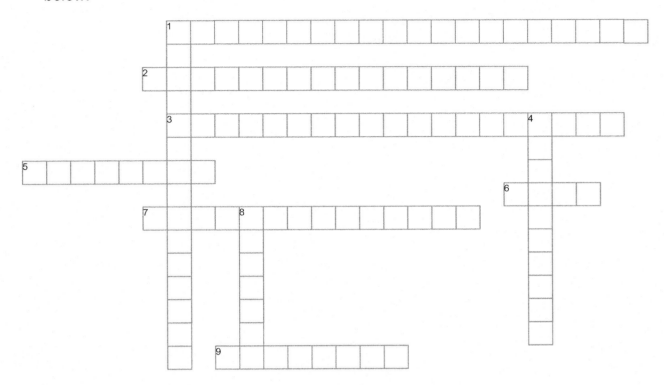

ACROSS

1. The study of the development of cognitive abilities across species and the continuity of abilities from nonhuman animals to humans.

2. The tendency for learned behavior to drift toward instinctual behavior over time.

3. The principle that subsequent retrieval of information is enhanced if cues received at the time of recall are consistent with those present at the time of encoding.

5. The biological transmission of traits from parents to offspring.

6. A rational reaction to an objectively identified external danger that may induce a person to flee or attack in self -defense.

7. Traits around which a person organizes his or her life. For example for Mother Teresa, this trait might have been self-sacrifice for the good of others.

9. The study of the causes and factors leading to the development of a disorder.

DOWN

1. The study of the development of cognitive abilities across species and the continuity of abilities from nonhuman animals to humans.

2. The tendency for learned behavior to drift toward instinctual behavior over time.

3. The principle that subsequent retrieval of information is enhanced if cues received at the time of recall are consistent with those present at the time of encoding.

5. The biological transmission of traits from parents to offspring.

6. A rational reaction to an objectively identified external danger that may induce a person to flee or attack in self -defense.

7. Traits around which a person organizes his or her life. For example for Mother Teresa, this trait might have been self-sacrifice for the good of others.

9. The study of the causes and factors leading to the development of a disorder.

A. Heredity
D. Instinctual drift
G. Content validity
J. Etiology

B. Insight
E. Comparative cognition
H. Cardinal traits

C. Encoding specificity
F. Cerebellum
I. Fear

16. *Using the Across and Down clues, write the correct words in the numbered grid below.*

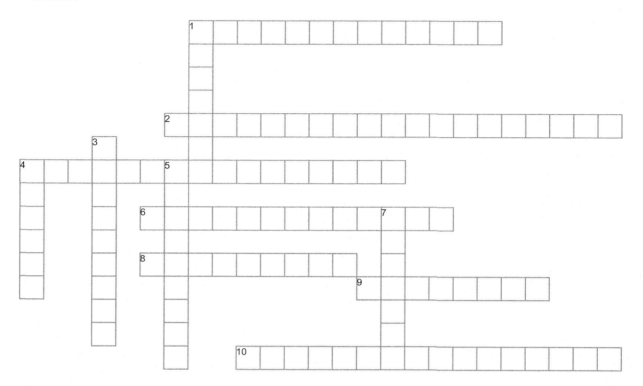

ACROSS

1. Study of the structure of mind and behavior; the view that all human mental experience can be understood as a combination of simple elements or events.

2. Learning in which the probability of a response is changed by a change in its consequences.

4. The recognition that objects exist independently of an individual's action or awareness; an important cognitive acquisition of infancy.

6. Seeks to clarify the typical communication patterns of the partners and then to improve the quality of their interaction.

8. Processes of knowing, including attending, remembering, and reasoning.

9. One of the branched fibers of neurons that receive incoming signals.

10. A procedure by which participants have an equal likelihood of being assigned to any condition within an experiment.

DOWN

1. Study of the structure of mind and behavior; the view that all human mental experience can be understood as a combination of simple elements or events.

2. Learning in which the probability of a response is changed by a change in its consequences.

4. The recognition that objects exist independently of an individual's action or awareness; an important cognitive acquisition of infancy.

6. Seeks to clarify the typical communication patterns of the partners and then to improve the quality of their interaction.

8. Processes of knowing, including attending, remembering, and reasoning.

9. One of the branched fibers of neurons that receive incoming signals.

10. A procedure by which participants have an equal likelihood of being assigned to any condition within an experiment.

A. Couple therapy
D. Operant conditioning
G. Structuralism
J. Opiate

B. Amnesia
E. Phonology
H. Cognition
K. Random assignment

C. Dendrite
F. Teratogen
I. Object permanence
L. Synapse

17. *Using the Across and Down clues, write the correct words in the numbered grid below.*

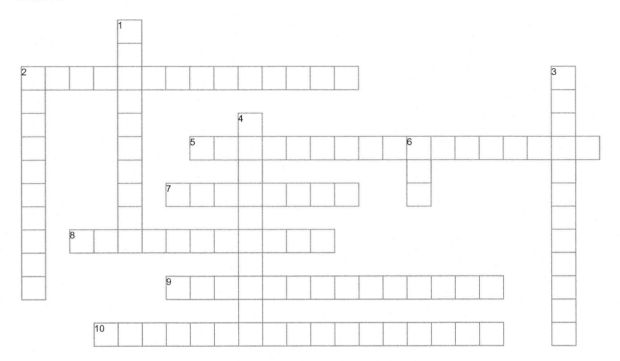

ACROSS

2. Thinking that is directed toward solving specific problems and that moves from an initial state to a goal state by means of a set of mental operations.

5. The tendency for groups to make decisions that are more extreme than the decisions that would be made by the members acting alone.

7. The learned, relatively stable tendency to respond to people, concepts, and events in an evaluative way.

8. Constancy or equilibrium of the internal conditions of the body.

9. A technique by which the therapist guides a patient toward discovering insights between present symptoms and past origins.

10. The aspect of intelligence that involves the ability to see complex relationships and solve problems; measured by tests of block designs and spatial visualization.

DOWN

2. Thinking that is directed toward solving specific problems and that moves from an initial state to a goal state by means of a set of mental operations.

5. The tendency for groups to make decisions that are more extreme than the decisions that would be made by the members acting alone.

7. The learned, relatively stable tendency to respond to people, concepts, and events in an evaluative way.

8. Constancy or equilibrium of the internal conditions of the body.

9. A technique by which the therapist guides a patient toward discovering insights between present symptoms and past origins.

10. The aspect of intelligence that involves the ability to see complex relationships and solve problems; measured by tests of block designs and spatial visualization.

A. Self esteem   B. Attitude   C. Homeostasis   D. Problem solving
E. Group polarization   F. REM   G. Perception   H. Fluid intelligence
I. Insight therapy   J. Motivation   K. Hypothalamus

18. *Using the Across and Down clues, write the correct words in the numbered grid below.*

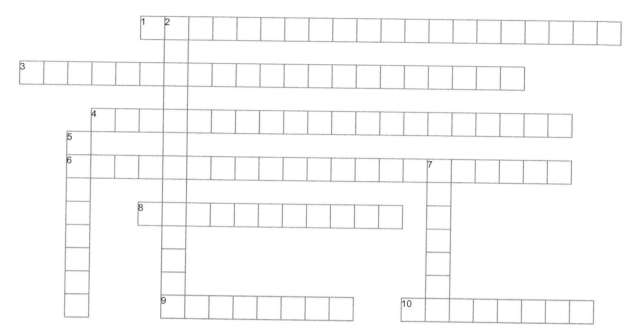

ACROSS

1. Type of therapy that assumes that a patient's problems have been caused by the psychological tension between unconscious impulses and the constraints of his or her life situation.

3. A type of learning in which a behavior (conditioned response) comes to be elicited by a stimulus (conditioned stimulus).

4. A disorder characterized by unexplained physical complaints in several categories over many years.

6. Type of intelligence defined as the abilities to perceive, appraise, and express emotions accurately and appropriately.

8. A basic law of learning that states that the power of a stimulus to evoke a response is strengthened when the response is followed by a reward and weakened when it is not followed by a reward.

9. People begin life with mental structures that provide constraints on how they experience the world.

10. The learned, relatively stable tendency to respond to people, concepts, and events in an evaluative way.

DOWN

1. Type of therapy that assumes that a patient's problems have been caused by the psychological tension between unconscious impulses and the constraints of his or her life situation.

3. A type of learning in which a behavior (conditioned response) comes to be elicited by a stimulus (conditioned stimulus).

4. A disorder characterized by unexplained physical complaints in several categories over many years.

6. Type of intelligence defined as the abilities to perceive, appraise, and express emotions accurately and appropriately.

8. A basic law of learning that states that the power of a stimulus to evoke a response is strengthened when the response is followed by a reward and weakened when it is not followed by a reward.

9. People begin life with mental structures that provide constraints on how they experience the world.

10. The learned, relatively stable tendency to respond to people, concepts, and events in an evaluative way.

A. Classical conditioning
D. Emotional intelligence
G. Law of effect
J. Socialization
B. Psychodynamic therapy
E. Heredity
H. Attitude
C. Nativist
F. Insight
I. Somatization disorder

19. *Using the Across and Down clues, write the correct words in the numbered grid below.*

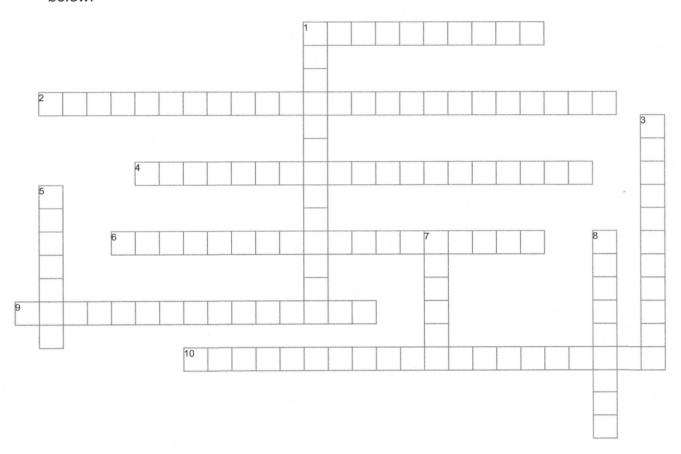

ACROSS

1. A socially defined pattern of behavior that is expected of a person who is functioning in a given setting or group.
2. A psychological model in which behavior is explained in terms of past experiences and motivational forces.
4. Focuses on the individual. Suggests that because everyone is unique and should be studied in an individual way, no general laws are possible.
6. A form of reasoning in which a conclusion is made about the probability of something happening based on the available evidence and experience.
9. A membrane running along the length of the cochlea.
10. The development of processes of knowing, including imagining, perceiving, reasoning, and problem solving.

DOWN

1. A socially defined pattern of behavior that is expected of a person who is functioning in a given setting or group.
2. A psychological model in which behavior is explained in terms of past experiences and motivational forces.
4. Focuses on the individual. Suggests that because everyone is unique and should be studied in an individual way, no general laws are possible.
6. A form of reasoning in which a conclusion is made about the probability of something happening based on the available evidence and experience.
9. A membrane running along the length of the cochlea.
10. The development of processes of knowing, including imagining, perceiving, reasoning, and problem solving.

A. Cognitive development
B. Obedience
C. Self concept
D. Social role
E. Psychodynamic perspective
F. Basilar membrane
G. Schizophrenia
H. Lexical
I. Idiographic research
J. Opiate
K. Inductive reasoning

20. *Using the Across and Down clues, write the correct words in the numbered grid below.*

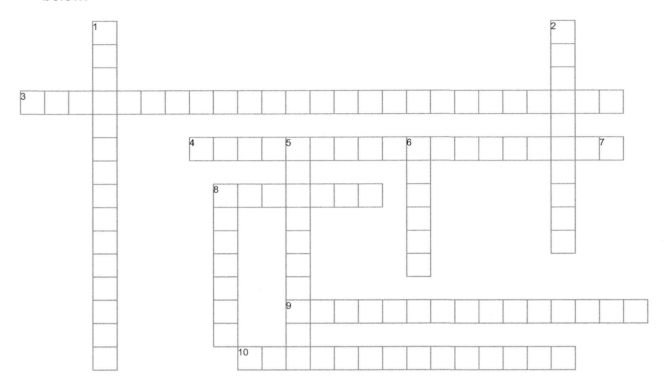

ACROSS

3. A behavioral therapy technique in which a client is taught to prevent the arousal of anxiety by confronting the feared stimulus while relaxed.

4. A form of thinking in which one draws a conclusion that is intended to follow logically from two or more statements or premises.

8. Minimal unit of speech in any given language that makes a meaningful difference in speech and production and reception.

9. The process through which individuals are informed about experimental procedures, risks, and benefits before they provide formal consent to become research participants.

10. The form of psychodynamic therapy developed by Freud; and intensive prolonged technique for exploring unconscious motivations and conflicts in neurotic, anxiety-ridden individuals.

DOWN

3. A behavioral therapy technique in which a client is taught to prevent the arousal of anxiety by confronting the feared stimulus while relaxed.

4. A form of thinking in which one draws a conclusion that is intended to follow logically from two or more statements or premises.

8. Minimal unit of speech in any given language that makes a meaningful difference in speech and production and reception.

9. The process through which individuals are informed about experimental procedures, risks, and benefits before they provide formal consent to become research participants.

10. The form of psychodynamic therapy developed by Freud; and intensive prolonged technique for exploring unconscious motivations and conflicts in neurotic, anxiety-ridden individuals.

A. Psychoanalysis   B. G   C. Informed consent
D. Retina   E. Puberty   F. Phoneme
G. Deductive reasoning   H. Content validity   I. Conformity
J. Empiricist   K. Systematic desensitization

21. *Using the Across and Down clues, write the correct words in the numbered grid below.*

ACROSS

3. A judgment based on the information readily available in memory.

6. The assumption that mental and behavioral reactions are determined by previous experiences.

7. The biological unit of heredity; discrete section of a chromosome responsible for transmission of traits.

8. A particular description of a choice; the perspective from which a choice is described or framed affects how a decision is made and which option is ultimately exercised.

9. Thinking that is directed toward solving specific problems and that moves from an initial state to a goal state by means of a set of mental operations.

10. The psychological perspective primarily concerned with observable behavior that can be objectively recorded.

DOWN

3. A judgment based on the information readily available in memory.

6. The assumption that mental and behavioral reactions are determined by previous experiences.

7. The biological unit of heredity; discrete section of a chromosome responsible for transmission of traits.

8. A particular description of a choice; the perspective from which a choice is described or framed affects how a decision is made and which option is ultimately exercised.

9. Thinking that is directed toward solving specific problems and that moves from an initial state to a goal state by means of a set of mental operations.

10. The psychological perspective primarily concerned with observable behavior that can be objectively recorded.

A. Fixation
D. Frame
G. Behaviorist perspective
J. Gene

B. Psychic determinism
E. Availability heuristic
H. OCD

C. Problem solving
F. Basilar membrane
I. Fixed interval

22. *Using the Across and Down clues, write the correct words in the numbered grid below.*

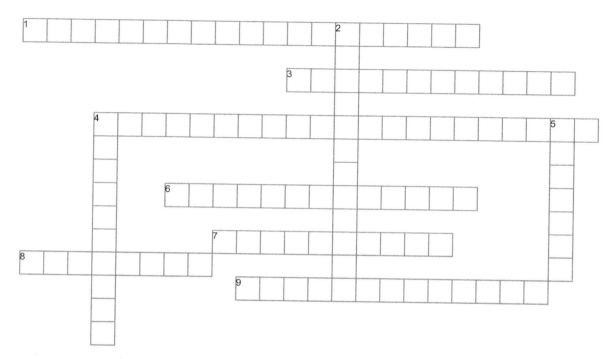

ACROSS

1. Conscious effort to encode or recover information through memory processes.
3. Researched the relationship between parents and their offspring by carrying out experiments on pea plants.
4. A summary of how frequently each score appears in a set of observations.
6. Seeks to clarify the typical communication patterns of the partners and then to improve the quality of their interaction.
7. The entire set of individuals to which generalizations will be made based on an experimental sample.
8. The legal (not clinical) designation for the state of an individual judged to be legally irresponsible or incompetent.
9. A surgical procedure performed on brain tissue to alleviate a psychological disorder.

DOWN

1. Conscious effort to encode or recover information through memory processes.
3. Researched the relationship between parents and their offspring by carrying out experiments on pea plants.
4. A summary of how frequently each score appears in a set of observations.
6. Seeks to clarify the typical communication patterns of the partners and then to improve the quality of their interaction.
7. The entire set of individuals to which generalizations will be made based on an experimental sample.
8. The legal (not clinical) designation for the state of an individual judged to be legally irresponsible or incompetent.
9. A surgical procedure performed on brain tissue to alleviate a psychological disorder.

A. Operant
D. Explicit use of memory
G. Population
J. Gregor Mendel

B. Fixed ratio
E. Frequency distribution
H. Couple therapy

C. Psychosurgery
F. Myelin sheath
I. Insanity

23. *Using the Across and Down clues, write the correct words in the numbered grid below.*

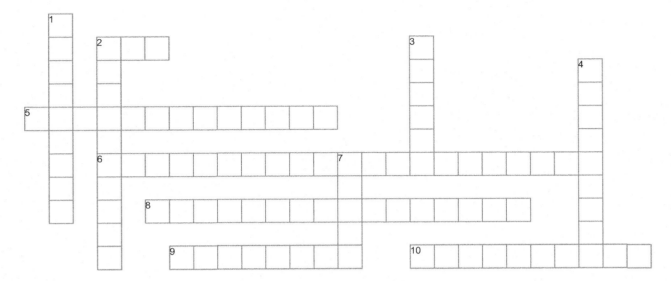

ACROSS

2. Magnetic resonance imaging. A technique for brain imaging that scans the brain using magnetic fields and radio waves.

5. The client is a whole nuclear family and each family member is treated as a member of a system of relationships.

6. A judgment based on the information readily available in memory.

8. The receptors for this information are tiny hairs in fluid-filled sacs and canals in the inner ear.

9. The process by which people form opinions, reach conclusions, and make critical evaluations of events and people based on available material; also, the product of the mental activity.

10. The extent to which people believe that their behaviors situations will bring about rewards.

DOWN

2. Magnetic resonance imaging. A technique for brain imaging that scans the brain using magnetic fields and radio waves.

5. The client is a whole nuclear family and each family member is treated as a member of a system of relationships.

6. A judgment based on the information readily available in memory.

8. The receptors for this information are tiny hairs in fluid-filled sacs and canals in the inner ear.

9. The process by which people form opinions, reach conclusions, and make critical evaluations of events and people based on available material; also, the product of the mental activity.

10. The extent to which people believe that their behaviors situations will bring about rewards.

A. Expectancy   ·B. Judgment   C. Vestibular system   D. Availability heuristic
E. Olfaction   F. Family therapy   G. Scheme   H. Trait
I. MRI   J. Meditation   K. Catharsis

24. *Using the Across and Down clues, write the correct words in the numbered grid below.*

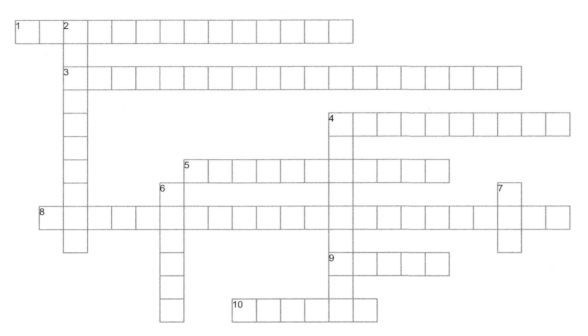

ACROSS

1. In the processes of perception, the physical object in the world.

3. The principle that subsequent retrieval of information is enhanced if cues received at the time of recall are consistent with those present at the time of encoding.

4. The approach to identifying causes of behavior that focuses on the functioning of the genes, the brain, the nervous system, and the endocrine system.

5. The psychological qualities of an individual that influence a variety of characteristic behavior patterns across different situations and over time.

8. A prediction made about some future behavior or event that modifies interactions to produce what is expected.

9. Enduring personal quality or attribute that influences behavior across situations.

10. Piaget's term for a cognitive structure that develops as infants and young children learn to interpret the world and adapt to their environment.

DOWN

1. In the processes of perception, the physical object in the world.

3. The principle that subsequent retrieval of information is enhanced if cues received at the time of recall are consistent with those present at the time of encoding.

4. The approach to identifying causes of behavior that focuses on the functioning of the genes, the brain, the nervous system, and the endocrine system.

5. The psychological qualities of an individual that influence a variety of characteristic behavior patterns across different situations and over time.

8. A prediction made about some future behavior or event that modifies interactions to produce what is expected.

9. Enduring personal quality or attribute that influences behavior across situations.

10. Piaget's term for a cognitive structure that develops as infants and young children learn to interpret the world and adapt to their environment.

A. Scheme
D. Hunger
G. Trait
J. Brain stem

B. REM
E. Biological
H. Sleep apnea
K. Self fulfilling prophecy

C. Personality
F. Distal stimulus
I. Encoding specificity

25. *Using the Across and Down clues, write the correct words in the numbered grid below.*

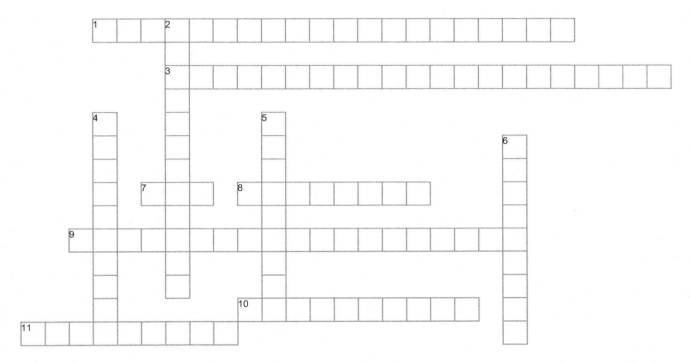

ACROSS

1. A measure of the correlation between test takers' performance on different halves (such as odd- and even-numbered items) of a test.

3. The process of learning new responses by watching the behavior of another.

7. A recording of the electrical activity of the brain.

8. Preprogrammed tendency that is essential to a species' survival.

9. The inability to remember important personal experiences, caused by psychological factors in the absence of any organic dysfunction.

10. Drug that depresses or slows down the activity of the central nervous system.

11. Intensive observation of an individual or small group of individuals.

DOWN

1. A measure of the correlation between test takers' performance on different halves (such as odd- and even-numbered items) of a test.

3. The process of learning new responses by watching the behavior of another.

7. A recording of the electrical activity of the brain.

8. Preprogrammed tendency that is essential to a species' survival.

9. The inability to remember important personal experiences, caused by psychological factors in the absence of any organic dysfunction.

10. Drug that depresses or slows down the activity of the central nervous system.

11. Intensive observation of an individual or small group of individuals.

A. Dissociative amnesia   B. Depressant   C. Observational learning
D. Iconic memory   E. Case study   F. Phenotype
G. Instinct   H. EEG   I. Catharsis
J. Split half reliability   K. Compliance

26. *Using the Across and Down clues, write the correct words in the numbered grid below.*

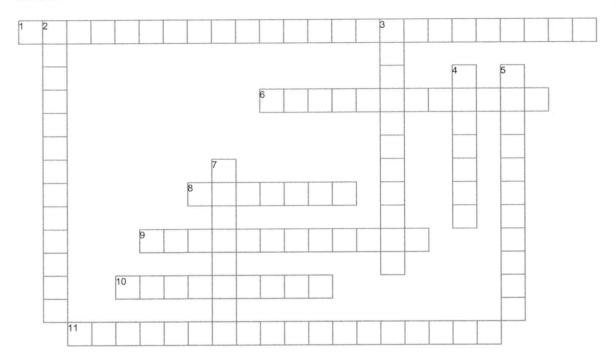

ACROSS

1. A statistic that indicates the degree of relationship between to variables. +1.0 is a perfect positive correlation, -1.0 is perfect negative correlation.

6. A drug that alters cognitions and perceptions and causes hallucinations.

8. An individual's discomfort and

9. A disorder that causes sleep walking.

10. Blind obedience is less a product of dispositional characteristics than the outcome of situational forces that could engulf anyone. (Milgram studies)

11. An aspect of creativity characterized by the ability to gather together different sources of information to solve a problem.

DOWN

1. A statistic that indicates the degree of relationship between to variables. +1.0 is a perfect positive correlation, -1.0 is perfect negative correlation.

6. A drug that alters cognitions and perceptions and causes hallucinations.

8. An individual's discomfort and

9. A disorder that causes sleep walking.

10. Blind obedience is less a product of dispositional characteristics than the outcome of situational forces that could engulf anyone. (Milgram studies)

11. An aspect of creativity characterized by the ability to gather together different sources of information to solve a problem.

A. Hallucinogen
D. Obedience
G. Personality
J. Chunking

B. Cochlea
E. Convergent thinking
H. Somnambulism
K. Egocentrism

C. Correlational coefficient
F. Shyness
I. Olfactory bulb

27. *Using the Across and Down clues, write the correct words in the numbered grid below.*

ACROSS

3. The process by which stimulation of a sensory receptor gives rise to neutral impulses that result in an experience, or awareness, of conditions inside or outside the body.

5. A social-cognitive approach to describing the ways the social perceiver uses information to generate causal explanations.

6. The region of the brain stem that regulates breathing, waking, and heartbeat.

7. The process of thinking in which conclusions are drawn from a set of facts; thinking directed toward a given goal or objective.

9. Research methodology that determines to what extent two variables, traits, or attributes are related.

10. The client is a whole nuclear family and each family member is treated as a member of a system of relationships.

11. The region of the brain attached to the brain stem that controls motor coordination, posture, and balance as well as the ability to learn control of body movements.

DOWN

3. The process by which stimulation of a sensory receptor gives rise to neutral impulses that result in an experience, or awareness, of conditions inside or outside the body.

5. A social-cognitive approach to describing the ways the social perceiver uses information to generate causal explanations.

6. The region of the brain stem that regulates breathing, waking, and heartbeat.

7. The process of thinking in which conclusions are drawn from a set of facts; thinking directed toward a given goal or objective.

9. Research methodology that determines to what extent two variables, traits, or attributes are related.

10. The client is a whole nuclear family and each family member is treated as a member of a system of relationships.

11. The region of the brain attached to the brain stem that controls motor coordination, posture, and balance as well as the ability to learn control of body movements.

A. Control group
D. Fixed interval
G. Cerebellum
J. Genome

B. Family therapy
E. Medulla
H. Reasoning
K. Sensation

C. Correlational research method
F. Attribution theory
I. Soma

28. *Using the Across and Down clues, write the correct words in the numbered grid below.*

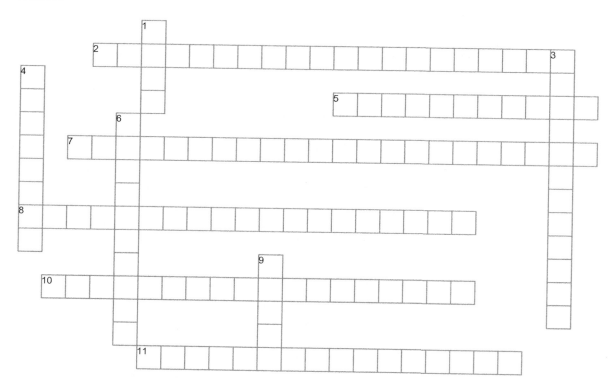

ACROSS

2. A research method in which groups of participants of different chronological ages are observed and compared at a given time.

5. The part of the limbic system that is involved in the acquisition of explicit memory.

7. A conditioning process in which an organism learns to respond differently to stimuli that differ from the conditioned stimulus on some dimension.

8. The inability to remember important personal experiences, caused by psychological factors in the absence of any organic dysfunction.

10. The branch of psychology that investigates the effects of drugs on behavior.

11. Chemical messenger released from a neuron that crosses the synapse from one neuron to another, stimulating the postsynaptic neuron.

DOWN

2. A research method in which groups of participants of different chronological ages are observed and compared at a given time.

5. The part of the limbic system that is involved in the acquisition of explicit memory.

7. A conditioning process in which an organism learns to respond differently to stimuli that differ from the conditioned stimulus on some dimension.

8. The inability to remember important personal experiences, caused by psychological factors in the absence of any organic dysfunction.

10. The branch of psychology that investigates the effects of drugs on behavior.

11. Chemical messenger released from a neuron that crosses the synapse from one neuron to another, stimulating the postsynaptic neuron.

A. Neurotransmitter
D. Dissociative amnesia
G. Trait
J. Hippocampus

B. Attitude
E. Stimulus discrimination
H. Psychopharmacology
K. Cross sectional design

C. Biological
F. Neuroscience
I. Norm

29. *Using the Across and Down clues, write the correct words in the numbered grid below.*

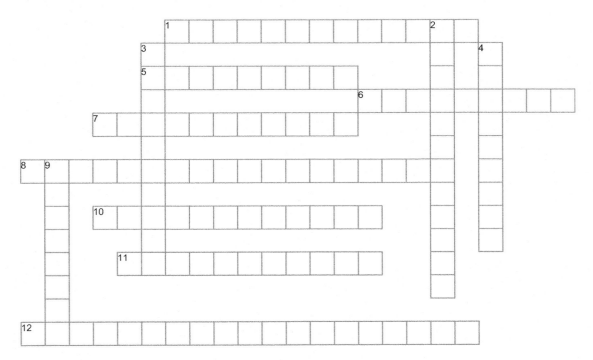

ACROSS

1. A schedule of reinforcement in which a reinforcer is delivered for the first response made after a variable number of responses whose average is predetermined.

5. The sense of smell.

6. Processes of knowing, including attending, remembering, and reasoning.

7. The part of the limbic system that is involved in the acquisition of explicit memory.

8. The assumption that mental and behavioral reactions are determined by previous experiences.

10. A group in an experiment that is not exposed to a treatment or does not experience a manipulation of the independent variable.

11. A person's mental model of his or her abilities and attributes.

12. The state of conflict someone experiences after deciding, taking an action, or being exposed to information that is contrary to prior beliefs, feelings, or values. Impels you to act to reduce the unpleasant feeling.

DOWN

1. A schedule of reinforcement in which a reinforcer is delivered for the first response made after a variable number of responses whose average is predetermined.

5. The sense of smell.

6. Processes of knowing, including attending, remembering, and reasoning.

7. The part of the limbic system that is involved in the acquisition of explicit memory.

8. The assumption that mental and behavioral reactions are determined by previous experiences.

10. A group in an experiment that is not exposed to a treatment or does not experience a manipulation of the independent variable.

11. A person's mental model of his or her abilities and attributes.

12. The state of conflict someone experiences after deciding, taking an action, or being exposed to information that is contrary to prior beliefs, feelings, or values. Impels you to act to reduce the unpleasant feeling.

A. Variable ratio
D. Cognitive dissonance
G. Superego
J. Cognition

B. Control group
E. Catharsis
H. Self concept
K. Psychic determinism

C. Compliance
F. Hippocampus
I. Iconic memory
L. Olfaction

30. *Using the Across and Down clues, write the correct words in the numbered grid below.*

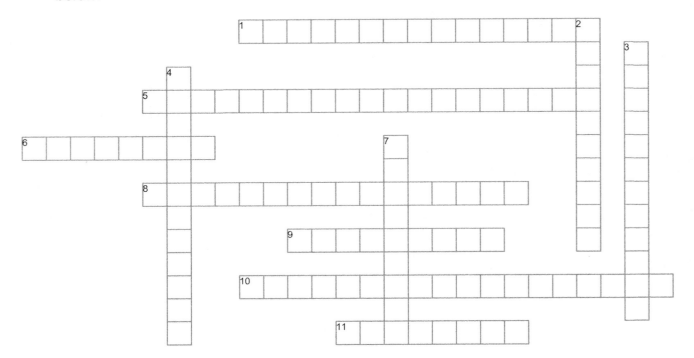

ACROSS

1. A mood disorder characterized by alternating periods of depression and mania.

5. A chronic, inflexible, maladaptive pattern of perceiving, thinking, and behaving that seriously impairs an individual's ability to function in social or other settings.

6. An altered state of awareness characterized by deep relaxation, susceptibility to suggestions, and changes in perception, memory, motivation, and self-control.

8. A schedule of reinforcement in which a reinforcer is delivered for the first response made after a variable period whose average is predetermined.

9. The sense of taste.

10. A disorder in which psychological conflict or stress brings about loss of motor or sensory function.

11. Preprogrammed tendency that is essential to a species' survival.

DOWN

1. A mood disorder characterized by alternating periods of depression and mania.

5. A chronic, inflexible, maladaptive pattern of perceiving, thinking, and behaving that seriously impairs an individual's ability to function in social or other settings.

6. An altered state of awareness characterized by deep relaxation, susceptibility to suggestions, and changes in perception, memory, motivation, and self-control.

8. A schedule of reinforcement in which a reinforcer is delivered for the first response made after a variable period whose average is predetermined.

9. The sense of taste.

10. A disorder in which psychological conflict or stress brings about loss of motor or sensory function.

11. Preprogrammed tendency that is essential to a species' survival.

A. Conversion disorder   B. Bipolar disorder   C. Hypnosis   D. Instinct
E. Catharsis   F. Heritability   G. Repression   H. Personality disorder
I. Gregor Mendel   J. Variable interval   K. Gustation

31. *Using the Across and Down clues, write the correct words in the numbered grid below.*

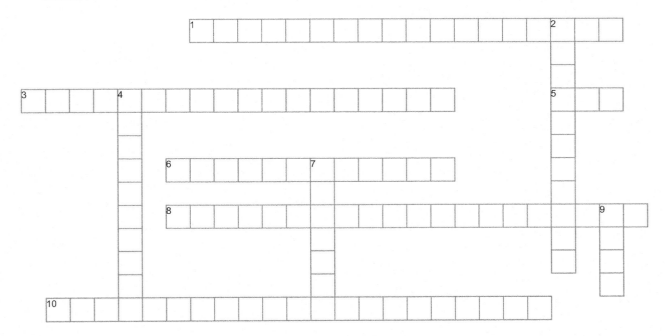

ACROSS

1. What people say, sign, and write, as well as the processes the go through to produce these messages.

3. A form of thinking in which one draws a conclusion that is intended to follow logically from two or more statements or premises.

5. A recording of the electrical activity of the brain.

6. Founded the first formal experimental psychology laboratory in 1879 in Leipzig, Germany.

8. Type of therapy that assumes that a patient's problems have been caused by the psychological tension between unconscious impulses and the constraints of his or her life situation.

10. The process of learning new responses by watching the behavior of another.

DOWN

1. What people say, sign, and write, as well as the processes the go through to produce these messages.

3. A form of thinking in which one draws a conclusion that is intended to follow logically from two or more statements or premises.

5. A recording of the electrical activity of the brain.

6. Founded the first formal experimental psychology laboratory in 1879 in Leipzig, Germany.

8. Type of therapy that assumes that a patient's problems have been caused by the psychological tension between unconscious impulses and the constraints of his or her life situation.

10. The process of learning new responses by watching the behavior of another.

A. Chromosome
D. Psychodynamic therapy
G. Deductive reasoning
J. Wilhelm Wundt

B. Language production
E. Observational learning
H. EEG

C. Interneuron
F. Medulla
I. Pons

32. *Using the Across and Down clues, write the correct words in the numbered grid below.*

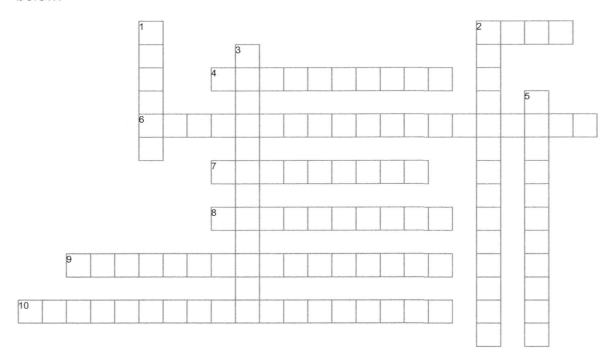

ACROSS

2. Posttraumatic stress disorder. An anxiety disorder characterized by the persistent re-experience of those traumatic events through distressing recollections, dreams, hallucinations, or flashbacks.

4. A sleep disorder characterized by an irresistible compulsion to sleep during the daytime.

6. Availability of information through memory processes without conscious effort to encode or recover information.

7. Environmental factors such as diseases and drugs that cause structural abnormalities in a developing fetus.

8. A schedule of reinforcement in which a reinforcer is delivered for the first response made after a fixed number of responses.

9. Sexual arousal is the motivational state of excitement and tension brought about by physiological and cognitive reactions to erotic stimuli.

10. A theory of personality that refers to the expertise people bring to their experience of life tasks.

DOWN

2. Posttraumatic stress disorder. An anxiety disorder characterized by the persistent re-experience of those traumatic events through distressing recollections, dreams, hallucinations, or flashbacks.

4. A sleep disorder characterized by an irresistible compulsion to sleep during the daytime.

6. Availability of information through memory processes without conscious effort to encode or recover information.

7. Environmental factors such as diseases and drugs that cause structural abnormalities in a developing fetus.

8. A schedule of reinforcement in which a reinforcer is delivered for the first response made after a fixed number of responses.

9. Sexual arousal is the motivational state of excitement and tension brought about by physiological and cognitive reactions to erotic stimuli.

10. A theory of personality that refers to the expertise people bring to their experience of life tasks.

A. Sexual motivation
D. PTSD
G. Narcolepsy
J. Manic episode

B. Homeostasis
E. Projective test
H. Phobia
K. Social intelligence

C. Fixed ratio
F. Implicit use of memory
I. Teratogen

33. *Using the Across and Down clues, write the correct words in the numbered grid below.*

ACROSS

3. The observation that personality ratings across time and among different observers are consistent while behavior ratings across situations are not consistent.

7. Belief about attributes and behaviors regarded as appropriate for males and females in a particular culture.

8. The process of reconfiguring items by grouping based on similarity or some other organizing principle.

9. The genetic structure an organism inherits from its parents.

10. The extent to which people believe that their behaviors situations will bring about rewards.

11. Constancy or equilibrium of the internal conditions of the body.

DOWN

3. The observation that personality ratings across time and among different observers are consistent while behavior ratings across situations are not consistent.

7. Belief about attributes and behaviors regarded as appropriate for males and females in a particular culture.

8. The process of reconfiguring items by grouping based on similarity or some other organizing principle.

9. The genetic structure an organism inherits from its parents.

10. The extent to which people believe that their behaviors situations will bring about rewards.

11. Constancy or equilibrium of the internal conditions of the body.

A. Genotype   B. Consistency paradox   C. Chunking   D. Judgment
E. Pragmatics   F. Expectancy   G. Nativist   H. Homeostasis
I. Gender stereotype   J. Aggression   K. Incentive

34. *Using the Across and Down clues, write the correct words in the numbered grid below.*

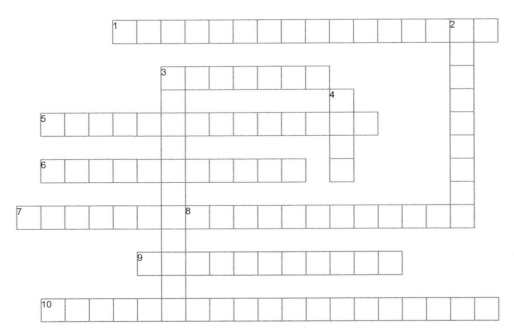

ACROSS

1. A type of psychotherapeutic treatment that attempts to change feelings and behaviors by changing the way a client thinks about or perceives significant life experience.
3. The gap between one neuron and another.
5. In the processes of perception, the physical object in the world.
6. The part of the limbic system that is involved in the acquisition of explicit memory.
7. The principle that subsequent retrieval of information is enhanced if cues received at the time of recall are consistent with those present at the time of encoding.
9. The degree to which a test produces similar scores each time it is used; stability or consistency of the scores produced by an instrument.
10. The subdivision of the ANS that deals with emergency response and the mobilization of energy.

DOWN

1. A type of psychotherapeutic treatment that attempts to change feelings and behaviors by changing the way a client thinks about or perceives significant life experience.
3. The gap between one neuron and another.
5. In the processes of perception, the physical object in the world.
6. The part of the limbic system that is involved in the acquisition of explicit memory.
7. The principle that subsequent retrieval of information is enhanced if cues received at the time of recall are consistent with those present at the time of encoding.
9. The degree to which a test produces similar scores each time it is used; stability or consistency of the scores produced by an instrument.
10. The subdivision of the ANS that deals with emergency response and the mobilization of energy.

A. Self concept   B. Cognitive therapy   C. Synapse   D. Encoding specificity
E. G   F. Rule   G. Reliability H. Phonology
I. Sympathetic division   J. Hippocampus   K. Distal stimulus

35. *Using the Across and Down clues, write the correct words in the numbered grid below.*

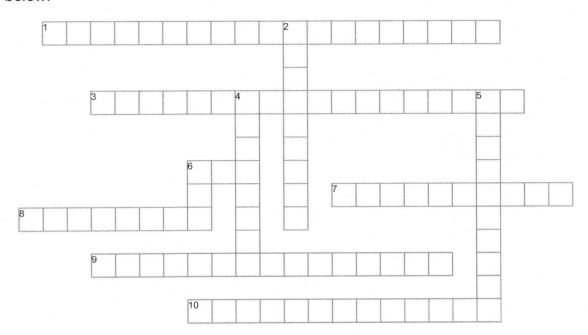

ACROSS

1. Produced in reaction to situations and is emotion driven.
3. A theory of personality that refers to the expertise people bring to their experience of life tasks.
6. Electroconvulsive therapy. The use of electroconvulsive shock as an effective treatment for severe depression.
7. The process of starting, directing, and maintaining physical and psychological activities; includes mechanisms involved in preferences for one activity over another and the vigor and persistence of responses.
8. The process of reconfiguring items by grouping based on similarity or some other organizing principle.
9. Founded a psychology laboratory at Cornell University in 1892, student of Wilhelm Wundt.
10. A surgical procedure performed on brain tissue to alleviate a psychological disorder.

DOWN

1. Produced in reaction to situations and is emotion driven.
3. A theory of personality that refers to the expertise people bring to their experience of life tasks.
6. Electroconvulsive therapy. The use of electroconvulsive shock as an effective treatment for severe depression.
7. The process of starting, directing, and maintaining physical and psychological activities; includes mechanisms involved in preferences for one activity over another and the vigor and persistence of responses.
8. The process of reconfiguring items by grouping based on similarity or some other organizing principle.
9. Founded a psychology laboratory at Cornell University in 1892, student of Wilhelm Wundt.
10. A surgical procedure performed on brain tissue to alleviate a psychological disorder.

A. Instinct   B. Motivation   C. Creativity   D. Chunking
E. Impulsive aggression   F. Gustation   G. EEG   H. Psychosurgery
I. ECT   J. Social intelligence   K. Edward Titchener

36. *Using the Across and Down clues, write the correct words in the numbered grid below.*

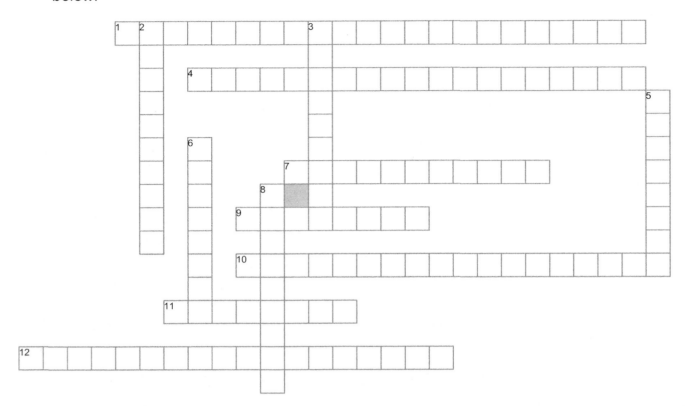

ACROSS

1. A prediction made about some future behavior or event that modifies interactions to produce what is expected.

4. The bodily changes, maturation, and growth that occur in an organism starting with conception and continuing across the life span.

7. The part of the limbic system that is involved in the acquisition of explicit memory.

9. The region of the brain that regulates higher cognitive and emotional functions.

10. The branch of psychology that investigates the effects of drugs on behavior.

11. A process based on experience that results in a relatively permanent change in behavior or behavioral potential.

12. Group effects that arise from individuals' desire to be like, accepted, and approved of by others.

DOWN

1. A prediction made about some future behavior or event that modifies interactions to produce what is expected.

4. The bodily changes, maturation, and growth that occur in an organism starting with conception and continuing across the life span.

7. The part of the limbic system that is involved in the acquisition of explicit memory.

9. The region of the brain that regulates higher cognitive and emotional functions.

10. The branch of psychology that investigates the effects of drugs on behavior.

11. A process based on experience that results in a relatively permanent change in behavior or behavioral potential.

12. Group effects that arise from individuals' desire to be like, accepted, and approved of by others.

A. Heredity
D. Psychopharmacology
G. Menarche
J. Physical development

B. Self fulfilling prophecy
E. Learning
H. Incentive
K. Reasoning

C. Empiricist
F. Normative influence
I. Cerebrum
L. Hippocampus

37. *Using the Across and Down clues, write the correct words in the numbered grid below.*

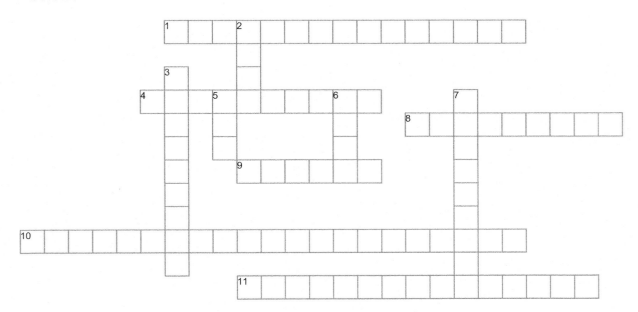

ACROSS

1. A type of behavioral therapy used to treat individuals attracted to harmful stimuli.

4. Drug that depresses or slows down the activity of the central nervous system.

8. A learned attitude toward a target object, involving negative affect (dislike or fear), negative beliefs (stereotypes), that justify the attitude, and a behavioral intention to avoid, control, dominate, or eliminate the target object.

9. Piaget's term for a cognitive structure that develops as infants and young children learn to interpret the world and adapt to their environment.

10. A summary of how frequently each score appears in a set of observations.

11. The network of glands that manufacture and secrete hormones into the bloodstream.

DOWN

1. A type of behavioral therapy used to treat individuals attracted to harmful stimuli.

4. Drug that depresses or slows down the activity of the central nervous system.

8. A learned attitude toward a target object, involving negative affect (dislike or fear), negative beliefs (stereotypes), that justify the attitude, and a behavioral intention to avoid, control, dominate, or eliminate the target object.

9. Piaget's term for a cognitive structure that develops as infants and young children learn to interpret the world and adapt to their environment.

10. A summary of how frequently each score appears in a set of observations.

11. The network of glands that manufacture and secrete hormones into the bloodstream.

A. Semantics
D. Reasoning
G. REM
J. Endocrine system

B. Frequency distribution
E. Depressant
H. Rule
K. Scheme

C. Norm
F. Prejudice
I. Aversion therapy

38. *Using the Across and Down clues, write the correct words in the numbered grid below.*

ACROSS

2. The psychological qualities of an individual that influence a variety of characteristic behavior patterns across different situations and over time.

4. A form of thinking in which one draws a conclusion that is intended to follow logically from two or more statements or premises.

8. A social-cognitive approach to describing the ways the social perceiver uses information to generate causal explanations.

9. Founded a psychology laboratory at Cornell University in 1892, student of Wilhelm Wundt.

10. The process of learning new responses by watching the behavior of another.

11. The area of psychological investigation concerned with understanding the nature of individual pathologies of mind, mood, and behavior.

DOWN

2. The psychological qualities of an individual that influence a variety of characteristic behavior patterns across different situations and over time.

4. A form of thinking in which one draws a conclusion that is intended to follow logically from two or more statements or premises.

8. A social-cognitive approach to describing the ways the social perceiver uses information to generate causal explanations.

9. Founded a psychology laboratory at Cornell University in 1892, student of Wilhelm Wundt.

10. The process of learning new responses by watching the behavior of another.

11. The area of psychological investigation concerned with understanding the nature of individual pathologies of mind, mood, and behavior.

A. Abnormal psychology
D. Population
G. Teratogen
J. LTM

B. Attribution theory
E. Observational learning
H. Endocrine system
K. Personality

C. Deductive reasoning
F. Edward Titchener
I. Genetics

39. *Using the Across and Down clues, write the correct words in the numbered grid below.*

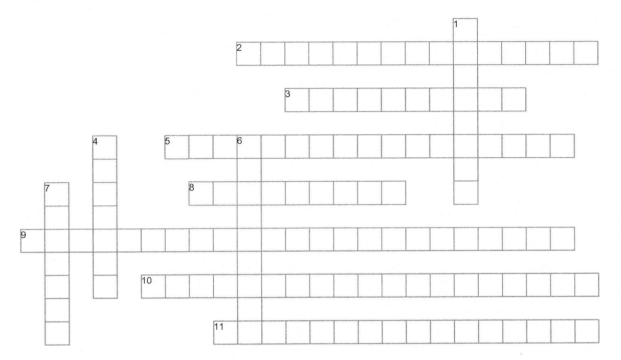

ACROSS

2. Specific personal features that help predict an individual's behavior but are less useful for understanding an individual's personality, such as food or dress preferences.

3. The expectation a group has for its members regarding acceptable and appropriate attitudes and behaviors.

5. Severe mental disorder in which a person experiences impairment manifested through thought, emotional, or perceptual difficulties.

8. Processes of knowing, including attending, remembering, and reasoning.

9. The use of specified procedures to evaluate the abilities, behaviors, and personal qualities of people.

10. Is a response elicited by some previously neutral stimulus that occurs as a result of pairing the neutral stimulus with an unconditioned stimulus.

11. Sexual arousal is the motivational state of excitement and tension brought about by physiological and cognitive reactions to erotic stimuli.

DOWN

2. Specific personal features that help predict an individual's behavior but are less useful for understanding an individual's personality, such as food or dress preferences.

3. The expectation a group has for its members regarding acceptable and appropriate attitudes and behaviors.

5. Severe mental disorder in which a person experiences impairment manifested through thought, emotional, or perceptual difficulties.

8. Processes of knowing, including attending, remembering, and reasoning.

9. The use of specified procedures to evaluate the abilities, behaviors, and personal qualities of people.

10. Is a response elicited by some previously neutral stimulus that occurs as a result of pairing the neutral stimulus with an unconditioned stimulus.

11. Sexual arousal is the motivational state of excitement and tension brought about by physiological and cognitive reactions to erotic stimuli.

A. Conditioned response
D. Etiology
G. Lexical
J. Insight

B. Psychological assessment
E. Cognition
H. Sexual motivation
K. Cognitive

C. Secondary traits
F. Social norm
I. Psychotic disorder

40. *Using the Across and Down clues, write the correct words in the numbered grid below.*

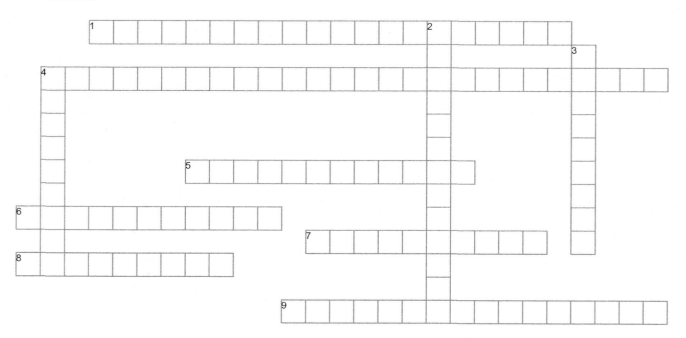

ACROSS

1. A personality disorder marked by a disturbance in the integration of identity, memory, or consciousness.

4. A therapeutic approach that combines the cognitive emphasis on thoughts and attitudes with the behavioral emphasis on changing performance.

5. The brain structure that regulates motivated behavior and homeostasis.

6. The part of the limbic system that is involved in the acquisition of explicit memory.

7. The expectation a group has for its members regarding acceptable and appropriate attitudes and behaviors.

8. The tendency to respond to a new problem in the manner used to respond to a previous problem.

9. Sexual arousal is the motivational state of excitement and tension brought about by physiological and cognitive reactions to erotic stimuli.

DOWN

1. A personality disorder marked by a disturbance in the integration of identity, memory, or consciousness.

4. A therapeutic approach that combines the cognitive emphasis on thoughts and attitudes with the behavioral emphasis on changing performance.

5. The brain structure that regulates motivated behavior and homeostasis.

6. The part of the limbic system that is involved in the acquisition of explicit memory.

7. The expectation a group has for its members regarding acceptable and appropriate attitudes and behaviors.

8. The tendency to respond to a new problem in the manner used to respond to a previous problem.

9. Sexual arousal is the motivational state of excitement and tension brought about by physiological and cognitive reactions to erotic stimuli.

A. Mental set
D. Cognitive behavioral therapy
G. Hippocampus
J. Structuralism

B. Dissociative disorder
E. Hypothalamus
H. Brain stem

C. Social norm
F. Cognitive
I. Sexual motivation

41. *Using the Across and Down clues, write the correct words in the numbered grid below.*

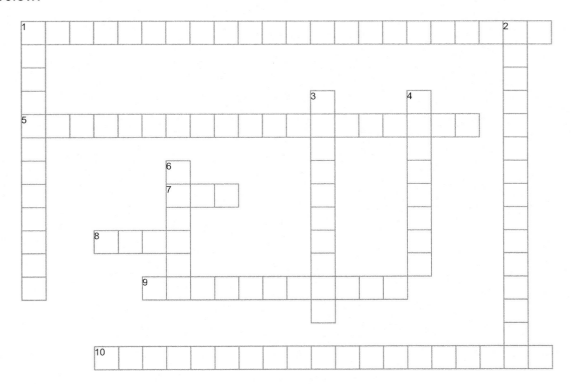

ACROSS

1. The label given to psychological abnormality by classifying and categorizing the observed behavior pattern into an approved diagnostic system.

5. A measure of reliability; the degree to which a test yields similar scores across its different parts, such as odd versus even items.

7. A recording of the electrical activity of the brain.

8. A rational reaction to an objectively identified external danger that may induce a person to flee or attack in self -defense.

9. The domain of the psyche that stores repressed urges and primitive impulses.

10. The bodily changes, maturation, and growth that occur in an organism starting with conception and continuing across the life span.

DOWN

1. The label given to psychological abnormality by classifying and categorizing the observed behavior pattern into an approved diagnostic system.

5. A measure of reliability; the degree to which a test yields similar scores across its different parts, such as odd versus even items.

7. A recording of the electrical activity of the brain.

8. A rational reaction to an objectively identified external danger that may induce a person to flee or attack in self -defense.

9. The domain of the psyche that stores repressed urges and primitive impulses.

10. The bodily changes, maturation, and growth that occur in an organism starting with conception and continuing across the life span.

A. Insanity
D. Internal consistency
G. Fixed ratio
J. EEG

B. Psychological diagnosis
E. Possible self
H. Neuron
K. Fear

C. Internalization
F. Unconscious
I. Physical development

42. *Using the Across and Down clues, write the correct words in the numbered grid below.*

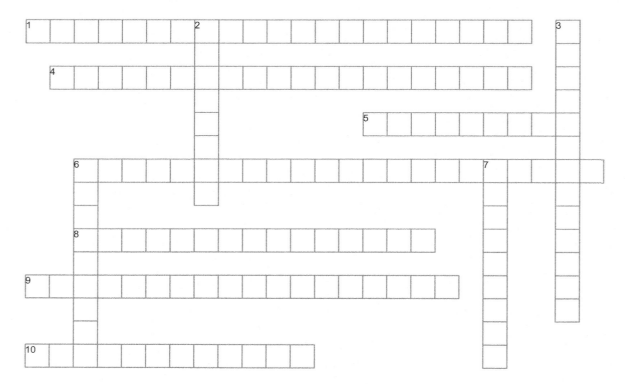

ACROSS

1. Statistical procedures that are used to summarize sets of scores with respect to central tendencies, variability, and correlations.

4. A self-report questionnaire used for personality assessment that includes a series of items about personal thoughts, feelings, and behaviors.

5. Cognitive strategies, or "rules of thumb," often used as shortcuts in solving a complex inferential task.

6. Is goal directed, and cognition based carried out with premeditated thought to achieve specific aims.

8. The network of glands that manufacture and secrete hormones into the bloodstream.

9. The region of the brain stem that alerts the cerebral cortex to incoming sensory signals and is responsible for maintaining consciousness and awakening from sleep.

10. Researched the relationship between parents and their offspring by carrying out experiments on pea plants.

DOWN

1. Statistical procedures that are used to summarize sets of scores with respect to central tendencies, variability, and correlations.

4. A self-report questionnaire used for personality assessment that includes a series of items about personal thoughts, feelings, and behaviors.

5. Cognitive strategies, or "rules of thumb," often used as shortcuts in solving a complex inferential task.

6. Is goal directed, and cognition based carried out with premeditated thought to achieve specific aims.

8. The network of glands that manufacture and secrete hormones into the bloodstream.

9. The region of the brain stem that alerts the cerebral cortex to incoming sensory signals and is responsible for maintaining consciousness and awakening from sleep.

10. Researched the relationship between parents and their offspring by carrying out experiments on pea plants.

A. Olfactory bulb
D. Instrumental aggression
G. Reticular formation
J. Gregor Mendel

B. Incentive
E. Heuristic
H. Descriptive statistics
K. Endocrine system

C. Thalamus
F. Personality inventory
I. Stimulant

43. *Using the Across and Down clues, write the correct words in the numbered grid below.*

ACROSS

3. Type of therapy that assumes that a patient's problems have been caused by the psychological tension between unconscious impulses and the constraints of his or her life situation.

4. A consistent relationship between a response and the changes in the environment that it produces.

5. Is a response elicited by some previously neutral stimulus that occurs as a result of pairing the neutral stimulus with an unconditioned stimulus.

6. Behaviors that cause psychological or physical harm to another individual.

9. The extent to which a test adequately measures the full range of the domain of interest.

10. A prediction made about some future behavior or event that modifies interactions to produce what is expected.

DOWN

3. Type of therapy that assumes that a patient's problems have been caused by the psychological tension between unconscious impulses and the constraints of his or her life situation.

4. A consistent relationship between a response and the changes in the environment that it produces.

5. Is a response elicited by some previously neutral stimulus that occurs as a result of pairing the neutral stimulus with an unconditioned stimulus.

6. Behaviors that cause psychological or physical harm to another individual.

9. The extent to which a test adequately measures the full range of the domain of interest.

10. A prediction made about some future behavior or event that modifies interactions to produce what is expected.

A. Reinforcement contingency
D. Cerebellum
G. Psychodynamic therapy
J. Superego

B. Self fulfilling prophecy
E. Aggression
H. Conditioned response

C. Content validity
F. Perception
I. Semantics

44. *Using the Across and Down clues, write the correct words in the numbered grid below.*

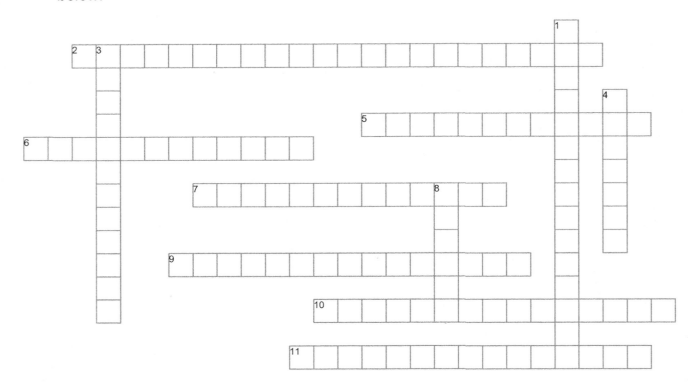

ACROSS

2. Research conducted with human subjects in which the investigator interacts directly with the subjects.

5. Author of "The Principles of Psychology."

6. The relative influence of genetics versus environment in determining patterns of behavior.

7. One of the biologically based characteristics that distinguish males from females.

9. The systematic use of principles of learning to increase the frequency of desired behaviors and

10. The extent to which a test adequately measures the full range of the domain of interest.

11. The skin senses that register sensations or pressure, warmth, and cold.

DOWN

2. Research conducted with human subjects in which the investigator interacts directly with the subjects.

5. Author of "The Principles of Psychology."

6. The relative influence of genetics versus environment in determining patterns of behavior.

7. One of the biologically based characteristics that distinguish males from females.

9. The systematic use of principles of learning to increase the frequency of desired behaviors and

10. The extent to which a test adequately measures the full range of the domain of interest.

11. The skin senses that register sensations or pressure, warmth, and cold.

A. Sex difference
D. Heritability
G. Limbic system
J. Clinical research method

B. William James
E. Neuron
H. PET scan
K. Social cognition

C. Cutaneous senses
F. Content validity
I. Behavior therapy

45. *Using the Across and Down clues, write the correct words in the numbered grid below.*

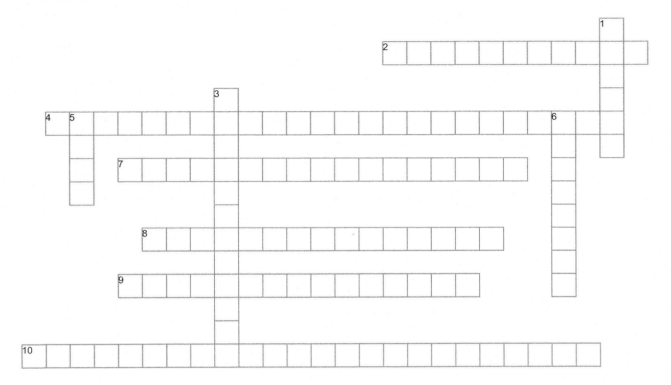

ACROSS

2. The part of the limbic system that is involved in the acquisition of explicit memory.

4. A psychological model in which behavior is explained in terms of past experiences and motivational forces.

7. A disorder characterized by a flight from home or work accompanied by a loss of ability to recall the personal past.

8. Founded a psychology laboratory at Cornell University in 1892, student of Wilhelm Wundt.

9. The process by which people select, interpret, and remember social information.

10. In operant conditioning, a pattern of delivering and withholding reinforcement.

DOWN

2. The part of the limbic system that is involved in the acquisition of explicit memory.

4. A psychological model in which behavior is explained in terms of past experiences and motivational forces.

7. A disorder characterized by a flight from home or work accompanied by a loss of ability to recall the personal past.

8. Founded a psychology laboratory at Cornell University in 1892, student of Wilhelm Wundt.

9. The process by which people select, interpret, and remember social information.

10. In operant conditioning, a pattern of delivering and withholding reinforcement.

A. Schedules of reinforcement
D. Psychodynamic perspective
G. Edward Titchener
J. Soma

B. Hippocampus
E. Hunger
H. Hypothalamus

C. Social cognition
F. Intimacy
I. Dissociative fugue

46. *Using the Across and Down clues, write the correct words in the numbered grid below.*

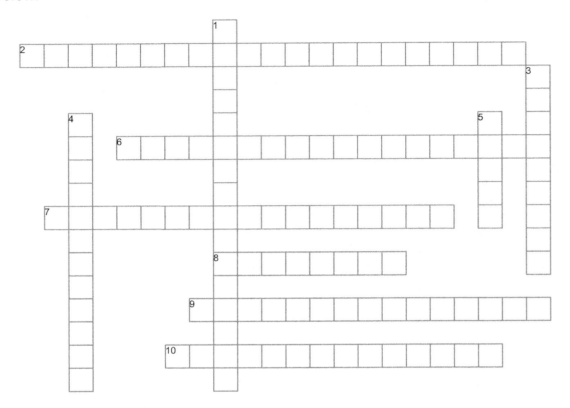

ACROSS

2. The process of learning new responses by watching the behavior of another.

6. Attempts to establish general laws and generalizations, and seeks to obtain objective knowledge through scientific methods.

7. The aspect of intelligence that involves the ability to see complex relationships and solve problems; measured by tests of block designs and spatial visualization.

8. The process of reconfiguring items by grouping based on similarity or some other organizing principle.

9. Distinct patter of personality characteristics used to assign people to categories; qualitative differences, rather than differences in degree, used to discriminate among people.

10. In the processes of perception, the physical object in the world.

DOWN

2. The process of learning new responses by watching the behavior of another.

6. Attempts to establish general laws and generalizations, and seeks to obtain objective knowledge through scientific methods.

7. The aspect of intelligence that involves the ability to see complex relationships and solve problems; measured by tests of block designs and spatial visualization.

8. The process of reconfiguring items by grouping based on similarity or some other organizing principle.

9. Distinct patter of personality characteristics used to assign people to categories; qualitative differences, rather than differences in degree, used to discriminate among people.

10. In the processes of perception, the physical object in the world.

A. Fluid intelligence
D. Catharsis
G. Trait
J. Distal stimulus

B. Observational learning
E. Personality type
H. Intelligence

C. Nomothetic research
F. Kinesthetic sense
I. Chunking

47. *Using the Across and Down clues, write the correct words in the numbered grid below.*

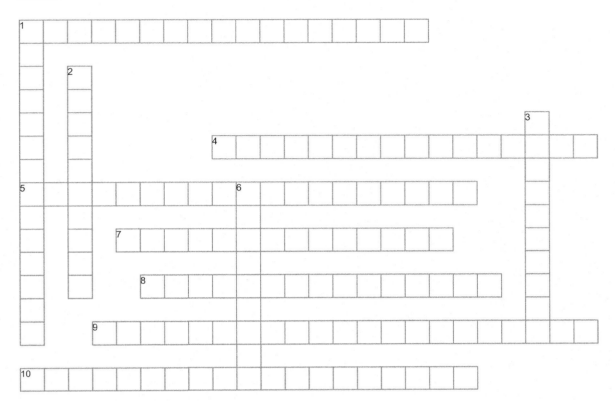

ACROSS

1. A biologically determined reinforcer, such as food and water.

4. Process that does not require attention; it can often be performed along with other tasks without interference.

5. Availability of information through memory processes without conscious effort to encode or recover information.

7. A bulblike structure at the branched ending of an axon that contains vesicles filled with neurotransmitters.

8. The therapeutic method in which a patient gives a running account of thoughts, wishes, physical sensations, and mental images as the occur.

9. Is the response elicited by an unconditioned stimulus without prior training or learning.

10. A technique used in therapy to substitute a new response for a maladaptive one by means of conditioning process.

DOWN

1. A biologically determined reinforcer, such as food and water.

4. Process that does not require attention; it can often be performed along with other tasks without interference.

5. Availability of information through memory processes without conscious effort to encode or recover information.

7. A bulblike structure at the branched ending of an axon that contains vesicles filled with neurotransmitters.

8. The therapeutic method in which a patient gives a running account of thoughts, wishes, physical sensations, and mental images as the occur.

9. Is the response elicited by an unconditioned stimulus without prior training or learning.

10. A technique used in therapy to substitute a new response for a maladaptive one by means of conditioning process.

A. Automatic process
D. Free association
G. Implicit use of memory
J. Unconditioned response

B. Centration
E. Counterconditioning
H. Terminal button
K. Perception

C. Polygenic trait
F. Primary reinforcer
I. Sensation

48. *Using the Across and Down clues, write the correct words in the numbered grid below.*

ACROSS

3. A cognitive theory of work motivation that proposes that workers are motivated to maintain fair and equitable relationships with other relevant persons.

6. The gap between one neuron and another.

9. The sense of taste.

10. Specific personal features that help predict an individual's behavior but are less useful for understanding an individual's personality, such as food or dress preferences.

11. One of the biologically based characteristics that distinguish males from females.

12. The facet of intelligence involving the knowledge a person has already acquired and the ability to access that knowledge; measures by vocabulary, arithmetic, and general information tests.

DOWN

3. A cognitive theory of work motivation that proposes that workers are motivated to maintain fair and equitable relationships with other relevant persons.

6. The gap between one neuron and another.

9. The sense of taste.

10. Specific personal features that help predict an individual's behavior but are less useful for understanding an individual's personality, such as food or dress preferences.

11. One of the biologically based characteristics that distinguish males from females.

12. The facet of intelligence involving the knowledge a person has already acquired and the ability to access that knowledge; measures by vocabulary, arithmetic, and general information tests.

A. Panic disorder
D. Control group
G. Self handicapping
J. Gustation

B. Sex difference
E. Teratogen
H. Synapse
K. Crystallized intelligence

C. Equity theory
F. Vestibular sense
I. ECT
L. Secondary traits

49. *Using the Across and Down clues, write the correct words in the numbered grid below.*

ACROSS

2. A mood disorder characterized by intense feelings of depression over an extended time, without the manic high phase of bipolar depression

4. An aspect of Rotter's expectancy theory; people's general expectancy about the extent to which the rewards they obtain are contingent on their own actions or on environmental factors.

6. Founded a psychology laboratory at Cornell University in 1892, student of Wilhelm Wundt.

8. The tendency for learned behavior to drift toward instinctual behavior over time.

9. A process based on experience that results in a relatively permanent change in behavior or behavioral potential.

10. The assumption that mental and behavioral reactions are determined by previous experiences.

DOWN

2. A mood disorder characterized by intense feelings of depression over an extended time, without the manic high phase of bipolar depression

4. An aspect of Rotter's expectancy theory; people's general expectancy about the extent to which the rewards they obtain are contingent on their own actions or on environmental factors.

6. Founded a psychology laboratory at Cornell University in 1892, student of Wilhelm Wundt.

8. The tendency for learned behavior to drift toward instinctual behavior over time.

9. A process based on experience that results in a relatively permanent change in behavior or behavioral potential.

10. The assumption that mental and behavioral reactions are determined by previous experiences.

A. Psychic determinism
D. Creativity
G. Phenotype
J. Locus of control

B. Law of effect
E. Major depressive disorder
H. Edward Titchener

C. Glia
F. Learning
I. Instinctual drift

50. *Using the Across and Down clues, write the correct words in the numbered grid below.*

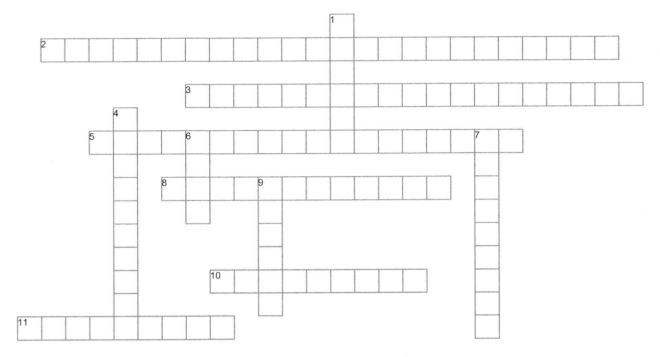

ACROSS

2. In operant conditioning, a pattern of delivering and withholding reinforcement.

3. A technique used in therapy to substitute a new response for a maladaptive one by means of conditioning process.

5. Group effects that arise from individuals' desire to be like, accepted, and approved of by others.

8. A group in an experiment that is not exposed to a treatment or does not experience a manipulation of the independent variable.

10. A learned attitude toward a target object, involving negative affect (dislike or fear), negative beliefs (stereotypes), that justify the attitude, and a behavioral intention to avoid, control, dominate, or eliminate the target object.

11. External stimulus or reward that motivates behavior although it does not related directly to biological needs.

DOWN

2. In operant conditioning, a pattern of delivering and withholding reinforcement.

3. A technique used in therapy to substitute a new response for a maladaptive one by means of conditioning process.

5. Group effects that arise from individuals' desire to be like, accepted, and approved of by others.

8. A group in an experiment that is not exposed to a treatment or does not experience a manipulation of the independent variable.

10. A learned attitude toward a target object, involving negative affect (dislike or fear), negative beliefs (stereotypes), that justify the attitude, and a behavioral intention to avoid, control, dominate, or eliminate the target object.

11. External stimulus or reward that motivates behavior although it does not related directly to biological needs.

A. Counterconditioning
D. Control group
G. Normative influence
J. Reflex

B. Case study
E. Motivation
H. Neuron
K. Schedules of reinforcement

C. Prejudice
F. Incentive
I. Axon

51. *Using the Across and Down clues, write the correct words in the numbered grid below.*

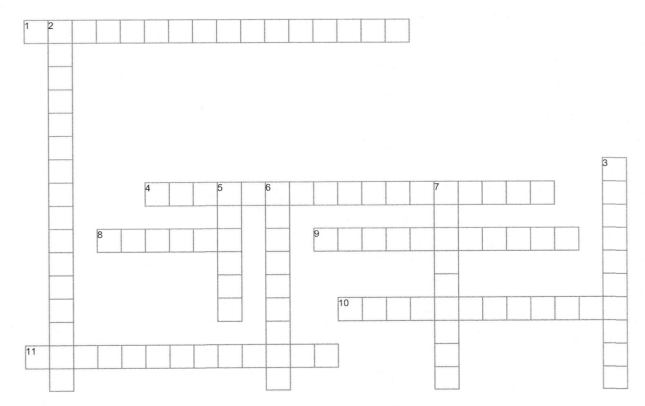

ACROSS

1. The branch of psychology that studies the effect of social variables on individual behavior, attitudes, perceptions, and motives.

4. The degree to which a test adequately measures an underlying construct.

8. A developmental disorder characterized by severe disruption of children's ability to form social bonds and use language.

9. The part of the limbic system that is involved in the acquisition of explicit memory.

10. The brain structure that serves as a relay station between the endocrine system and the CNS.

11. A severe form of psychopathology characterized by the breakdown of integrated personality functioning, withdrawal from reality, emotional distortions, and disturbed thoughts.

DOWN

1. The branch of psychology that studies the effect of social variables on individual behavior, attitudes, perceptions, and motives.

4. The degree to which a test adequately measures an underlying construct.

8. A developmental disorder characterized by severe disruption of children's ability to form social bonds and use language.

9. The part of the limbic system that is involved in the acquisition of explicit memory.

10. The brain structure that serves as a relay station between the endocrine system and the CNS.

11. A severe form of psychopathology characterized by the breakdown of integrated personality functioning, withdrawal from reality, emotional distortions, and disturbed thoughts.

A. Construct validity
B. Depressant
C. Sample
D. Incentive
E. Social psychology
F. Schizophrenia
G. Reasoning
H. Object permanence
I. Autism
J. Hippocampus
K. Hypothalamus

52. *Using the Across and Down clues, write the correct words in the numbered grid below.*

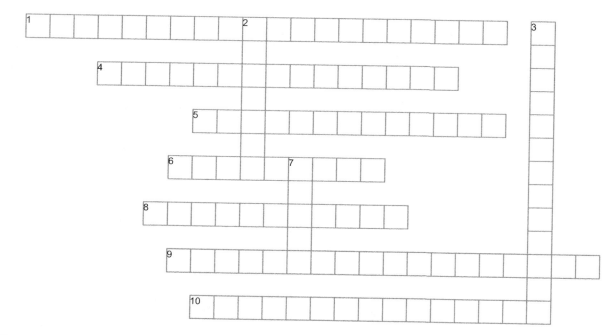

ACROSS

1. The hypothesis that the structure of the language and individual speaks has an impact on the way in which that individual thinks about the world.

4. Founded a psychology laboratory at Cornell University in 1892, student of Wilhelm Wundt.

5. The lifelong process whereby an individual's behavioral patterns, values, standards, skills, attitudes, and motives are shaped to conform to those regarded as desirable in a particular society.

6. Processes of knowing, including attending, remembering, and reasoning.

8. The part of the limbic system that is involved in the acquisition of explicit memory.

9. A research design in which the same participants are observed repeatedly, sometimes over many years.

10. The process by which people select, interpret, and remember social information.

DOWN

1. The hypothesis that the structure of the language and individual speaks has an impact on the way in which that individual thinks about the world.

4. Founded a psychology laboratory at Cornell University in 1892, student of Wilhelm Wundt.

5. The lifelong process whereby an individual's behavioral patterns, values, standards, skills, attitudes, and motives are shaped to conform to those regarded as desirable in a particular society.

6. Processes of knowing, including attending, remembering, and reasoning.

8. The part of the limbic system that is involved in the acquisition of explicit memory.

9. A research design in which the same participants are observed repeatedly, sometimes over many years.

10. The process by which people select, interpret, and remember social information.

A. Trait
E. Hallucination
I. CAT Scan

B. Cognition
F. Linguistic relativity
J. Edward Titchener

C. Hippocampus
G. Longitudinal design

D. Socialization
H. Social cognition

53. *Using the Across and Down clues, write the correct words in the numbered grid below.*

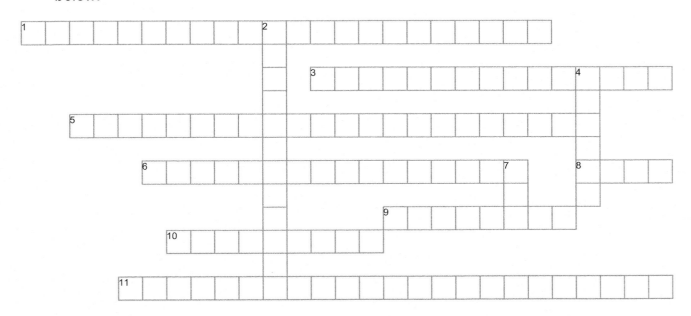

ACROSS

1. Research conducted with human subjects in which the investigator interacts directly with the subjects.

3. The network of glands that manufacture and secrete hormones into the bloodstream.

5. The processes that put sensory information together to give the perception of a coherent scene over the whole visual field.

6. The receptors for this information are tiny hairs in fluid-filled sacs and canals in the inner ear.

8. A disorder of childhood characterized by inattention and hyperactivity-impulsivity.

9. The study of the inheritance of physical and psychological traits from ancestors.

10. Cognitive strategies, or "rules of thumb," often used as shortcuts in solving a complex inferential task.

11. The subdivision of the ANS that monitors the routine operation of the body's internal functions and conserves and restores body energy.

DOWN

1. Research conducted with human subjects in which the investigator interacts directly with the subjects.

3. The network of glands that manufacture and secrete hormones into the bloodstream.

5. The processes that put sensory information together to give the perception of a coherent scene over the whole visual field.

6. The receptors for this information are tiny hairs in fluid-filled sacs and canals in the inner ear.

8. A disorder of childhood characterized by inattention and hyperactivity-impulsivity.

9. The study of the inheritance of physical and psychological traits from ancestors.

10. Cognitive strategies, or "rules of thumb," often used as shortcuts in solving a complex inferential task.

11. The subdivision of the ANS that monitors the routine operation of the body's internal functions and conserves and restores body energy.

A. Somnambulism
B. Genetics
C. Vestibular system
D. Syntax
E. Endocrine system
F. Parasympathetic division
G. Perceptual organization
H. ADHD
I. MRI
J. Clinical research method
K. Heuristic

54. *Using the Across and Down clues, write the correct words in the numbered grid below.*

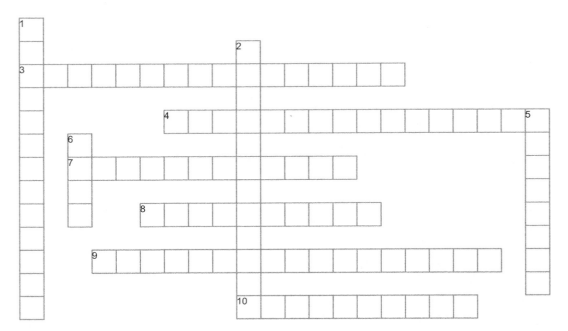

ACROSS

3. The period of rest during which a new nerve impulse cannot be activated in a segment of an axon.

4. Process that does not require attention; it can often be performed along with other tasks without interference.

7. A cognitive theory of work motivation that proposes that workers are motivated to maintain fair and equitable relationships with other relevant persons.

8. The entire set of individuals to which generalizations will be made based on an experimental sample.

9. A group in an experiment that is exposed to a treatment or experiences a manipulation of the independent variable.

10. A generalized evaluative attitude toward the self that influences both moods and behavior and that exerts a powerful effect on a range of personal and social behaviors.

DOWN

3. The period of rest during which a new nerve impulse cannot be activated in a segment of an axon.

4. Process that does not require attention; it can often be performed along with other tasks without interference.

7. A cognitive theory of work motivation that proposes that workers are motivated to maintain fair and equitable relationships with other relevant persons.

8. The entire set of individuals to which generalizations will be made based on an experimental sample.

9. A group in an experiment that is exposed to a treatment or experiences a manipulation of the independent variable.

10. A generalized evaluative attitude toward the self that influences both moods and behavior and that exerts a powerful effect on a range of personal and social behaviors.

A. Experimental group
B. Equity theory
C. Refractory period
D. Self esteem
E. Superego
F. Gene
G. Population
H. Variable ratio
I. Automatic process
J. Hypothalamus

55. *Using the Across and Down clues, write the correct words in the numbered grid below.*

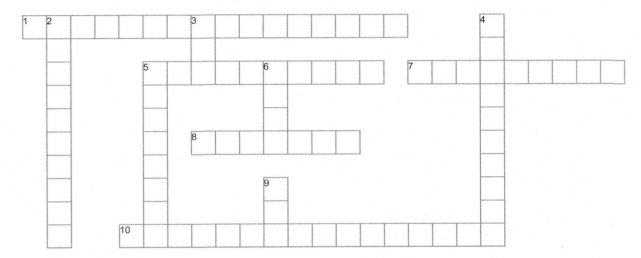

ACROSS

1. The period of rest during which a new nerve impulse cannot be activated in a segment of an axon.

5. A form of consciousness alteration designed to enhance self-knowledge and well-being by achieving a deep state of tranquility.

7. The study of the sounds that are put together to form words.

8. An individual's discomfort and

10. Sexual arousal is the motivational state of excitement and tension brought about by physiological and cognitive reactions to erotic stimuli.

DOWN

1. The period of rest during which a new nerve impulse cannot be activated in a segment of an axon.

5. A form of consciousness alteration designed to enhance self-knowledge and well-being by achieving a deep state of tranquility.

7. The study of the sounds that are put together to form words.

8. An individual's discomfort and

10. Sexual arousal is the motivational state of excitement and tension brought about by physiological and cognitive reactions to erotic stimuli.

A. LTM
E. OCD
I. Phonology

B. Centration
F. Axon
J. Sexual motivation

C. Shyness
G. Expectancy
K. Menarche

D. Refractory period
H. Meditation

56. *Using the Across and Down clues, write the correct words in the numbered grid below.*

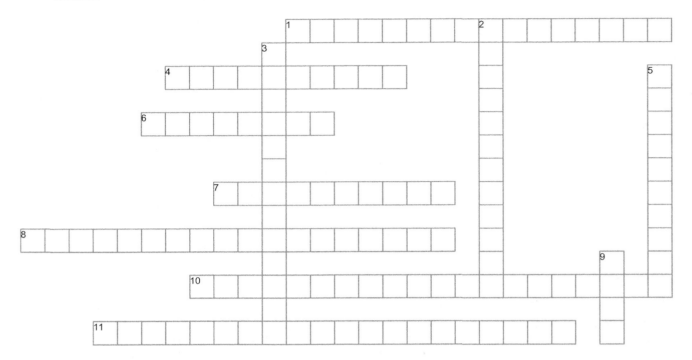

ACROSS

1. Chemical messenger released from a neuron that crosses the synapse from one neuron to another, stimulating the postsynaptic neuron.

4. The extent to which people believe that their behaviors situations will bring about rewards.

6. The process of reconfiguring items by grouping based on similarity or some other organizing principle.

7. Drug that depresses or slows down the activity of the central nervous system.

8. Attempts to establish general laws and generalizations, and seeks to obtain objective knowledge through scientific methods.

10. The development of processes of knowing, including imagining, perceiving, reasoning, and problem solving.

11. A personality disorder marked by a disturbance in the integration of identity, memory, or consciousness.

DOWN

1. Chemical messenger released from a neuron that crosses the synapse from one neuron to another, stimulating the postsynaptic neuron.

4. The extent to which people believe that their behaviors situations will bring about rewards.

6. The process of reconfiguring items by grouping based on similarity or some other organizing principle.

7. Drug that depresses or slows down the activity of the central nervous system.

8. Attempts to establish general laws and generalizations, and seeks to obtain objective knowledge through scientific methods.

10. The development of processes of knowing, including imagining, perceiving, reasoning, and problem solving.

11. A personality disorder marked by a disturbance in the integration of identity, memory, or consciousness.

A. Nomothetic research   B. Chunking   C. Empiricist
D. Neurotransmitter   E. Dissociative disorder F. Fear
G. Neuroscience   H. Depressant   I. Schizophrenia
J. Cognitive development   K. Expectancy

57. *Using the Across and Down clues, write the correct words in the numbered grid below.*

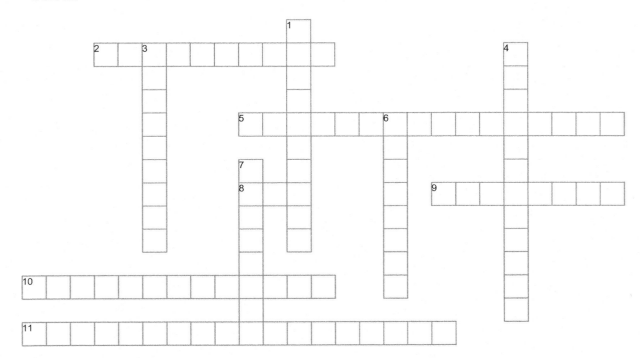

ACROSS

2. The age-related physical and behavioral changes characteristic of a species; the process of growth typical of all members of a species who are reared in the specie's usual habitat.

5. A disorder defined by a large discrepancy between individuals' measured IQ and their actual performance.

8. The reality-based aspect of the self that arbitrates the conflict between id impulses and superego demands.

9. According to Freud, a state in which a person remains attached to objects or activities more appropriate for an earlier stage of psychosexual development.

10. An anxiety disorder in which sufferers experience unexpected, severe panic attacks that begin with a feeling of intense apprehension, fear, or terror.

11. A disorder in which people have physical illnesses or complaints that cannot be fully explained by actual medical conditions.

DOWN

2. The age-related physical and behavioral changes characteristic of a species; the process of growth typical of all members of a species who are reared in the specie's usual habitat.

5. A disorder defined by a large discrepancy between individuals' measured IQ and their actual performance.

8. The reality-based aspect of the self that arbitrates the conflict between id impulses and superego demands.

9. According to Freud, a state in which a person remains attached to objects or activities more appropriate for an earlier stage of psychosexual development.

10. An anxiety disorder in which sufferers experience unexpected, severe panic attacks that begin with a feeling of intense apprehension, fear, or terror.

11. A disorder in which people have physical illnesses or complaints that cannot be fully explained by actual medical conditions.

A. Nativist   B. Learning disorder   C. Teratogen   D. Fixation
E. Panic disorder   F. Somatoform disorder   G. Ego   H. Hypothalamus
I. Social role   J. Cerebrum   K. Maturation

58. *Using the Across and Down clues, write the correct words in the numbered grid below.*

ACROSS

2. A type of learning in which a behavior (conditioned response) comes to be elicited by a stimulus (conditioned stimulus).

3. A general treatment strategy involving changing behavior by modifying its consequences.

4. The approach to identifying causes of behavior that focuses on the functioning of the genes, the brain, the nervous system, and the endocrine system.

6. A generalized evaluative attitude toward the self that influences both moods and behavior and that exerts a powerful effect on a range of personal and social behaviors.

8. The negative reaction of people to an individual or group because of some assumed inferiority or source of difference that is degraded.

9. A disorder in which psychological conflict or stress brings about loss of motor or sensory function.

DOWN

2. A type of learning in which a behavior (conditioned response) comes to be elicited by a stimulus (conditioned stimulus).

3. A general treatment strategy involving changing behavior by modifying its consequences.

4. The approach to identifying causes of behavior that focuses on the functioning of the genes, the brain, the nervous system, and the endocrine system.

6. A generalized evaluative attitude toward the self that influences both moods and behavior and that exerts a powerful effect on a range of personal and social behaviors.

8. The negative reaction of people to an individual or group because of some assumed inferiority or source of difference that is degraded.

9. A disorder in which psychological conflict or stress brings about loss of motor or sensory function.

A. Contingency management
D. Synapse
G. Biological
J. Conversion disorder

B. Classical conditioning
E. Self esteem
H. Edward Titchener

C. Sample
F. Groupthink
I. Stigma

59. *Using the Across and Down clues, write the correct words in the numbered grid below.*

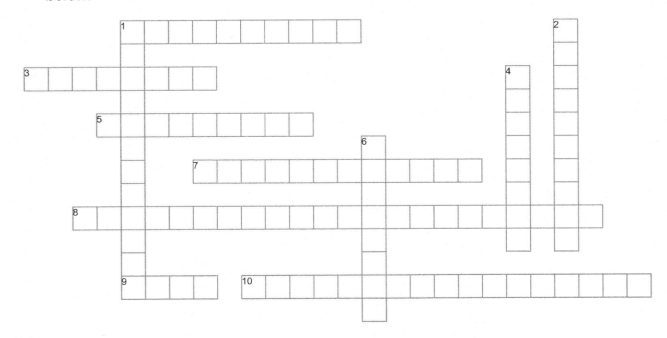

ACROSS

1. A thread-like structure found in the nucleus of cells and made of protein and DNA

3. A process based on experience that results in a relatively permanent change in behavior or behavioral potential.

5. The brain structure that regulates the body's basic life processes.

7. A disorder that causes sleep walking.

8. Research effort designed to describe what is characteristic of a specific age or developmental stage.

9. Posttraumatic stress disorder. An anxiety disorder characterized by the persistent re-experience of those traumatic events through distressing recollections, dreams, hallucinations, or flashbacks.

10. An aspect of creativity characterized by an ability to produce unusual but appropriate response to problems.

DOWN

1. A thread-like structure found in the nucleus of cells and made of protein and DNA

3. A process based on experience that results in a relatively permanent change in behavior or behavioral potential.

5. The brain structure that regulates the body's basic life processes.

7. A disorder that causes sleep walking.

8. Research effort designed to describe what is characteristic of a specific age or developmental stage.

9. Posttraumatic stress disorder. An anxiety disorder characterized by the persistent re-experience of those traumatic events through distressing recollections, dreams, hallucinations, or flashbacks.

10. An aspect of creativity characterized by an ability to produce unusual but appropriate response to problems.

A. PTSD
D. Superego
G. Learning
J. Maturation

B. Normative investigation
E. Control group
H. Divergent thinking
K. Brain stem

C. Somnambulism
F. Chromosome
I. Heredity

60. *Using the Across and Down clues, write the correct words in the numbered grid below.*

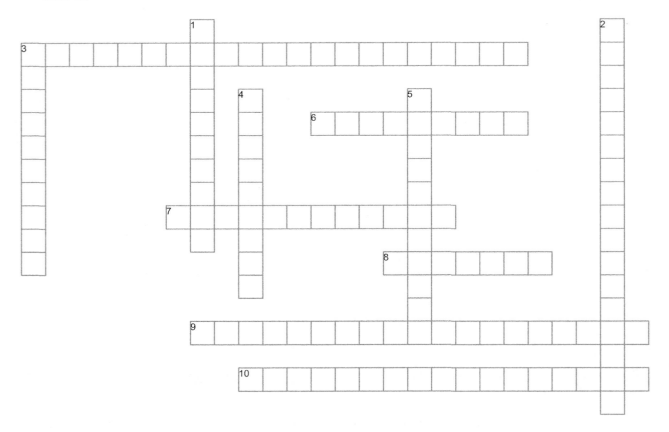

ACROSS

3. A general treatment strategy involving changing behavior by modifying its consequences.

6. Blind obedience is less a product of dispositional characteristics than the outcome of situational forces that could engulf anyone. (Milgram studies)

7. The global capacity to profit from experience and to go beyond given information about the environment.

8. A complex pattern of changes, including physiological arousal, feelings, cognitive processes, and behavioral reactions, made in response to a situation perceived to be personally significant.

9. Availability of information through memory processes without conscious effort to encode or recover information.

10. A biologically determined reinforcer, such as food and water.

DOWN

3. A general treatment strategy involving changing behavior by modifying its consequences.

6. Blind obedience is less a product of dispositional characteristics than the outcome of situational forces that could engulf anyone. (Milgram studies)

7. The global capacity to profit from experience and to go beyond given information about the environment.

8. A complex pattern of changes, including physiological arousal, feelings, cognitive processes, and behavioral reactions, made in response to a situation perceived to be personally significant.

9. Availability of information through memory processes without conscious effort to encode or recover information.

10. A biologically determined reinforcer, such as food and water.

A. Hippocampus
D. Depressant
G. Implicit use of memory
J. Contingency management

B. Obedience
E. Inference
H. Emotion
K. Primary reinforcer

C. Creativity
F. Intelligence
I. Psychotic disorder

61. *Using the Across and Down clues, write the correct words in the numbered grid below.*

ACROSS

3. The study of the inheritance of physical and psychological traits from ancestors.

4. The mental capacity to encode, store, and retrieve information.

6. The label given to psychological abnormality by classifying and categorizing the observed behavior pattern into an approved diagnostic system.

8. The negative reaction of people to an individual or group because of some assumed inferiority or source of difference that is degraded.

9. Distinct patter of personality characteristics used to assign people to categories; qualitative differences, rather than differences in degree, used to discriminate among people.

10. Posttraumatic stress disorder. An anxiety disorder characterized by the persistent re-experience of those traumatic events through distressing recollections, dreams, hallucinations, or flashbacks.

DOWN

3. The study of the inheritance of physical and psychological traits from ancestors.

4. The mental capacity to encode, store, and retrieve information.

6. The label given to psychological abnormality by classifying and categorizing the observed behavior pattern into an approved diagnostic system.

8. The negative reaction of people to an individual or group because of some assumed inferiority or source of difference that is degraded.

9. Distinct patter of personality characteristics used to assign people to categories; qualitative differences, rather than differences in degree, used to discriminate among people.

10. Posttraumatic stress disorder. An anxiety disorder characterized by the persistent re-experience of those traumatic events through distressing recollections, dreams, hallucinations, or flashbacks.

A. Stigma
D. Cochlea
G. Psychological diagnosis
J. Genetics

B. Retina
E. Opiate
H. PTSD
K. Personality type

C. Shyness
F. Structuralism
I. Memory

62. *Using the Across and Down clues, write the correct words in the numbered grid below.*

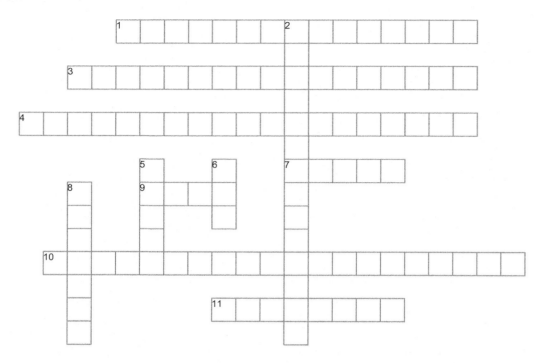

ACROSS

1. The sense that tells how one's own body is oriented in the world with respect to gravity.

3. Centers around the concept of a whole person in the continual process of changing and of becoming.

4. A measure of reliability; the degree to which a test yields similar scores across its different parts, such as odd versus even items.

7. A particular description of a choice; the perspective from which a choice is described or framed affects how a decision is made and which option is ultimately exercised.

9. Behavioral guideline for acting in a certain way in a certain instance.

10. A statistical estimate of the degree of inheritance of a given trait or behavior, asses by the degree of similarity between individuals who vary in their extent of genetic similarity.

11. The study of the causes and factors leading to the development of a disorder.

DOWN

1. The sense that tells how one's own body is oriented in the world with respect to gravity.

3. Centers around the concept of a whole person in the continual process of changing and of becoming.

4. A measure of reliability; the degree to which a test yields similar scores across its different parts, such as odd versus even items.

7. A particular description of a choice; the perspective from which a choice is described or framed affects how a decision is made and which option is ultimately exercised.

9. Behavioral guideline for acting in a certain way in a certain instance.

10. A statistical estimate of the degree of inheritance of a given trait or behavior, asses by the degree of similarity between individuals who vary in their extent of genetic similarity.

11. The study of the causes and factors leading to the development of a disorder.

A. Humanistic therapy   B. Amnesia   C. Etiology   D. Vestibular sense
E. Internal consistency   F. Heritability estimate   G. Locus of control   H. Frame
I. Rule   J. EEG   K. Trait

63. *Using the Across and Down clues, write the correct words in the numbered grid below.*

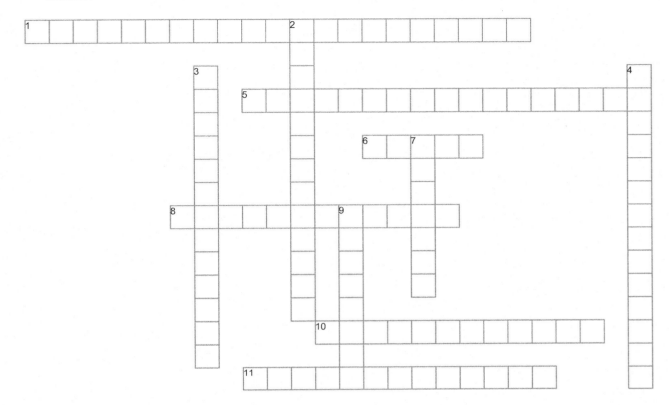

ACROSS

1. A summary of how frequently each score appears in a set of observations.

5. The aspect of intelligence that involves the ability to see complex relationships and solve problems; measured by tests of block designs and spatial visualization.

6. A particular description of a choice; the perspective from which a choice is described or framed affects how a decision is made and which option is ultimately exercised.

8. Author of "The Principles of Psychology."

10. The relative influence of genetics versus environment in determining patterns of behavior.

11. The perspective on mind and behavior that focuses on the examination of their functions in an organism's interactions with the environment.

DOWN

1. A summary of how frequently each score appears in a set of observations.

5. The aspect of intelligence that involves the ability to see complex relationships and solve problems; measured by tests of block designs and spatial visualization.

6. A particular description of a choice; the perspective from which a choice is described or framed affects how a decision is made and which option is ultimately exercised.

8. Author of "The Principles of Psychology."

10. The relative influence of genetics versus environment in determining patterns of behavior.

11. The perspective on mind and behavior that focuses on the examination of their functions in an organism's interactions with the environment.

A. Judgment
D. Hallucination
G. Amnesia
J. Fluid intelligence

B. Functionalism
E. Frame
H. Structuralism
K. Heritability

C. Frequency distribution
F. William James
I. Gestalt therapy

64. *Using the Across and Down clues, write the correct words in the numbered grid below.*

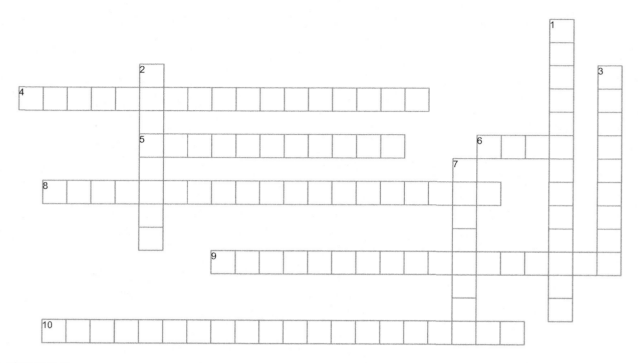

ACROSS

4. Severe mental disorder in which a person experiences impairment manifested through thought, emotional, or perceptual difficulties.

5. An extreme fear of being in public places or open spaces from which escape may be difficult or embarrassing.

6. The cell body of a neuron, containing the nucleus and cytoplasm.

8. The bodily changes, maturation, and growth that occur in an organism starting with conception and continuing across the life span.

9. The tendency for groups to make decisions that are more extreme than the decisions that would be made by the members acting alone.

10. The part of the nervous system consisting of the brain and spinal cord.

DOWN

4. Severe mental disorder in which a person experiences impairment manifested through thought, emotional, or perceptual difficulties.

5. An extreme fear of being in public places or open spaces from which escape may be difficult or embarrassing.

6. The cell body of a neuron, containing the nucleus and cytoplasm.

8. The bodily changes, maturation, and growth that occur in an organism starting with conception and continuing across the life span.

9. The tendency for groups to make decisions that are more extreme than the decisions that would be made by the members acting alone.

10. The part of the nervous system consisting of the brain and spinal cord.

A. Soma
D. Group polarization
G. Instinct
J. Morality

B. Central traits
E. Central nervous system
H. Psychotic disorder

C. Agoraphobia
F. Cognition
I. Physical development

65. *Using the Across and Down clues, write the correct words in the numbered grid below.*

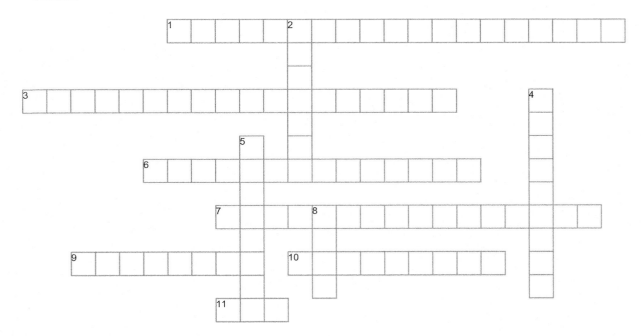

ACROSS

1. The principle that subsequent retrieval of information is enhanced if cues received at the time of recall are consistent with those present at the time of encoding.

3. A disorder in which psychological conflict or stress brings about loss of motor or sensory function.

6. A method of personality assessment in which an individual is presented with a standardized set of ambiguous, abstract stimuli and asked to interpret their meanings.

7. The systematic procedures and measurement instruments used by trained professionals to assess and individual's functioning, aptitudes, abilities, or mental states.

9. The extent to which a test measures what it was intended to measure.

10. The study of the sounds that are put together to form words.

11. Rapid eye movements. A behavioral sign of the phase of sleep during which the sleeper is likely to be experiencing dreamlike mental activity.

DOWN

1. The principle that subsequent retrieval of information is enhanced if cues received at the time of recall are consistent with those present at the time of encoding.

3. A disorder in which psychological conflict or stress brings about loss of motor or sensory function.

6. A method of personality assessment in which an individual is presented with a standardized set of ambiguous, abstract stimuli and asked to interpret their meanings.

7. The systematic procedures and measurement instruments used by trained professionals to assess and individual's functioning, aptitudes, abilities, or mental states.

9. The extent to which a test measures what it was intended to measure.

10. The study of the sounds that are put together to form words.

11. Rapid eye movements. A behavioral sign of the phase of sleep during which the sleeper is likely to be experiencing dreamlike mental activity.

A. Encoding specificity   B. Phonology   C. Obedience   D. Formal assessment
E. Insight   F. Validity   G. Projective test   H. Conversion disorder
I. REM   J. ADHD   K. Genotype

66. *Using the Across and Down clues, write the correct words in the numbered grid below.*

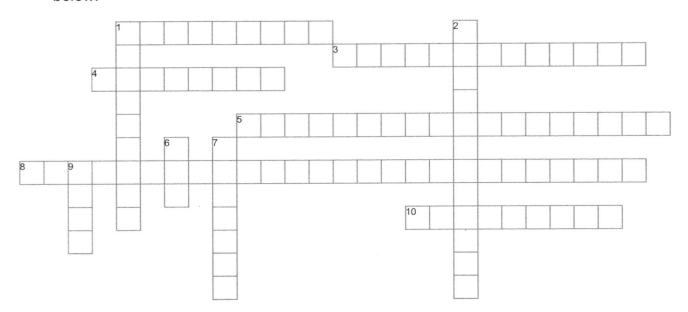

ACROSS

1. The observable characteristics of an organism, resulting from the interaction between the organism's genotype and its environment.

3. The field of psychology that specializes in mental testing.

4. The region of the brain that regulates higher cognitive and emotional functions.

5. What people say, sign, and write, as well as the processes the go through to produce these messages.

8. A therapeutic approach that combines the cognitive emphasis on thoughts and attitudes with the behavioral emphasis on changing performance.

10. Environmental factors such as diseases and drugs that cause structural abnormalities in a developing fetus.

DOWN

1. The observable characteristics of an organism, resulting from the interaction between the organism's genotype and its environment.

3. The field of psychology that specializes in mental testing.

4. The region of the brain that regulates higher cognitive and emotional functions.

5. What people say, sign, and write, as well as the processes the go through to produce these messages.

8. A therapeutic approach that combines the cognitive emphasis on thoughts and attitudes with the behavioral emphasis on changing performance.

10. Environmental factors such as diseases and drugs that cause structural abnormalities in a developing fetus.

A. Phenotype
D. DID
G. Psychometrics
J. Gene

B. Prejudice
E. Cerebrum
H. Teratogen
K. Control group

C. Language production
F. PET scan
I. Cognitive behavioral therapy

67. *Using the Across and Down clues, write the correct words in the numbered grid below.*

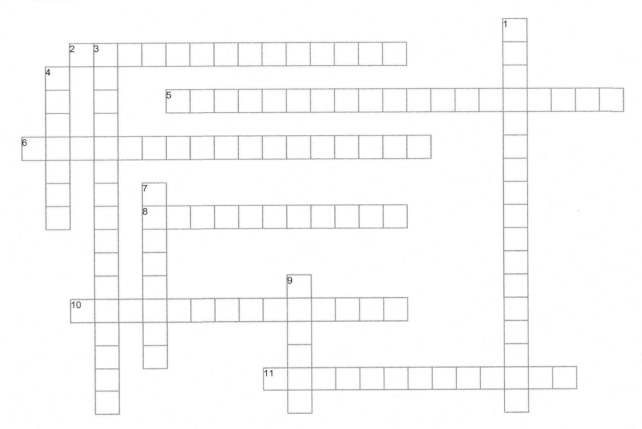

ACROSS

2. Thinking that is directed toward solving specific problems and that moves from an initial state to a goal state by means of a set of mental operations.

5. Availability of information through memory processes without conscious effort to encode or recover information.

6. Centers around the concept of a whole person in the continual process of changing and of becoming.

8. The domain of the psyche that stores repressed urges and primitive impulses.

10. The process of choosing between alternatives; selecting or rejecting available options.

11. The center where odor-sensitive receptors send their signals, located just below the frontal lobes of the cortex.

DOWN

2. Thinking that is directed toward solving specific problems and that moves from an initial state to a goal state by means of a set of mental operations.

5. Availability of information through memory processes without conscious effort to encode or recover information.

6. Centers around the concept of a whole person in the continual process of changing and of becoming.

8. The domain of the psyche that stores repressed urges and primitive impulses.

10. The process of choosing between alternatives; selecting or rejecting available options.

11. The center where odor-sensitive receptors send their signals, located just below the frontal lobes of the cortex.

A. Medulla
D. Implicit use of memory
G. Humanistic therapy
J. Problem solving

B. Humanist
E. Unconscious
H. Decision making
K. Olfactory bulb

C. Sample
F. Refractory period
I. Experimental group

68. *Using the Across and Down clues, write the correct words in the numbered grid below.*

ACROSS

1. A membrane running along the length of the cochlea.
3. The network of glands that manufacture and secrete hormones into the bloodstream.
4. The genetic information for an organism, stored in the DNA of its chromosomes.
8. Process that does not require attention; it can often be performed along with other tasks without interference.
9. Brain neuron that relays massages from sensory neurons to other interneurons or to motor neurons.
10. A socially defined pattern of behavior that is expected of a person who is functioning in a given setting or group.

DOWN

1. A membrane running along the length of the cochlea.
3. The network of glands that manufacture and secrete hormones into the bloodstream.
4. The genetic information for an organism, stored in the DNA of its chromosomes.
8. Process that does not require attention; it can often be performed along with other tasks without interference.
9. Brain neuron that relays massages from sensory neurons to other interneurons or to motor neurons.
10. A socially defined pattern of behavior that is expected of a person who is functioning in a given setting or group.

A. Neuron
B. Scheme
C. Social role
D. Automatic process
E. Genetics
F. Interneuron
G. Genome
H. Repression
I. Basilar membrane
J. Endocrine system

69. *Using the Across and Down clues, write the correct words in the numbered grid below.*

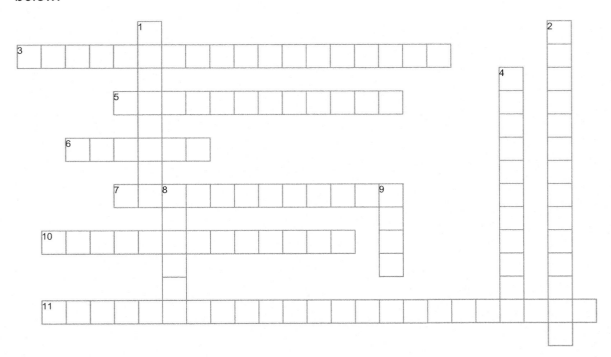

ACROSS

3. The branch of psychology that investigates the effects of drugs on behavior.

5. A drug that alters cognitions and perceptions and causes hallucinations.

6. The layer at the back of the eye that contains photoreceptors and converts light energy to neural responses.

7. The brain structure that regulates motivated behavior and homeostasis.

10. The field of psychology that specializes in mental testing.

11. A research technique in which unobtrusive observations are made of behaviors that occur in natural environments.

DOWN

3. The branch of psychology that investigates the effects of drugs on behavior.

5. A drug that alters cognitions and perceptions and causes hallucinations.

6. The layer at the back of the eye that contains photoreceptors and converts light energy to neural responses.

7. The brain structure that regulates motivated behavior and homeostasis.

10. The field of psychology that specializes in mental testing.

11. A research technique in which unobtrusive observations are made of behaviors that occur in natural environments.

A. Psychopharmacology
D. Self concept
G. Hypothalamus
J. Morality

B. Naturalistic observation
E. Hallucinogen
H. Soma
K. Psychometrics

C. Locus of control
F. Phobia
I. Retina

70. *Using the Across and Down clues, write the correct words in the numbered grid below.*

ACROSS

3. Sometimes necessary when revealing certain information to the patient would bias the results.

6. A form of consciousness alteration designed to enhance self-knowledge and well-being by achieving a deep state of tranquility.

7. Founded a psychology laboratory at Cornell University in 1892, student of Wilhelm Wundt.

8. The scientific study of the brain and of the links between brain activity and behavior.

9. The area of psychology that focuses on the environmental determinants of learning and behavior.

10. Brain neuron that relays massages from sensory neurons to other interneurons or to motor neurons.

11. A behavior emitted by an organism that can be characterized in terms of the observable effects it has on the environment.

DOWN

3. Sometimes necessary when revealing certain information to the patient would bias the results.

6. A form of consciousness alteration designed to enhance self-knowledge and well-being by achieving a deep state of tranquility.

7. Founded a psychology laboratory at Cornell University in 1892, student of Wilhelm Wundt.

8. The scientific study of the brain and of the links between brain activity and behavior.

9. The area of psychology that focuses on the environmental determinants of learning and behavior.

10. Brain neuron that relays massages from sensory neurons to other interneurons or to motor neurons.

11. A behavior emitted by an organism that can be characterized in terms of the observable effects it has on the environment.

A. Operant   B. Behavior analysis   C. Attention   D. Family therapy
E. Neuroscience   F. Compliance   G. Conservation   H. Interneuron
I. Edward Titchener J. Intentional deception K. Meditation

71. *Using the Across and Down clues, write the correct words in the numbered grid below.*

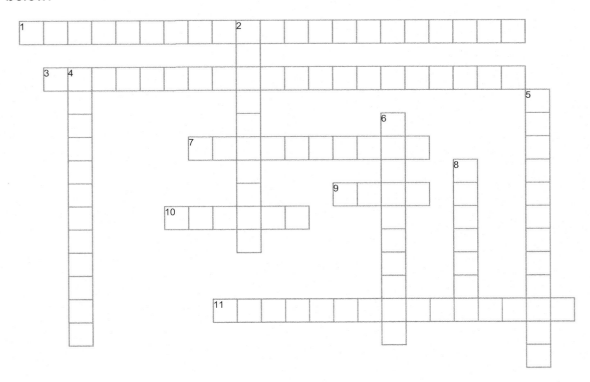

ACROSS

1. A general treatment strategy involving changing behavior by modifying its consequences.

3. Type of therapy that assumes that a patient's problems have been caused by the psychological tension between unconscious impulses and the constraints of his or her life situation.

7. Deliberate efforts to change attitudes.

9. The cells that hold neurons together and facilitate neural transmission, remove damaged and dead neurons, and prevent poisonous substances in the blood from reaching the brain.

10. The way in which words are strung together to form sentences.

11. The therapeutic method in which a patient gives a running account of thoughts, wishes, physical sensations, and mental images as the occur.

DOWN

1. A general treatment strategy involving changing behavior by modifying its consequences.

3. Type of therapy that assumes that a patient's problems have been caused by the psychological tension between unconscious impulses and the constraints of his or her life situation.

7. Deliberate efforts to change attitudes.

9. The cells that hold neurons together and facilitate neural transmission, remove damaged and dead neurons, and prevent poisonous substances in the blood from reaching the brain.

10. The way in which words are strung together to form sentences.

11. The therapeutic method in which a patient gives a running account of thoughts, wishes, physical sensations, and mental images as the occur.

A. Conformity
B. Motivation
C. Medulla
D. Glia
E. Free association
F. Somnambulism
G. Syntax
H. Persuasion
I. Contingency management
J. Iconic memory
K. Psychodynamic therapy

72. *Using the Across and Down clues, write the correct words in the numbered grid below.*

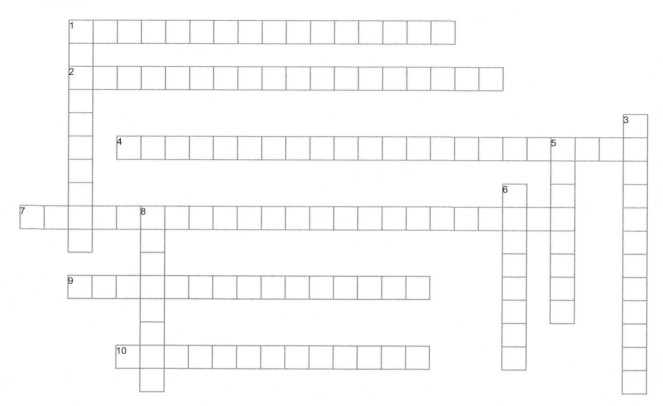

ACROSS

1. The process of developing, in anticipation of failure, behavioral reactions and explanations that minimize ability deficits as possible attributions for the failure

2. A disorder in which psychological conflict or stress brings about loss of motor or sensory function.

4. A prediction made about some future behavior or event that modifies interactions to produce what is expected.

7. The part of the nervous system composed of the spinal and cranial nerves that connect the body's sensory receptors to the CNS and the CNS to the muscles and glands.

9. Founded a psychology laboratory at Cornell University in 1892, student of Wilhelm Wundt.

10. A surgical procedure performed on brain tissue to alleviate a psychological disorder.

DOWN

1. The process of developing, in anticipation of failure, behavioral reactions and explanations that minimize ability deficits as possible attributions for the failure

2. A disorder in which psychological conflict or stress brings about loss of motor or sensory function.

4. A prediction made about some future behavior or event that modifies interactions to produce what is expected.

7. The part of the nervous system composed of the spinal and cranial nerves that connect the body's sensory receptors to the CNS and the CNS to the muscles and glands.

9. Founded a psychology laboratory at Cornell University in 1892, student of Wilhelm Wundt.

10. A surgical procedure performed on brain tissue to alleviate a psychological disorder.

A. Self fulfilling prophecy
D. Hormones
G. Humanist
J. Peripheral nervous system

B. Psychosurgery
E. Hypothalamus
H. Attitude
K. Edward Titchener

C. Social norm
F. Conversion disorder
I. Self handicapping

73. *Using the Across and Down clues, write the correct words in the numbered grid below.*

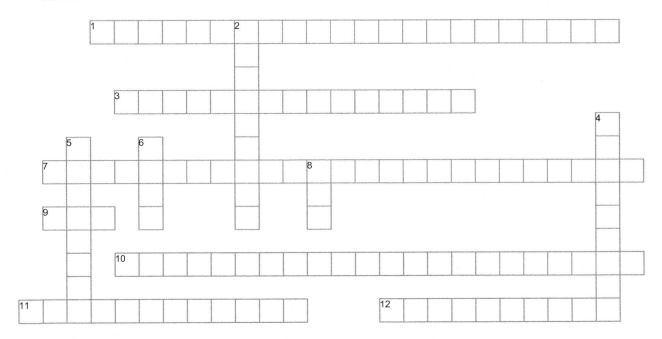

ACROSS

1. The psychological perspective primarily concerned with observable behavior that can be objectively recorded.

3. A mood disorder characterized by alternating periods of depression and mania.

7. A behavioral therapy technique in which a client is taught to prevent the arousal of anxiety by confronting the feared stimulus while relaxed.

9. The physical basis for the transmission of genetic information.

10. Is goal directed, and cognition based carried out with premeditated thought to achieve specific aims.

11. One of the ideal selves that a person would like to become, the selves a person could become, and the selves a person is afraid of becoming; components of the cognitive sense of self.

12. The tendency for people to adopt the behaviors, attitudes, and values of the members of a reference group.

DOWN

1. The psychological perspective primarily concerned with observable behavior that can be objectively recorded.

3. A mood disorder characterized by alternating periods of depression and mania.

7. A behavioral therapy technique in which a client is taught to prevent the arousal of anxiety by confronting the feared stimulus while relaxed.

9. The physical basis for the transmission of genetic information.

10. Is goal directed, and cognition based carried out with premeditated thought to achieve specific aims.

11. One of the ideal selves that a person would like to become, the selves a person could become, and the selves a person is afraid of becoming; components of the cognitive sense of self.

12. The tendency for people to adopt the behaviors, attitudes, and values of the members of a reference group.

A. ECT
D. Olfaction
G. Behaviorist perspective
J. Phonology

B. DNA
E. Systematic desensitization
H. Bipolar disorder
K. Hypnosis

C. Instrumental aggression
F. Possible self
I. Gene
L. Conformity

74. Using the Across and Down clues, write the correct words in the numbered grid below.

ACROSS

1. A severe form of psychopathology characterized by the breakdown of integrated personality functioning, withdrawal from reality, emotional distortions, and disturbed thoughts.
4. Conscious effort to encode or recover information through memory processes.
6. A mood disturbance such as severe depression or depression alternating with mania.
7. The subdivision of the PNS that controls the body's involuntary motor responses.
8. One's sense of maleness or femaleness; usually includes awareness and acceptance of one's biological sex.
9. The part of the nervous system consisting of the brain and spinal cord.

DOWN

1. A severe form of psychopathology characterized by the breakdown of integrated personality functioning, withdrawal from reality, emotional distortions, and disturbed thoughts.
4. Conscious effort to encode or recover information through memory processes.
6. A mood disturbance such as severe depression or depression alternating with mania.
7. The subdivision of the PNS that controls the body's involuntary motor responses.
8. One's sense of maleness or femaleness; usually includes awareness and acceptance of one's biological sex.
9. The part of the nervous system consisting of the brain and spinal cord.

A. Mental set
D. Gender identity
G. Mood disorder
J. Cognitive

B. Explicit use of memory
E. Retina
H. Autonomic nervous system

C. Compliance
F. Schizophrenia
I. Central nervous system

75. *Using the Across and Down clues, write the correct words in the numbered grid below.*

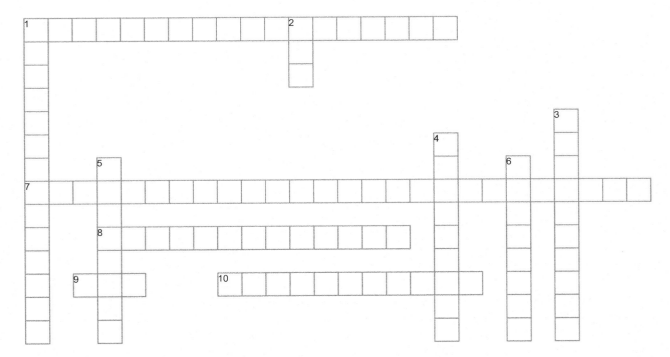

ACROSS

1. The assumption that mental and behavioral reactions are determined by previous experiences.

7. A therapeutic approach that combines the cognitive emphasis on thoughts and attitudes with the behavioral emphasis on changing performance.

8. The center where odor-sensitive receptors send their signals, located just below the frontal lobes of the cortex.

9. The physical basis for the transmission of genetic information.

10. The psychological qualities of an individual that influence a variety of characteristic behavior patterns across different situations and over time.

DOWN

1. The assumption that mental and behavioral reactions are determined by previous experiences.

7. A therapeutic approach that combines the cognitive emphasis on thoughts and attitudes with the behavioral emphasis on changing performance.

8. The center where odor-sensitive receptors send their signals, located just below the frontal lobes of the cortex.

9. The physical basis for the transmission of genetic information.

10. The psychological qualities of an individual that influence a variety of characteristic behavior patterns across different situations and over time.

A. Brain stem
D. Personality
G. Aggression
J. Chunking

B. DNA
E. REM
H. Olfactory bulb
K. Cognitive behavioral therapy

C. Placebo control
F. Insomnia
I. Psychic determinism

76. *Using the Across and Down clues, write the correct words in the numbered grid below.*

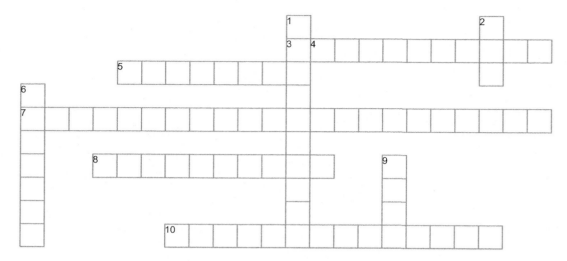

ACROSS

3. In cognitive development, the inability of a young child at the preoperational stage to take the perceptive of another person.

5. According to Freud, a state in which a person remains attached to objects or activities more appropriate for an earlier stage of psychosexual development.

7. The subdivision of the PNS that controls the body's involuntary motor responses.

8. The tendency for people to adopt the behaviors, attitudes, and values of the members of a reference group.

10. The process of shaping a message depending on the audience for which it is intended.

DOWN

3. In cognitive development, the inability of a young child at the preoperational stage to take the perceptive of another person.

5. According to Freud, a state in which a person remains attached to objects or activities more appropriate for an earlier stage of psychosexual development.

7. The subdivision of the PNS that controls the body's involuntary motor responses.

8. The tendency for people to adopt the behaviors, attitudes, and values of the members of a reference group.

10. The process of shaping a message depending on the audience for which it is intended.

A. DID
D. Centration
G. Conformity
J. Audience design

B. Egocentrism
E. Rule
H. Autonomic nervous system

C. CAT Scan
F. Fixation
I. G

77. *Using the Across and Down clues, write the correct words in the numbered grid below.*

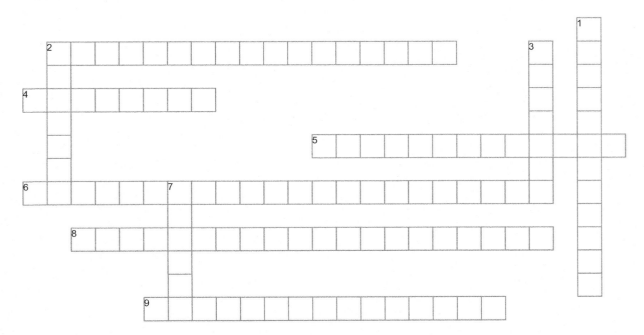

ACROSS

2. The diminishing responsiveness of sensory systems to prolonged stimulus input; allows a more rapid reaction to new (different) sources of information.

4. The capacity to make a full commitment - sexual, emotional, and moral - to another person.

5. One of the biologically based characteristics that distinguish males from females.

6. The psychological perspective primarily concerned with observable behavior that can be objectively recorded.

8. The development of processes of knowing, including imagining, perceiving, reasoning, and problem solving.

9. The sense that tells how one's own body is oriented in the world with respect to gravity.

DOWN

2. The diminishing responsiveness of sensory systems to prolonged stimulus input; allows a more rapid reaction to new (different) sources of information.

4. The capacity to make a full commitment - sexual, emotional, and moral - to another person.

5. One of the biologically based characteristics that distinguish males from females.

6. The psychological perspective primarily concerned with observable behavior that can be objectively recorded.

8. The development of processes of knowing, including imagining, perceiving, reasoning, and problem solving.

9. The sense that tells how one's own body is oriented in the world with respect to gravity.

A. Behaviorist perspective
D. Intimacy
G. Synapse
J. Iconic memory

B. Cognitive development
E. Opiate
H. Vestibular sense

C. Phoneme
F. Sex difference
I. Sensory adaptation

78. *Using the Across and Down clues, write the correct words in the numbered grid below.*

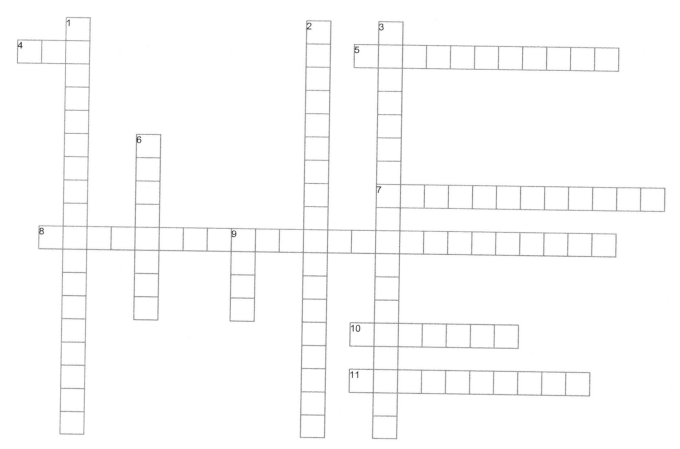

ACROSS

4. The reality-based aspect of the self that arbitrates the conflict between id impulses and superego demands.

5. The experience of more than one disorder at the same time.

7. Memory system in the visual domain that allows large amounts of information to be stored for very brief durations.

8. In operant conditioning, a pattern of delivering and withholding reinforcement.

10. An individual's discomfort and

11. A socially defined pattern of behavior that is expected of a person who is functioning in a given setting or group.

DOWN

4. The reality-based aspect of the self that arbitrates the conflict between id impulses and superego demands.

5. The experience of more than one disorder at the same time.

7. Memory system in the visual domain that allows large amounts of information to be stored for very brief durations.

8. In operant conditioning, a pattern of delivering and withholding reinforcement.

10. An individual's discomfort and

11. A socially defined pattern of behavior that is expected of a person who is functioning in a given setting or group.

A. Soma
D. Foundational theory
G. Amygdala
J. Social role

B. Schedules of reinforcement
E. Ego
H. Iconic memory
K. Language production

C. Comorbidity
F. Consistency paradox
I. Shyness

79. *Using the Across and Down clues, write the correct words in the numbered grid below.*

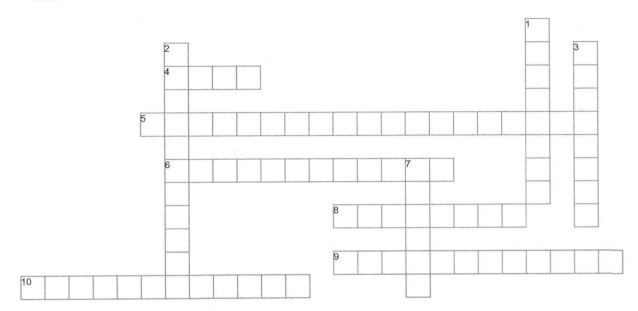

ACROSS

4. The extended fiber of a neuron through which nerve impulses travel from the soma to the terminal buttons.

5. Is a response elicited by some previously neutral stimulus that occurs as a result of pairing the neutral stimulus with an unconditioned stimulus.

6. A cognitive theory of work motivation that proposes that workers are motivated to maintain fair and equitable relationships with other relevant persons.

8. Preprogrammed tendency that is essential to a species' survival.

9. A disorder that causes sleep walking.

10. A commitment beyond one's self and one's partner to family, work, society, and future generations; typically, a crucial state in development in one's 30's and 40's.

DOWN

4. The extended fiber of a neuron through which nerve impulses travel from the soma to the terminal buttons.

5. Is a response elicited by some previously neutral stimulus that occurs as a result of pairing the neutral stimulus with an unconditioned stimulus.

6. A cognitive theory of work motivation that proposes that workers are motivated to maintain fair and equitable relationships with other relevant persons.

8. Preprogrammed tendency that is essential to a species' survival.

9. A disorder that causes sleep walking.

10. A commitment beyond one's self and one's partner to family, work, society, and future generations; typically, a crucial state in development in one's 30's and 40's.

A. Retina
E. Law of effect
I. Conditioned response
B. Equity theory
F. Instinct
J. Axon
C. Insanity
G. Generativity
D. Somnambulism
H. Heredity

80. *Using the Across and Down clues, write the correct words in the numbered grid below.*

ACROSS

3. The chronological age at which most children show a level of physical or mental development.

6. The learned, relatively stable tendency to respond to people, concepts, and events in an evaluative way.

7. Centers around the concept of a whole person in the continual process of changing and of becoming.

8. The process of reconfiguring items by grouping based on similarity or some other organizing principle.

10. The observation that personality ratings across time and among different observers are consistent while behavior ratings across situations are not consistent.

11. The branch of psychology that investigates the effects of drugs on behavior.

DOWN

3. The chronological age at which most children show a level of physical or mental development.

6. The learned, relatively stable tendency to respond to people, concepts, and events in an evaluative way.

7. Centers around the concept of a whole person in the continual process of changing and of becoming.

8. The process of reconfiguring items by grouping based on similarity or some other organizing principle.

10. The observation that personality ratings across time and among different observers are consistent while behavior ratings across situations are not consistent.

11. The branch of psychology that investigates the effects of drugs on behavior.

A. Humanistic therapy
E. Attitude
I. Sleep apnea
B. Behavior analysis
F. Psychopharmacology
J. Chunking
C. Groupthink
G. Hypnosis
K. Amygdala
D. Consistency paradox
H. Developmental age

81. *Using the Across and Down clues, write the correct words in the numbered grid below.*

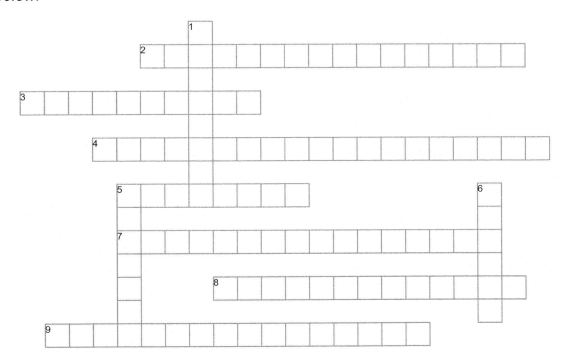

ACROSS

2. Mental disorder in which a person does not have signs of brain abnormalities and does not display grossly irrational thinking or violate basic norms

3. Drug that depresses or slows down the activity of the central nervous system.

4. Conscious effort to encode or recover information through memory processes.

5. Preprogrammed tendency that is essential to a species' survival.

7. Sexual arousal is the motivational state of excitement and tension brought about by physiological and cognitive reactions to erotic stimuli.

8. An anxiety disorder in which sufferers experience unexpected, severe panic attacks that begin with a feeling of intense apprehension, fear, or terror.

9. The receptors for this information are tiny hairs in fluid-filled sacs and canals in the inner ear.

DOWN

2. Mental disorder in which a person does not have signs of brain abnormalities and does not display grossly irrational thinking or violate basic norms

3. Drug that depresses or slows down the activity of the central nervous system.

4. Conscious effort to encode or recover information through memory processes.

5. Preprogrammed tendency that is essential to a species' survival.

7. Sexual arousal is the motivational state of excitement and tension brought about by physiological and cognitive reactions to erotic stimuli.

8. An anxiety disorder in which sufferers experience unexpected, severe panic attacks that begin with a feeling of intense apprehension, fear, or terror.

9. The receptors for this information are tiny hairs in fluid-filled sacs and canals in the inner ear.

A. Neurotic disorder
D. Vestibular system
G. Panic disorder
J. Depressant

B. Insight
E. Humanist
H. Hunger

C. Explicit use of memory
F. Sexual motivation
I. Instinct

82. *Using the Across and Down clues, write the correct words in the numbered grid below.*

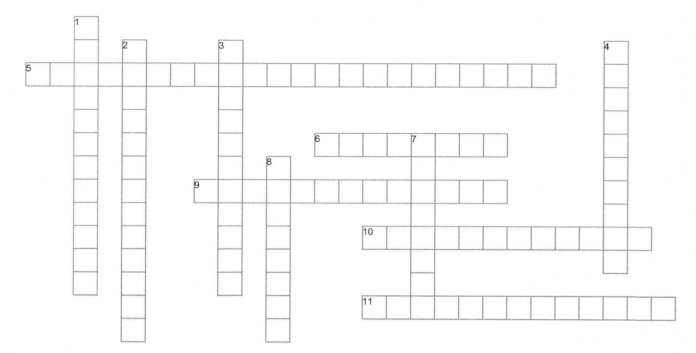

ACROSS

5. Research effort designed to describe what is characteristic of a specific age or developmental stage.

6. The process by which people form opinions, reach conclusions, and make critical evaluations of events and people based on available material; also, the product of the mental activity.

9. The client is a whole nuclear family and each family member is treated as a member of a system of relationships.

10. A drug that alters cognitions and perceptions and causes hallucinations.

11. A surgical procedure performed on brain tissue to alleviate a psychological disorder.

DOWN

5. Research effort designed to describe what is characteristic of a specific age or developmental stage.

6. The process by which people form opinions, reach conclusions, and make critical evaluations of events and people based on available material; also, the product of the mental activity.

9. The client is a whole nuclear family and each family member is treated as a member of a system of relationships.

10. A drug that alters cognitions and perceptions and causes hallucinations.

11. A surgical procedure performed on brain tissue to alleviate a psychological disorder.

A. Judgment
D. Hallucinogen
G. Normative investigation
J. Family therapy

B. Morality
E. Sleep apnea
H. Heritability
K. Fixation

C. Hallucination
F. Psychosurgery
I. Personality

83. *Using the Across and Down clues, write the correct words in the numbered grid below.*

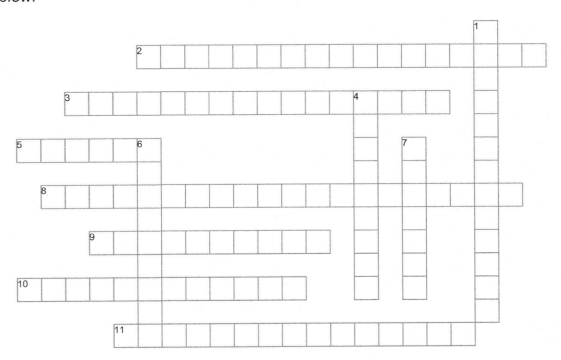

ACROSS

2. Centers around the concept of a whole person in the continual process of changing and of becoming.

3. Process that does not require attention; it can often be performed along with other tasks without interference.

5. The negative reaction of people to an individual or group because of some assumed inferiority or source of difference that is degraded.

8. A disorder characterized by unexplained physical complaints in several categories over many years.

9. Preoperational children's tendency to focus their attention on only one aspect of a situation and disregard other relevant aspects.

10. A mood disturbance such as severe depression or depression alternating with mania.

11. The process through which individuals are informed about experimental procedures, risks, and benefits before they provide formal consent to become research participants.

DOWN

2. Centers around the concept of a whole person in the continual process of changing and of becoming.

3. Process that does not require attention; it can often be performed along with other tasks without interference.

5. The negative reaction of people to an individual or group because of some assumed inferiority or source of difference that is degraded.

8. A disorder characterized by unexplained physical complaints in several categories over many years.

9. Preoperational children's tendency to focus their attention on only one aspect of a situation and disregard other relevant aspects.

10. A mood disturbance such as severe depression or depression alternating with mania.

11. The process through which individuals are informed about experimental procedures, risks, and benefits before they provide formal consent to become research participants.

A. Variable ratio
D. Informed consent
G. Mood disorder
J. Attention

B. Centration
E. Cognitive
H. Somatization disorder
K. Automatic process

C. Humanistic therapy
F. Emotion
I. Stigma

84. *Using the Across and Down clues, write the correct words in the numbered grid below.*

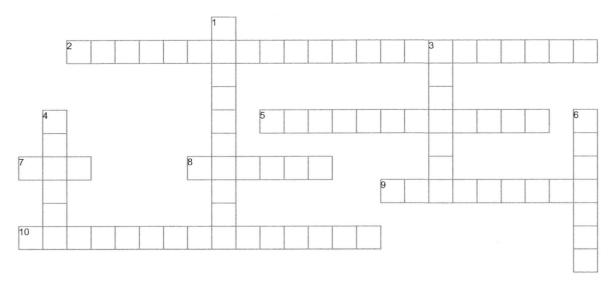

ACROSS

2. The psychological perspective primarily concerned with observable behavior that can be objectively recorded.

5. A drug that alters cognitions and perceptions and causes hallucinations.

7. Dissociative identity disorder. A dissociative mental disorder in which two or more distinct personalities exist within the same individual; formerly known as multiple personality disorder.

8. A subset of a population selected as participants in an experiment.

9. Blind obedience is less a product of dispositional characteristics than the outcome of situational forces that could engulf anyone. (Milgram studies)

10. A membrane running along the length of the cochlea.

DOWN

2. The psychological perspective primarily concerned with observable behavior that can be objectively recorded.

5. A drug that alters cognitions and perceptions and causes hallucinations.

7. Dissociative identity disorder. A dissociative mental disorder in which two or more distinct personalities exist within the same individual; formerly known as multiple personality disorder.

8. A subset of a population selected as participants in an experiment.

9. Blind obedience is less a product of dispositional characteristics than the outcome of situational forces that could engulf anyone. (Milgram studies)

10. A membrane running along the length of the cochlea.

A. Obedience
D. Behaviorist perspective
G. Basilar membrane
J. Hallucinogen

B. Sample
E. Compliance
H. Stigma

C. Phoneme
F. DID
I. Puberty

85. *Using the Across and Down clues, write the correct words in the numbered grid below.*

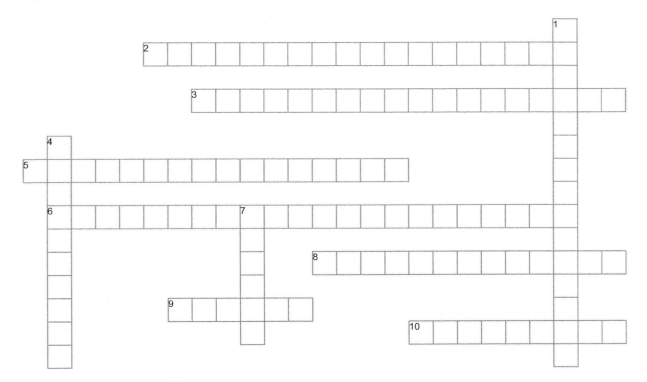

ACROSS

2. The branch of psychology that investigates the effects of drugs on behavior.

3. The area of psychological investigation concerned with understanding the nature of individual pathologies of mind, mood, and behavior.

5. A disorder defined by a large discrepancy between individuals' measured IQ and their actual performance.

6. Research conducted with human subjects in which the investigator interacts directly with the subjects.

8. The field of psychology that specializes in mental testing.

9. Piaget's term for a cognitive structure that develops as infants and young children learn to interpret the world and adapt to their environment.

10. The sense of smell.

DOWN

2. The branch of psychology that investigates the effects of drugs on behavior.

3. The area of psychological investigation concerned with understanding the nature of individual pathologies of mind, mood, and behavior.

5. A disorder defined by a large discrepancy between individuals' measured IQ and their actual performance.

6. Research conducted with human subjects in which the investigator interacts directly with the subjects.

8. The field of psychology that specializes in mental testing.

9. Piaget's term for a cognitive structure that develops as infants and young children learn to interpret the world and adapt to their environment.

10. The sense of smell.

A. Reflex
D. Scheme
G. Abnormal psychology
J. Psychopharmacology

B. Psychometrics
E. Olfaction
H. Hypochondriasis

C. Perception
F. Clinical research method
I. Learning disorder

86. *Using the Across and Down clues, write the correct words in the numbered grid below.*

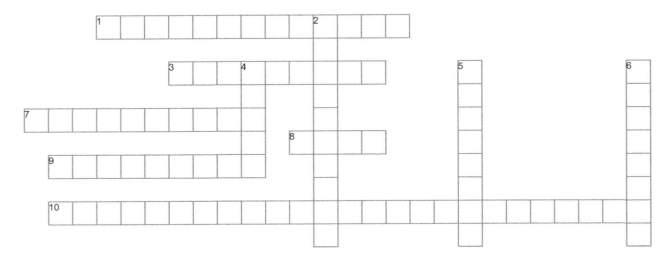

ACROSS

1. The client is a whole nuclear family and each family member is treated as a member of a system of relationships.

3. The sense of taste.

7. A sleep disorder of the upper respiratory system that causes the person to stop breathing while asleep.

8. Standard based on measurement of a large group of people; used for comparing the scores of an individual with those of others within a well-defined group.

9. The tendency to respond to a new problem in the manner used to respond to a previous problem.

10. A behavioral therapy technique in which a client is taught to prevent the arousal of anxiety by confronting the feared stimulus while relaxed.

DOWN

1. The client is a whole nuclear family and each family member is treated as a member of a system of relationships.

3. The sense of taste.

7. A sleep disorder of the upper respiratory system that causes the person to stop breathing while asleep.

8. Standard based on measurement of a large group of people; used for comparing the scores of an individual with those of others within a well-defined group.

9. The tendency to respond to a new problem in the manner used to respond to a previous problem.

10. A behavioral therapy technique in which a client is taught to prevent the arousal of anxiety by confronting the feared stimulus while relaxed.

A. Judgment
D. Reinforcer
G. Trait
J. Sleep apnea

B. Family therapy
E. Validity
H. Mental set

C. Gustation
F. Systematic desensitization
I. Norm

87. *Using the Across and Down clues, write the correct words in the numbered grid below.*

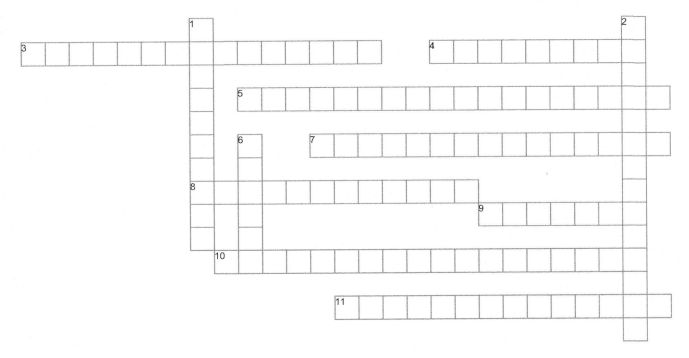

ACROSS

3. Founded a psychology laboratory at Cornell University in 1892, student of Wilhelm Wundt.

4. The process of expressing strongly felt but usually repressed emotions.

5. Attempts to establish general laws and generalizations, and seeks to obtain objective knowledge through scientific methods.

7. The therapeutic method in which a patient gives a running account of thoughts, wishes, physical sensations, and mental images as the occur.

8. According to Piaget, the understanding that physical properties do not change when nothing is added or taken away, even though appearances may change.

9. A failure of memory caused by physical injury, disease, drug use, or psychological trauma.

10. The theory that there are three types of color receptors that produce the primary color sensations of red, green, and blue.

11. Characteristic that is influenced by more than one gene.

DOWN

3. Founded a psychology laboratory at Cornell University in 1892, student of Wilhelm Wundt.

4. The process of expressing strongly felt but usually repressed emotions.

5. Attempts to establish general laws and generalizations, and seeks to obtain objective knowledge through scientific methods.

7. The therapeutic method in which a patient gives a running account of thoughts, wishes, physical sensations, and mental images as the occur.

8. According to Piaget, the understanding that physical properties do not change when nothing is added or taken away, even though appearances may change.

9. A failure of memory caused by physical injury, disease, drug use, or psychological trauma.

10. The theory that there are three types of color receptors that produce the primary color sensations of red, green, and blue.

11. Characteristic that is influenced by more than one gene.

A. Psychoanalysis B. Hunger C. Nomothetic research D. Biological
E. Polygenic trait F. Conservation G. Catharsis H. Trichromatic theory
I. Free association J. Edward Titchener K. Amnesia

88. *Using the Across and Down clues, write the correct words in the numbered grid below.*

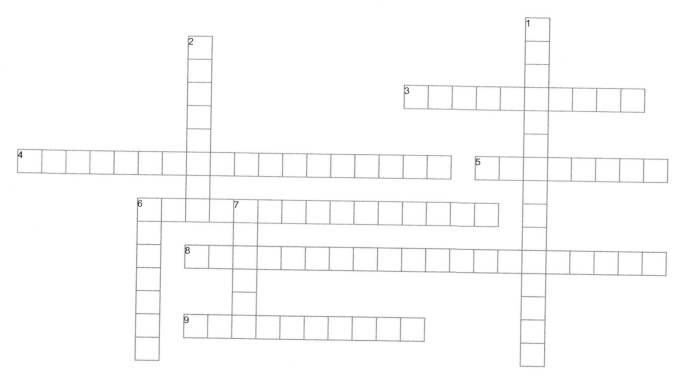

ACROSS

3. Any stimulus that, when made contingent on a response, respectively increases or decreases the probability of that response.

4. An aspect of creativity characterized by the ability to gather together different sources of information to solve a problem.

5. The biological transmission of traits from parents to offspring.

6. According to Lev Vygotsky, the process through which children absorb knowledge from the social environment.

8. Sometimes necessary when revealing certain information to the patient would bias the results.

9. Rules for participation in conversations; social conventions for communicating, sequencing sentences, and responding appropriately to others.

DOWN

3. Any stimulus that, when made contingent on a response, respectively increases or decreases the probability of that response.

4. An aspect of creativity characterized by the ability to gather together different sources of information to solve a problem.

5. The biological transmission of traits from parents to offspring.

6. According to Lev Vygotsky, the process through which children absorb knowledge from the social environment.

8. Sometimes necessary when revealing certain information to the patient would bias the results.

9. Rules for participation in conversations; social conventions for communicating, sequencing sentences, and responding appropriately to others.

A. Intentional deception   B. Insight   C. Exposure therapy   D. Pragmatics
E. Reinforcer   F. Internalization   G. Judgment   H. Convergent thinking
I. Heredity   J. Retina

89. *Using the Across and Down clues, write the correct words in the numbered grid below.*

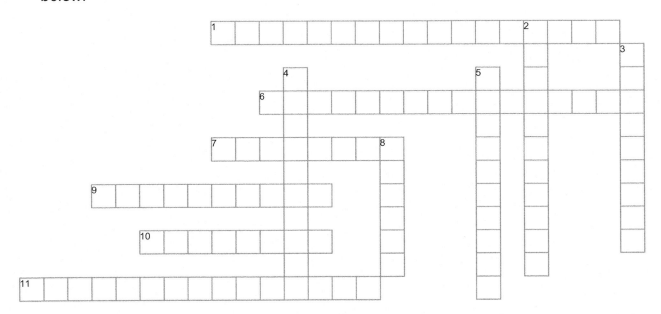

ACROSS

1. A disorder characterized by a flight from home or work accompanied by a loss of ability to recall the personal past.

6. Belief about attributes and behaviors regarded as appropriate for males and females in a particular culture.

7. The process of reconfiguring items by grouping based on similarity or some other organizing principle.

9. The age-related physical and behavioral changes characteristic of a species; the process of growth typical of all members of a species who are reared in the specie's usual habitat.

10. The capacity to make a full commitment - sexual, emotional, and moral - to another person.

11. A membrane running along the length of the cochlea.

DOWN

1. A disorder characterized by a flight from home or work accompanied by a loss of ability to recall the personal past.

6. Belief about attributes and behaviors regarded as appropriate for males and females in a particular culture.

7. The process of reconfiguring items by grouping based on similarity or some other organizing principle.

9. The age-related physical and behavioral changes characteristic of a species; the process of growth typical of all members of a species who are reared in the specie's usual habitat.

10. The capacity to make a full commitment - sexual, emotional, and moral - to another person.

11. A membrane running along the length of the cochlea.

A. Dissociative fugue   B. Basilar membrane   C. Obedience   D. Gender stereotype
E. Chunking   F. Maturation   G. Reinforcer   H. Genome
I. Pragmatics   J. Intimacy   K. Unconscious

90. *Using the Across and Down clues, write the correct words in the numbered grid below.*

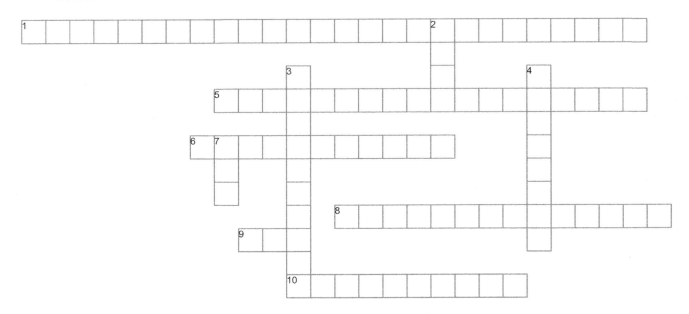

ACROSS

1. A therapeutic approach that combines the cognitive emphasis on thoughts and attitudes with the behavioral emphasis on changing performance.

5. A research design in which the same participants are observed repeatedly, sometimes over many years.

6. The experience of more than one disorder at the same time.

8. An experimental condition in which treatment is not administered; it is used in cases where a placebo effect might occur.

9. Magnetic resonance imaging. A technique for brain imaging that scans the brain using magnetic fields and radio waves.

10. A sleep disorder characterized by an irresistible compulsion to sleep during the daytime.

DOWN

1. A therapeutic approach that combines the cognitive emphasis on thoughts and attitudes with the behavioral emphasis on changing performance.

5. A research design in which the same participants are observed repeatedly, sometimes over many years.

6. The experience of more than one disorder at the same time.

8. An experimental condition in which treatment is not administered; it is used in cases where a placebo effect might occur.

9. Magnetic resonance imaging. A technique for brain imaging that scans the brain using magnetic fields and radio waves.

10. A sleep disorder characterized by an irresistible compulsion to sleep during the daytime.

A. Narcolepsy
D. MRI
G. Placebo control
J. Delusion

B. Cognitive behavioral therapy
E. Longitudinal design
H. OCD

C. Aggression
F. Comorbidity
I. Axon

91. *Using the Across and Down clues, write the correct words in the numbered grid below.*

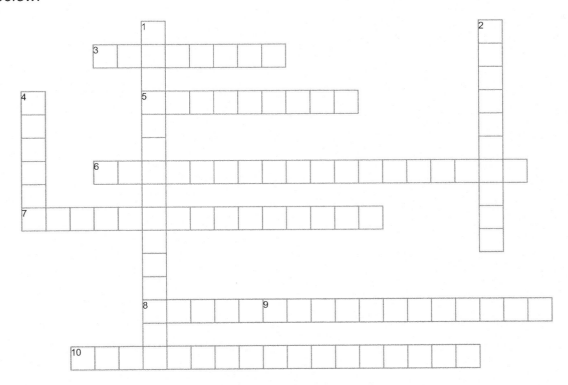

ACROSS

3. One of the branched fibers of neurons that receive incoming signals.

5. Missing information filled in on the basis of a sample of evidence or on the basis of prior beliefs and theories.

6. The assumption that mental and behavioral reactions are determined by previous experiences.

7. A type of behavioral therapy used to treat individuals attracted to harmful stimuli.

8. An aspect of creativity characterized by an ability to produce unusual but appropriate response to problems.

10. A social-cognitive approach to describing the ways the social perceiver uses information to generate causal explanations.

DOWN

1. Mental disorder marked by psychological arousal, feeling of tension, and intense apprehension without apparent reason.

2. A thread-like structure found in the nucleus of cells and made of protein and DNA

4. The negative reaction of people to an individual or group because of some assumed inferiority or source of difference that is degraded.

9. According to Charles Spearman, the factor of general intelligence underlying all intelligent performance.

A. Aversion therapy   B. Divergent thinking   C. Anxiety disorder   D. Psychic determinism
E. Stigma   F. Dendrite   G. Attribution theory   H. G
I. Inference   J. Chromosome

92. *Using the Across and Down clues, write the correct words in the numbered grid below.*

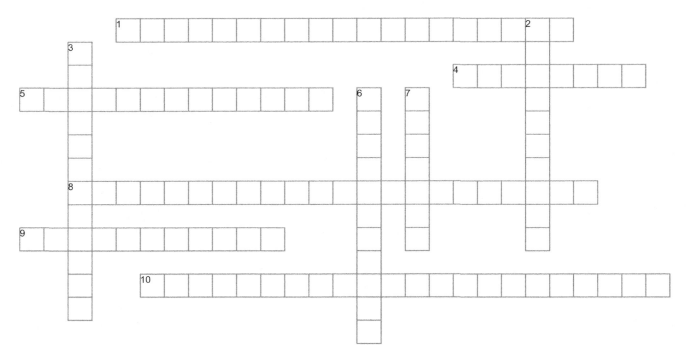

ACROSS

1. A measure of reliability; the degree to which a test yields similar scores across its different parts, such as odd versus even items.

4. The study of the inheritance of physical and psychological traits from ancestors.

5. The client is a whole nuclear family and each family member is treated as a member of a system of relationships.

8. The psychological perspective primarily concerned with observable behavior that can be objectively recorded.

9. The degree to which a test produces similar scores each time it is used; stability or consistency of the scores produced by an instrument.

10. Group effects that arise from individuals' desire to be correct and right and to understand how best to act in a given situation.

DOWN

2. The ability to generate ideas or products that are both novel and appropriate to the circumstances.

3. A disorder that causes sleep walking.

6. The theory that different frequency tones produce maximum activation at different locations along the basilar membrane.

7. A failure of memory caused by physical injury, disease, drug use, or psychological trauma.

A. Place theory
D. Creativity
G. Family therapy
J. Genetics

B. Amnesia
E. Somnambulism
H. Internal consistency

C. Behaviorist perspective
F. Reliability
I. Informational influence

93. *Using the Across and Down clues, write the correct words in the numbered grid below.*

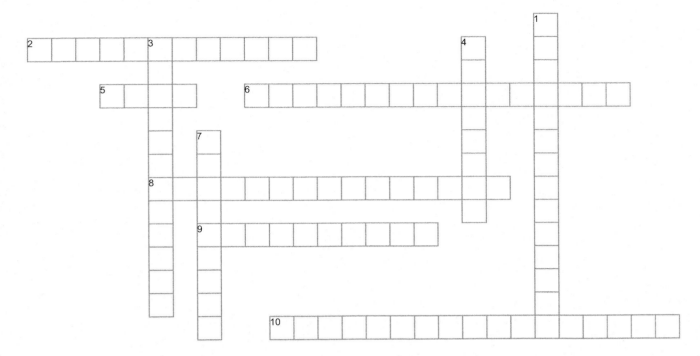

ACROSS

2. The region of the brain that regulates emotional behavior, basic motivational urges, and memory, as well as major physiological functions.

5. The biological unit of heredity; discrete section of a chromosome responsible for transmission of traits.

6. The optical image on the retina.

8. The sense that tells how one's own body is oriented in the world with respect to gravity.

9. A socially defined pattern of behavior that is expected of a person who is functioning in a given setting or group.

10. A group in an experiment that is exposed to a treatment or experiences a manipulation of the independent variable.

DOWN

1. An aspect of Rotter's expectancy theory; people's general expectancy about the extent to which the rewards they obtain are contingent on their own actions or on environmental factors.

3. According to Piaget, the understanding that physical properties do not change when nothing is added or taken away, even though appearances may change.

4. People begin life with mental structures that provide constraints on how they experience the world.

7. Intensive observation of an individual or small group of individuals.

A. Proximal stimulus
E. Vestibular sense
I. Gene

B. Social role
F. Conservation
J. Nativist

C. Case study
G. Locus of control

D. Experimental group
H. Limbic system

94. *Using the Across and Down clues, write the correct words in the numbered grid below.*

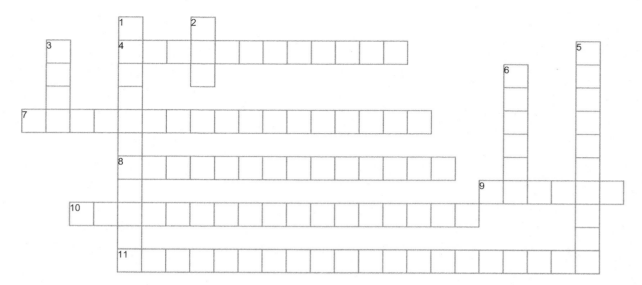

ACROSS

4. The global capacity to profit from experience and to go beyond given information about the environment.

7. The diminishing responsiveness of sensory systems to prolonged stimulus input; allows a more rapid reaction to new (different) sources of information.

8. The process of shaping a message depending on the audience for which it is intended.

9. The genetic information for an organism, stored in the DNA of its chromosomes.

10. A group in an experiment that is exposed to a treatment or experiences a manipulation of the independent variable.

11. A measure of the correlation between test takers' performance on different halves (such as odd- and even-numbered items) of a test.

DOWN

1. The part of the limbic system that is involved in the acquisition of explicit memory.

2. Rapid eye movements. A behavioral sign of the phase of sleep during which the sleeper is likely to be experiencing dreamlike mental activity.

3. Behavioral guideline for acting in a certain way in a certain instance.

5. The tendency for people to adopt the behaviors, attitudes, and values of the members of a reference group.

6. Drug that suppresses physical sensation and response to stimulation.

A. Hippocampus B. Split half reliability C. Conformity D. Experimental group
E. Rule F. Audience design G. Opiate H. Genome
I. Intelligence J. Sensory adaptation K. REM

95. *Using the Across and Down clues, write the correct words in the numbered grid below.*

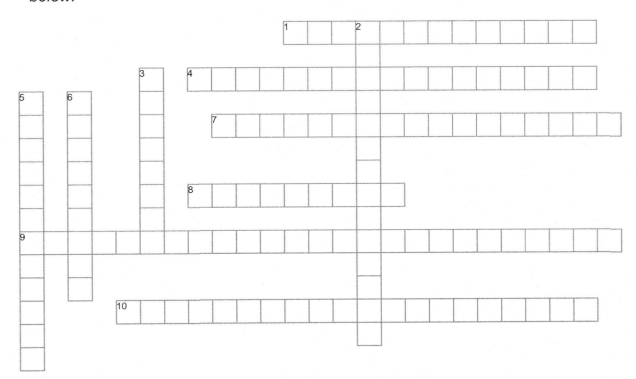

ACROSS

1. Seeks to clarify the typical communication patterns of the partners and then to improve the quality of their interaction.

4. A disorder characterized by a flight from home or work accompanied by a loss of ability to recall the personal past.

7. An aspect of creativity characterized by an ability to produce unusual but appropriate response to problems.

8. A learned attitude toward a target object, involving negative affect (dislike or fear), negative beliefs (stereotypes), that justify the attitude, and a behavioral intention to avoid, control, dominate, or eliminate the target object.

9. A behavioral therapy technique in which a client is taught to prevent the arousal of anxiety by confronting the feared stimulus while relaxed.

10. A disorder characterized by unexplained physical complaints in several categories over many years.

DOWN

2. An experimental condition in which treatment is not administered; it is used in cases where a placebo effect might occur.

3. The region of the brain that regulates higher cognitive and emotional functions.

5. Insulating material that surrounds axons and increases the speed of neural transmission.

6. The process of expressing strongly felt but usually repressed emotions.

A. Somatization disorder
D. Dissociative fugue
G. Systematic desensitization
J. Couple therapy

B. Myelin sheath
E. Catharsis
H. Cerebrum

C. Placebo control
F. Prejudice
I. Divergent thinking

96. *Using the Across and Down clues, write the correct words in the numbered grid below.*

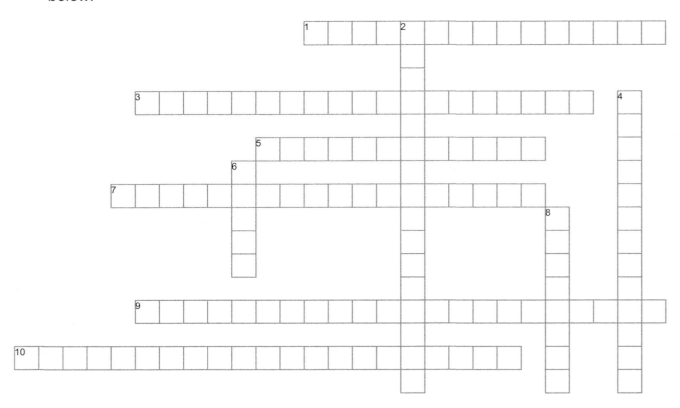

ACROSS

1. The therapeutic method in which a patient gives a running account of thoughts, wishes, physical sensations, and mental images as the occur.

3. Conscious effort to encode or recover information through memory processes.

5. The brain structure that regulates motivated behavior and homeostasis.

7. An aspect of creativity characterized by the ability to gather together different sources of information to solve a problem.

9. A conditioning process in which an organism learns to respond differently to stimuli that differ from the conditioned stimulus on some dimension.

10. Statistical procedures that allow researchers to determine whether the results they obtain support their hypotheses or can be attributed to chance variation.

DOWN

2. Process that does not require attention; it can often be performed along with other tasks without interference.

4. Different versions of a test used to assess test reliability; the change of forms reduces effects of direct practice, memory, or the desire of an individual to appear consistent on the same items.

6. Internal state that arises in response to a disequilibrium in an animal's physiological needs.

8. The brain structure that relays sensory impulses to the cerebral cortex.

A. Convergent thinking
B. Explicit use of memory
C. Hypothalamus
D. Inferential statistics
E. Drive
F. Thalamus
G. Parallel forms
H. Free association
I. Automatic process
J. Stimulus discrimination

97. *Using the Across and Down clues, write the correct words in the numbered grid below.*

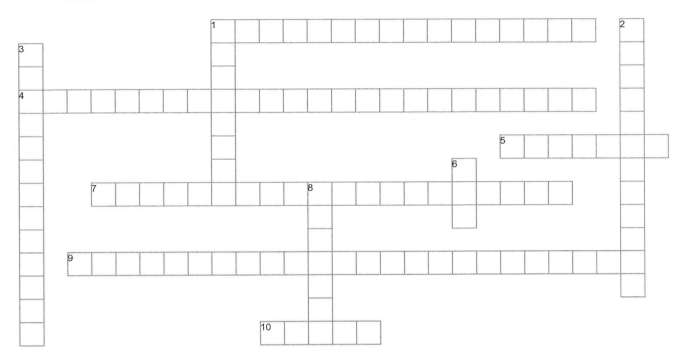

ACROSS

1. The process of developing, in anticipation of failure, behavioral reactions and explanations that minimize ability deficits as possible attributions for the failure

4. A consistent relationship between a response and the changes in the environment that it produces.

5. Meaning is the dictionary meaning of a word

7. Type of therapy that assumes that a patient's problems have been caused by the psychological tension between unconscious impulses and the constraints of his or her life situation.

9. The facet of intelligence involving the knowledge a person has already acquired and the ability to access that knowledge; measures by vocabulary, arithmetic, and general information tests.

10. A particular description of a choice; the perspective from which a choice is described or framed affects how a decision is made and which option is ultimately exercised.

DOWN

1. The part of the personality that corresponds roughly to the idea of conscience, the inner voice of should and should nots.

2. Author of "The Principles of Psychology."

3. Different versions of a test used to assess test reliability; the change of forms reduces effects of direct practice, memory, or the desire of an individual to appear consistent on the same items.

6. A recording of the electrical activity of the brain.

8. A failure of memory caused by physical injury, disease, drug use, or psychological trauma.

A. Parallel forms
D. Reinforcement contingency
G. Amnesia
J. Self handicapping

B. Psychodynamic therapy
E. William James
H. Frame
K. Superego

C. Crystallized intelligence
F. Lexical
I. EEG

98. *Using the Across and Down clues, write the correct words in the numbered grid below.*

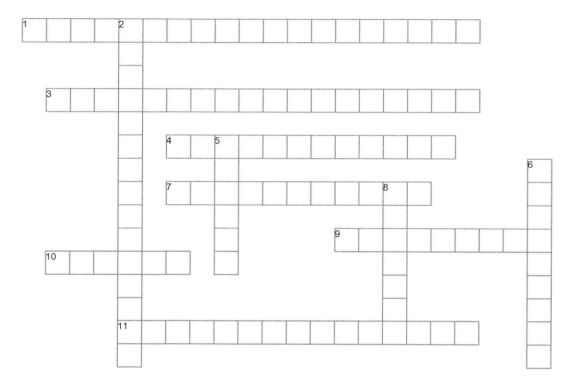

ACROSS

1. The subdivision of the ANS that deals with emergency response and the mobilization of energy.

3. A theory of personality that refers to the expertise people bring to their experience of life tasks.

4. The brain structure that serves as a relay station between the endocrine system and the CNS.

7. In cognitive development, the inability of a young child at the preoperational stage to take the perceptive of another person.

9. The process by which stimulation of a sensory receptor gives rise to neutral impulses that result in an experience, or awareness, of conditions inside or outside the body.

10. The mental capacity to encode, store, and retrieve information.

11. Founded a psychology laboratory at Cornell University in 1892, student of Wilhelm Wundt.

DOWN

2. Mental disorder marked by psychological arousal, feeling of tension, and intense apprehension without apparent reason.

5. A persistent and irrational fear of a specific object, activity, or situation that is excessive and unreasonable, given the reality of the threat.

6. The study of the sounds that are put together to form words.

8. The gap between one neuron and another.

A. Memory
E. Social intelligence
I. Sensation

B. Synapse
F. Phobia
J. Edward Titchener

C. Anxiety disorder
G. Phonology
K. Sympathetic division

D. Egocentrism
H. Hypothalamus

99. *Using the Across and Down clues, write the correct words in the numbered grid below.*

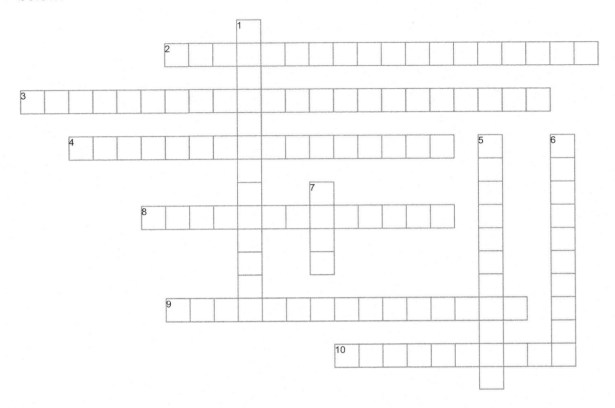

ACROSS

2. The assumption that mental and behavioral reactions are determined by previous experiences.

3. A conditioning process in which an organism learns to respond differently to stimuli that differ from the conditioned stimulus on some dimension.

4. Sexual arousal is the motivational state of excitement and tension brought about by physiological and cognitive reactions to erotic stimuli.

8. Traits that represent major characteristics of a person, such as honesty or optimism.

9. Founded a psychology laboratory at Cornell University in 1892, student of Wilhelm Wundt.

10. A socially defined pattern of behavior that is expected of a person who is functioning in a given setting or group.

DOWN

1. A severe form of psychopathology characterized by the breakdown of integrated personality functioning, withdrawal from reality, emotional distortions, and disturbed thoughts.

5. The theory that different frequency tones produce maximum activation at different locations along the basilar membrane.

6. A thread-like structure found in the nucleus of cells and made of protein and DNA

7. Posttraumatic stress disorder. An anxiety disorder characterized by the persistent re-experience of those traumatic events through distressing recollections, dreams, hallucinations, or flashbacks.

A. Schizophrenia
D. PTSD
G. Central traits
J. Chromosome

B. Psychic determinism
E. Place theory
H. Stimulus discrimination

C. Edward Titchener
F. Sexual motivation
I. Social role

100. *Using the Across and Down clues, write the correct words in the numbered grid below.*

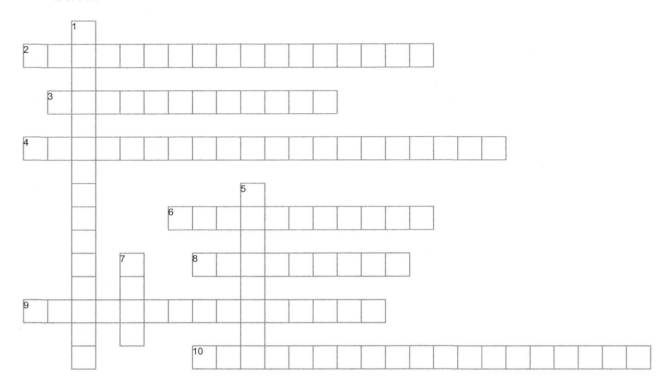

ACROSS

2. The degree to which a test adequately measures an underlying construct.

3. A group in an experiment that is not exposed to a treatment or does not experience a manipulation of the independent variable.

4. The study of the development of cognitive abilities across species and the continuity of abilities from nonhuman animals to humans.

6. The domain of the psyche that stores repressed urges and primitive impulses.

8. The brain structure that regulates the body's basic life processes.

9. The therapeutic method in which a patient gives a running account of thoughts, wishes, physical sensations, and mental images as the occur.

10. The bodily changes, maturation, and growth that occur in an organism starting with conception and continuing across the life span.

DOWN

1. The process through which individuals are informed about experimental procedures, risks, and benefits before they provide formal consent to become research participants.

5. A system of beliefs and values that ensures that individuals will keep their obligations to others in society and will behave in ways that do not interfere with the rights and interests of others.

7. A rational reaction to an objectively identified external danger that may induce a person to flee or attack in self -defense.

A. Unconscious
D. Comparative cognition
G. Informed consent
J. Construct validity

B. Brain stem
E. Physical development
H. Fear

C. Free association
F. Control group
I. Morality

1. *Using the Across and Down clues, write the correct words in the numbered grid below.*

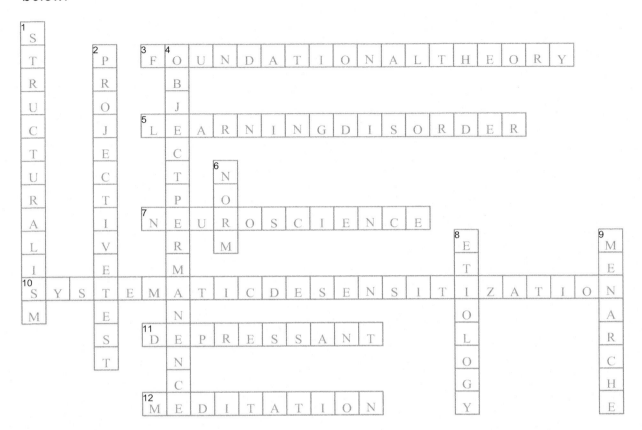

ACROSS

3. Framework for initial understanding formulated by children to explain their experiences of the world.

5. A disorder defined by a large discrepancy between individuals' measured IQ and their actual performance.

7. The scientific study of the brain and of the links between brain activity and behavior.

10. A behavioral therapy technique in which a client is taught to prevent the arousal of anxiety by confronting the feared stimulus while relaxed.

11. Drug that depresses or slows down the activity of the central nervous system.

12. A form of consciousness alteration designed to enhance self-knowledge and well-being by achieving a deep state of tranquility.

DOWN

3. Framework for initial understanding formulated by children to explain their experiences of the world.

5. A disorder defined by a large discrepancy between individuals' measured IQ and their actual performance.

7. The scientific study of the brain and of the links between brain activity and behavior.

10. A behavioral therapy technique in which a client is taught to prevent the arousal of anxiety by confronting the feared stimulus while relaxed.

11. Drug that depresses or slows down the activity of the central nervous system.

12. A form of consciousness alteration designed to enhance self-knowledge and well-being by achieving a deep state of tranquility.

A. Meditation
D. Structuralism
G. Depressant
J. Menarche

B. Learning disorder
E. Neuroscience
H. Foundational theory
K. Projective test

C. Object permanence
F. Systematic desensitization
I. Norm
L. Etiology

2. *Using the Across and Down clues, write the correct words in the numbered grid below.*

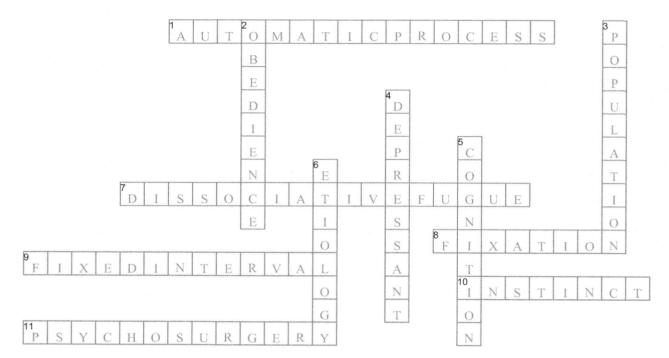

ACROSS

1. Process that does not require attention; it can often be performed along with other tasks without interference.

7. A disorder characterized by a flight from home or work accompanied by a loss of ability to recall the personal past.

8. According to Freud, a state in which a person remains attached to objects or activities more appropriate for an earlier stage of psychosexual development.

9. A schedule of reinforcement in which a reinforcer is delivered for the first response made after a fixed period.

10. Preprogrammed tendency that is essential to a species' survival.

11. A surgical procedure performed on brain tissue to alleviate a psychological disorder.

DOWN

1. Process that does not require attention; it can often be performed along with other tasks without interference.

7. A disorder characterized by a flight from home or work accompanied by a loss of ability to recall the personal past.

8. According to Freud, a state in which a person remains attached to objects or activities more appropriate for an earlier stage of psychosexual development.

9. A schedule of reinforcement in which a reinforcer is delivered for the first response made after a fixed period.

10. Preprogrammed tendency that is essential to a species' survival.

11. A surgical procedure performed on brain tissue to alleviate a psychological disorder.

A. Population   B. Fixed interval   C. Depressant   D. Fixation
E. Psychosurgery   F. Etiology   G. Obedience   H. Automatic process
I. Instinct   J. Dissociative fugue   K. Cognition

3. *Using the Across and Down clues, write the correct words in the numbered grid below.*

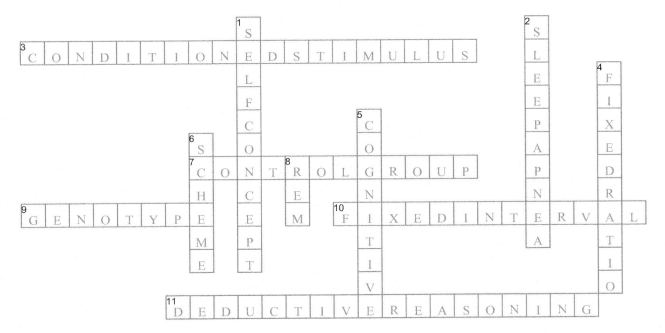

ACROSS

3. Is a previously neutral stimulus that comes to elicit a conditioned response.

7. A group in an experiment that is not exposed to a treatment or does not experience a manipulation of the independent variable.

9. The genetic structure an organism inherits from its parents.

10. A schedule of reinforcement in which a reinforcer is delivered for the first response made after a fixed period.

11. A form of thinking in which one draws a conclusion that is intended to follow logically from two or more statements or premises.

DOWN

3. Is a previously neutral stimulus that comes to elicit a conditioned response.

7. A group in an experiment that is not exposed to a treatment or does not experience a manipulation of the independent variable.

9. The genetic structure an organism inherits from its parents.

10. A schedule of reinforcement in which a reinforcer is delivered for the first response made after a fixed period.

11. A form of thinking in which one draws a conclusion that is intended to follow logically from two or more statements or premises.

A. Genotype
D. REM
G. Sleep apnea
J. Control group

B. Fixed interval
E. Cognitive
H. Scheme
K. Deductive reasoning

C. Conditioned stimulus
F. Fixed ratio
I. Self concept

4. Using the Across and Down clues, write the correct words in the numbered grid below.

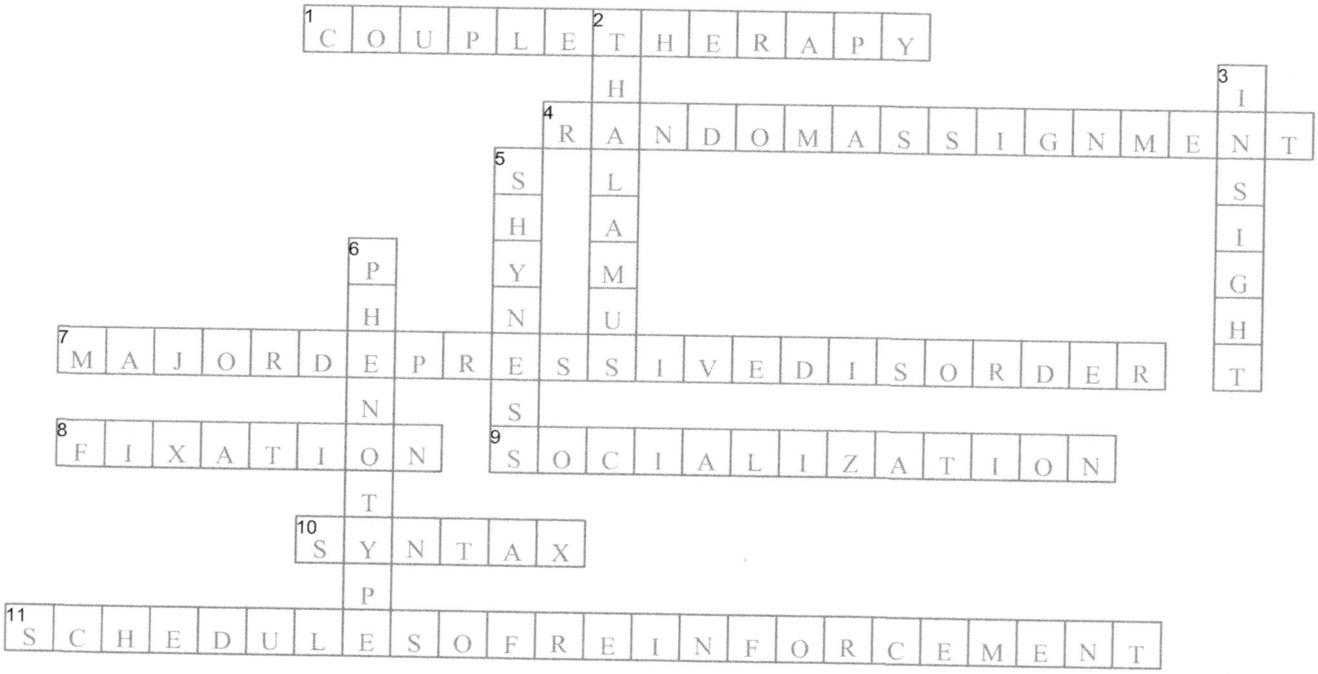

Crossword grid (filled):

- 1 Across: COUPLE THERAPY
- 2 Down: THALAMUS
- 3 Down: INSIGHT
- 4 Across: RANDOM ASSIGNMENT
- 5 Down: SHYNESS
- 6 Down: PHENOTYPE
- 7 Across: MAJOR DEPRESSIVE DISORDER
- 8 Across: FIXATION
- 9 Across: SOCIALIZATION
- 10 Across: SYNTAX
- 11 Across: SCHEDULES OF REINFORCEMENT

ACROSS

1. Seeks to clarify the typical communication patterns of the partners and then to improve the quality of their interaction.

4. A procedure by which participants have an equal likelihood of being assigned to any condition within an experiment.

7. A mood disorder characterized by intense feelings of depression over an extended time, without the manic high phase of bipolar depression

8. According to Freud, a state in which a person remains attached to objects or activities more appropriate for an earlier stage of psychosexual development.

9. The lifelong process whereby an individual's behavioral patterns, values, standards, skills, attitudes, and motives are shaped to conform to those regarded as desirable in a particular society.

10. The way in which words are strung together to form sentences.

11. In operant conditioning, a pattern of delivering and withholding reinforcement.

DOWN

1. Seeks to clarify the typical communication patterns of the partners and then to improve the quality of their interaction.

4. A procedure by which participants have an equal likelihood of being assigned to any condition within an experiment.

7. A mood disorder characterized by intense feelings of depression over an extended time, without the manic high phase of bipolar depression

8. According to Freud, a state in which a person remains attached to objects or activities more appropriate for an earlier stage of psychosexual development.

9. The lifelong process whereby an individual's behavioral patterns, values, standards, skills, attitudes, and motives are shaped to conform to those regarded as desirable in a particular society.

10. The way in which words are strung together to form sentences.

11. In operant conditioning, a pattern of delivering and withholding reinforcement.

A. Syntax
D. Random assignment
G. Socialization
J. Phenotype
B. Fixation
E. Insight
H. Shyness
K. Couple therapy
C. Thalamus
F. Schedules of reinforcement
I. Major depressive disorder

5. *Using the Across and Down clues, write the correct words in the numbered grid below.*

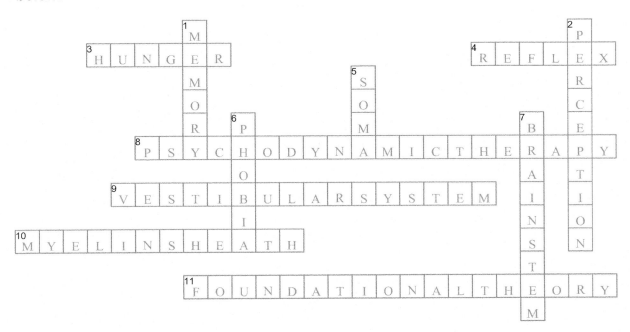

ACROSS

3. The body is sensitive to the source of pressure in the stomach, gastric pressure will cause a person to full while an inflated balloon will not.

4. An unlearned response elicited by specific stimuli that have biological relevance for an organism.

8. Type of therapy that assumes that a patient's problems have been caused by the psychological tension between unconscious impulses and the constraints of his or her life situation.

9. The receptors for this information are tiny hairs in fluid-filled sacs and canals in the inner ear.

10. Insulating material that surrounds axons and increases the speed of neural transmission.

11. Framework for initial understanding formulated by children to explain their experiences of the world.

DOWN

3. The body is sensitive to the source of pressure in the stomach, gastric pressure will cause a person to full while an inflated balloon will not.

4. An unlearned response elicited by specific stimuli that have biological relevance for an organism.

8. Type of therapy that assumes that a patient's problems have been caused by the psychological tension between unconscious impulses and the constraints of his or her life situation.

9. The receptors for this information are tiny hairs in fluid-filled sacs and canals in the inner ear.

10. Insulating material that surrounds axons and increases the speed of neural transmission.

11. Framework for initial understanding formulated by children to explain their experiences of the world.

A. Foundational theory
D. Brain stem
G. Hunger
J. Psychodynamic therapy

B. Reflex
E. Phobia
H. Memory
K. Myelin sheath

C. Perception
F. Vestibular system
I. Soma

6. *Using the Across and Down clues, write the correct words in the numbered grid below.*

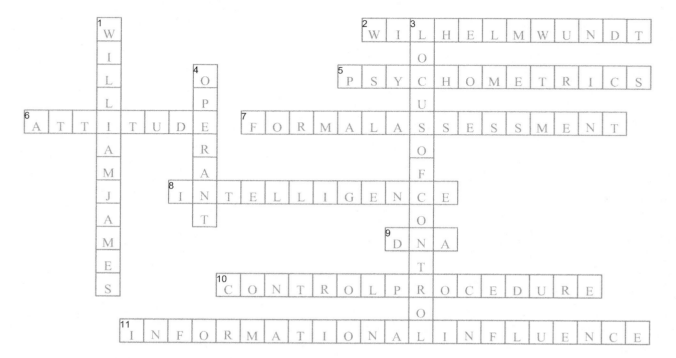

ACROSS

2. Founded the first formal experimental psychology laboratory in 1879 in Leipzig, Germany.

5. The field of psychology that specializes in mental testing.

6. The learned, relatively stable tendency to respond to people, concepts, and events in an evaluative way.

7. The systematic procedures and measurement instruments used by trained professionals to assess and individual's functioning, aptitudes, abilities, or mental states.

8. The global capacity to profit from experience and to go beyond given information about the environment.

9. The physical basis for the transmission of genetic information.

10. Consistent procedure for giving instructions, scoring responses, and holding all other variables constant except those being systematically varied.

11. Group effects that arise from individuals' desire to be correct and right and to understand how best to act in a given situation.

DOWN

2. Founded the first formal experimental psychology laboratory in 1879 in Leipzig, Germany.

5. The field of psychology that specializes in mental testing.

6. The learned, relatively stable tendency to respond to people, concepts, and events in an evaluative way.

7. The systematic procedures and measurement instruments used by trained professionals to assess and individual's functioning, aptitudes, abilities, or mental states.

8. The global capacity to profit from experience and to go beyond given information about the environment.

9. The physical basis for the transmission of genetic information.

10. Consistent procedure for giving instructions, scoring responses, and holding all other variables constant except those being systematically varied.

11. Group effects that arise from individuals' desire to be correct and right and to understand how best to act in a given situation.

A. Wilhelm Wundt
D. DNA
G. Attitude
J. Intelligence

B. Operant
E. Locus of control
H. Control procedure
K. Psychometrics

C. Formal assessment
F. William James
I. Informational influence

7. *Using the Across and Down clues, write the correct words in the numbered grid below.*

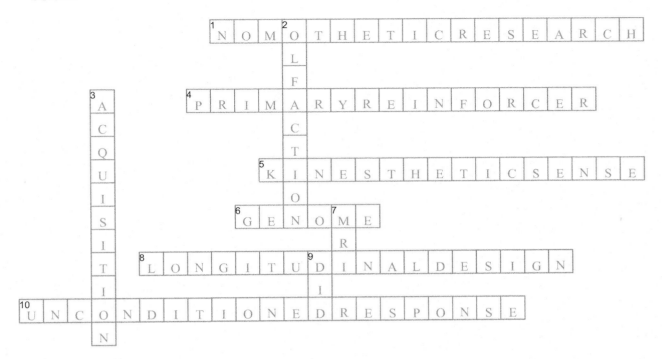

ACROSS

1. Attempts to establish general laws and generalizations, and seeks to obtain objective knowledge through scientific methods.

4. A biologically determined reinforcer, such as food and water.

5. The sense concerned with bodily position and movement of the body parts relative to one another.

6. The genetic information for an organism, stored in the DNA of its chromosomes.

8. A research design in which the same participants are observed repeatedly, sometimes over many years.

10. Is the response elicited by an unconditioned stimulus without prior training or learning.

DOWN

1. Attempts to establish general laws and generalizations, and seeks to obtain objective knowledge through scientific methods.

4. A biologically determined reinforcer, such as food and water.

5. The sense concerned with bodily position and movement of the body parts relative to one another.

6. The genetic information for an organism, stored in the DNA of its chromosomes.

8. A research design in which the same participants are observed repeatedly, sometimes over many years.

10. Is the response elicited by an unconditioned stimulus without prior training or learning.

A. Unconditioned response
D. Genome
G. MRI
J. Olfaction

B. Acquisition
E. Longitudinal design
H. Nomothetic research

C. Kinesthetic sense
F. Primary reinforcer
I. DID

8. *Using the Across and Down clues, write the correct words in the numbered grid below.*

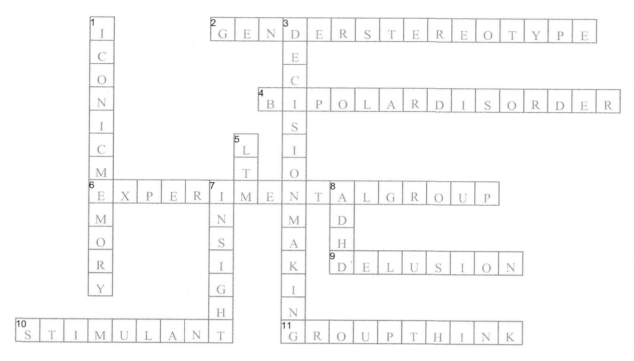

ACROSS

2. Belief about attributes and behaviors regarded as appropriate for males and females in a particular culture.

4. A mood disorder characterized by alternating periods of depression and mania.

6. A group in an experiment that is exposed to a treatment or experiences a manipulation of the independent variable.

9. False or irrational belief maintained despite clear evidence to the contrary.

10. Drug that causes arousal, increased activity, and euphoria.

11. The tendency of a decision-making group to filter out undesirable input so that a consensus may be reached, especially if it is in line with the leader's viewpoint.

DOWN

2. Belief about attributes and behaviors regarded as appropriate for males and females in a particular culture.

4. A mood disorder characterized by alternating periods of depression and mania.

6. A group in an experiment that is exposed to a treatment or experiences a manipulation of the independent variable.

9. False or irrational belief maintained despite clear evidence to the contrary.

10. Drug that causes arousal, increased activity, and euphoria.

11. The tendency of a decision-making group to filter out undesirable input so that a consensus may be reached, especially if it is in line with the leader's viewpoint.

A. Experimental group
E. Stimulant
I. Decision making

B. ADHD
F. Bipolar disorder
J. Insight

C. Groupthink
G. Delusion
K. Iconic memory

D. LTM
H. Gender stereotype

9. *Using the Across and Down clues, write the correct words in the numbered grid below.*

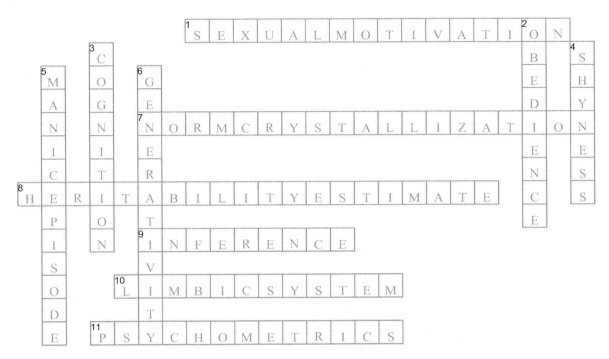

ACROSS

1. Sexual arousal is the motivational state of excitement and tension brought about by physiological and cognitive reactions to erotic stimuli.

7. The convergence of the expectations of a group of individuals into a common perspective as they talk and carry out activities together.

8. A statistical estimate of the degree of inheritance of a given trait or behavior, asses by the degree of similarity between individuals who vary in their extent of genetic similarity.

9. Missing information filled in on the basis of a sample of evidence or on the basis of prior beliefs and theories.

10. The region of the brain that regulates emotional behavior, basic motivational urges, and memory, as well as major physiological functions.

11. The field of psychology that specializes in mental testing.

DOWN

1. Sexual arousal is the motivational state of excitement and tension brought about by physiological and cognitive reactions to erotic stimuli.

7. The convergence of the expectations of a group of individuals into a common perspective as they talk and carry out activities together.

8. A statistical estimate of the degree of inheritance of a given trait or behavior, asses by the degree of similarity between individuals who vary in their extent of genetic similarity.

9. Missing information filled in on the basis of a sample of evidence or on the basis of prior beliefs and theories.

10. The region of the brain that regulates emotional behavior, basic motivational urges, and memory, as well as major physiological functions.

11. The field of psychology that specializes in mental testing.

A. Sexual motivation
E. Psychometrics
I. Generativity
B. Heritability estimate
F. Norm crystallization
J. Shyness
C. Manic episode
G. Limbic system
K. Obedience
D. Cognition
H. Inference

10. *Using the Across and Down clues, write the correct words in the numbered grid below.*

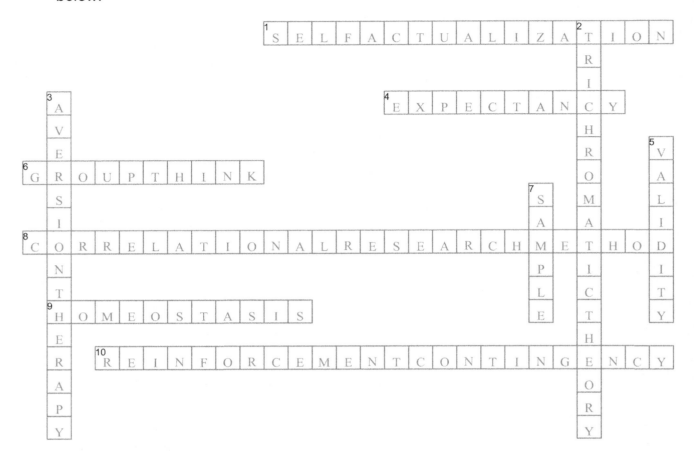

ACROSS

1. A concept in personality psychology referring to a person's constant striving to realize his or her potential and to develop inherent talents and capabilities.

4. The extent to which people believe that their behaviors situations will bring about rewards.

6. The tendency of a decision-making group to filter out undesirable input so that a consensus may be reached, especially if it is in line with the leader's viewpoint.

8. Research methodology that determines to what extent two variables, traits, or attributes are related.

9. Constancy or equilibrium of the internal conditions of the body.

10. A consistent relationship between a response and the changes in the environment that it produces.

DOWN

1. A concept in personality psychology referring to a person's constant striving to realize his or her potential and to develop inherent talents and capabilities.

4. The extent to which people believe that their behaviors situations will bring about rewards.

6. The tendency of a decision-making group to filter out undesirable input so that a consensus may be reached, especially if it is in line with the leader's viewpoint.

8. Research methodology that determines to what extent two variables, traits, or attributes are related.

9. Constancy or equilibrium of the internal conditions of the body.

10. A consistent relationship between a response and the changes in the environment that it produces.

A. Correlational research method   B. Sample   C. Homeostasis
D. Reinforcement contingency   E. Self actualization   F. Expectancy
G. Aversion therapy   H. Groupthink   I. Trichromatic theory
J. Validity

11. *Using the Across and Down clues, write the correct words in the numbered grid below.*

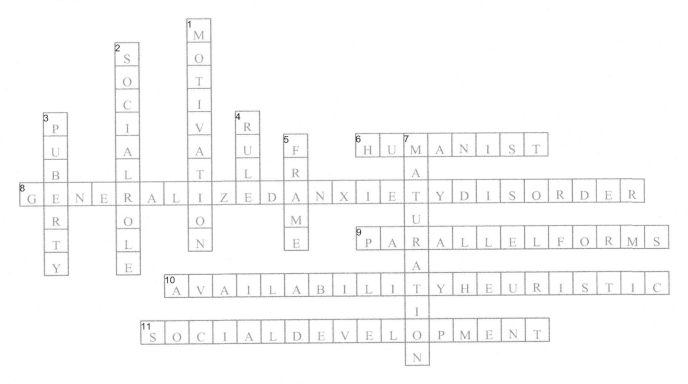

ACROSS

6. A psychological model that emphasizes an individual's phenomenal world and inherent capacity for making rational choices and developing to maximum potential.

8. An anxiety disorder in which an individual feels anxious and worried most of the time for at least six months when not threatened by any specific danger or object.

9. Different versions of a test used to assess test reliability; the change of forms reduces effects of direct practice, memory, or the desire of an individual to appear consistent on the same items.

10. A judgment based on the information readily available in memory.

11. The ways in which individual's social interactions and expectations change across the life span.

DOWN

6. A psychological model that emphasizes an individual's phenomenal world and inherent capacity for making rational choices and developing to maximum potential.

8. An anxiety disorder in which an individual feels anxious and worried most of the time for at least six months when not threatened by any specific danger or object.

9. Different versions of a test used to assess test reliability; the change of forms reduces effects of direct practice, memory, or the desire of an individual to appear consistent on the same items.

10. A judgment based on the information readily available in memory.

11. The ways in which individual's social interactions and expectations change across the life span.

A. Frame
D. Humanist
G. Availability heuristic
J. Generalized anxiety disorder

B. Social role
E. Maturation
H. Rule
K. Puberty

C. Parallel forms
F. Social development
I. Motivation

12. *Using the Across and Down clues, write the correct words in the numbered grid below.*

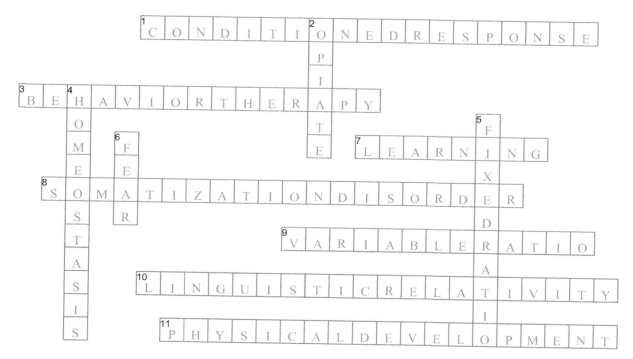

ACROSS

1. Is a response elicited by some previously neutral stimulus that occurs as a result of pairing the neutral stimulus with an unconditioned stimulus.

3. The systematic use of principles of learning to increase the frequency of desired behaviors and

7. A process based on experience that results in a relatively permanent change in behavior or behavioral potential.

8. A disorder characterized by unexplained physical complaints in several categories over many years.

9. A schedule of reinforcement in which a reinforcer is delivered for the first response made after a variable number of responses whose average is predetermined.

10. The hypothesis that the structure of the language and individual speaks has an impact on the way in which that individual thinks about the world.

11. The bodily changes, maturation, and growth that occur in an organism starting with conception and continuing across the life span.

DOWN

1. Is a response elicited by some previously neutral stimulus that occurs as a result of pairing the neutral stimulus with an unconditioned stimulus.

3. The systematic use of principles of learning to increase the frequency of desired behaviors and

7. A process based on experience that results in a relatively permanent change in behavior or behavioral potential.

8. A disorder characterized by unexplained physical complaints in several categories over many years.

9. A schedule of reinforcement in which a reinforcer is delivered for the first response made after a variable number of responses whose average is predetermined.

10. The hypothesis that the structure of the language and individual speaks has an impact on the way in which that individual thinks about the world.

11. The bodily changes, maturation, and growth that occur in an organism starting with conception and continuing across the life span.

A. Variable ratio
D. Opiate
G. Behavior therapy
J. Fear

B. Somatization disorder
E. Linguistic relativity
H. Fixed ratio
K. Learning

C. Physical development
F. Conditioned response
I. Homeostasis

13. *Using the Across and Down clues, write the correct words in the numbered grid below.*

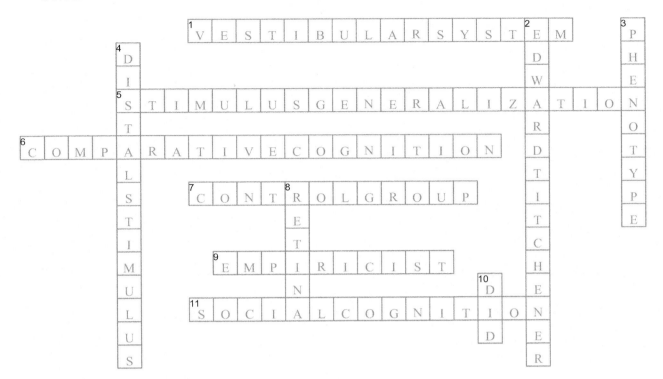

ACROSS

1. The receptors for this information are tiny hairs in fluid-filled sacs and canals in the inner ear.

5. The automatic extension of conditioned responding to similar stimuli that have never been paired with the unconditioned stimulus.

6. The study of the development of cognitive abilities across species and the continuity of abilities from nonhuman animals to humans.

7. A group in an experiment that is not exposed to a treatment or does not experience a manipulation of the independent variable.

9. People begin life with their mind as a blank tablet, and the mind acquires information through experiences with the world.

11. The process by which people select, interpret, and remember social information.

DOWN

1. The receptors for this information are tiny hairs in fluid-filled sacs and canals in the inner ear.

5. The automatic extension of conditioned responding to similar stimuli that have never been paired with the unconditioned stimulus.

6. The study of the development of cognitive abilities across species and the continuity of abilities from nonhuman animals to humans.

7. A group in an experiment that is not exposed to a treatment or does not experience a manipulation of the independent variable.

9. People begin life with their mind as a blank tablet, and the mind acquires information through experiences with the world.

11. The process by which people select, interpret, and remember social information.

A. Stimulus generalization
D. Control group
G. Distal stimulus
J. Social cognition

B. Phenotype
E. Comparative cognition
H. Empiricist
K. DID

C. Retina
F. Vestibular system
I. Edward Titchener

14. *Using the Across and Down clues, write the correct words in the numbered grid below.*

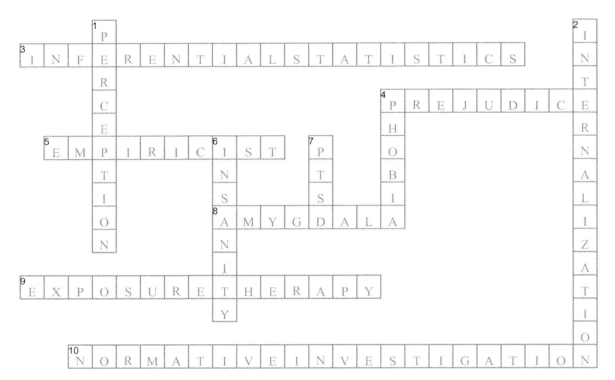

ACROSS

3. Statistical procedures that allow researchers to determine whether the results they obtain support their hypotheses or can be attributed to chance variation.

4. A learned attitude toward a target object, involving negative affect (dislike or fear), negative beliefs (stereotypes), that justify the attitude, and a behavioral intention to avoid, control, dominate, or eliminate the target object.

5. People begin life with their mind as a blank tablet, and the mind acquires information through experiences with the world.

8. The part of the limbic system that controls emotions, aggression, and the formation of emotional memory.

9. A behavioral technique in which clients are exposed to the objects or situations that cause them anxiety.

10. Research effort designed to describe what is characteristic of a specific age or developmental stage.

DOWN

3. Statistical procedures that allow researchers to determine whether the results they obtain support their hypotheses or can be attributed to chance variation.

4. A learned attitude toward a target object, involving negative affect (dislike or fear), negative beliefs (stereotypes), that justify the attitude, and a behavioral intention to avoid, control, dominate, or eliminate the target object.

5. People begin life with their mind as a blank tablet, and the mind acquires information through experiences with the world.

8. The part of the limbic system that controls emotions, aggression, and the formation of emotional memory.

9. A behavioral technique in which clients are exposed to the objects or situations that cause them anxiety.

10. Research effort designed to describe what is characteristic of a specific age or developmental stage.

A. Exposure therapy
D. Internalization
G. Prejudice
J. Empiricist

B. Phobia
E. Perception
H. Normative investigation
K. Amygdala

C. Insanity
F. Inferential statistics
I. PTSD

15. *Using the Across and Down clues, write the correct words in the numbered grid below.*

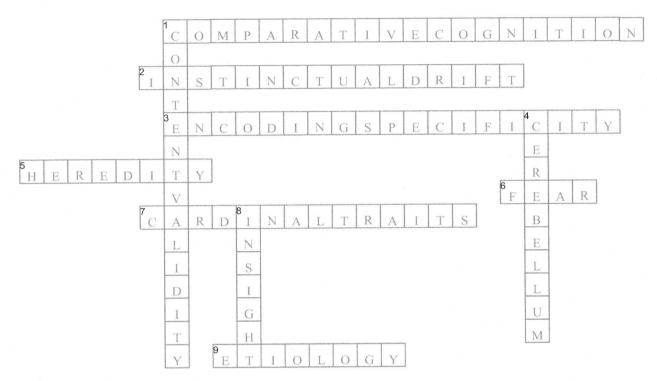

ACROSS

1. The study of the development of cognitive abilities across species and the continuity of abilities from nonhuman animals to humans.

2. The tendency for learned behavior to drift toward instinctual behavior over time.

3. The principle that subsequent retrieval of information is enhanced if cues received at the time of recall are consistent with those present at the time of encoding.

5. The biological transmission of traits from parents to offspring.

6. A rational reaction to an objectively identified external danger that may induce a person to flee or attack in self -defense.

7. Traits around which a person organizes his or her life. For example for Mother Teresa, this trait might have been self-sacrifice for the good of others.

9. The study of the causes and factors leading to the development of a disorder.

DOWN

1. The study of the development of cognitive abilities across species and the continuity of abilities from nonhuman animals to humans.

2. The tendency for learned behavior to drift toward instinctual behavior over time.

3. The principle that subsequent retrieval of information is enhanced if cues received at the time of recall are consistent with those present at the time of encoding.

5. The biological transmission of traits from parents to offspring.

6. A rational reaction to an objectively identified external danger that may induce a person to flee or attack in self -defense.

7. Traits around which a person organizes his or her life. For example for Mother Teresa, this trait might have been self-sacrifice for the good of others.

9. The study of the causes and factors leading to the development of a disorder.

A. Heredity
D. Instinctual drift
G. Content validity
J. Etiology

B. Insight
E. Comparative cognition
H. Cardinal traits

C. Encoding specificity
F. Cerebellum
I. Fear

16. *Using the Across and Down clues, write the correct words in the numbered grid below.*

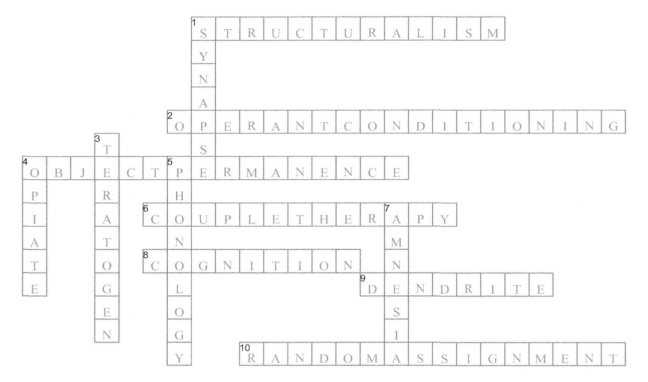

ACROSS

1. Study of the structure of mind and behavior; the view that all human mental experience can be understood as a combination of simple elements or events.

2. Learning in which the probability of a response is changed by a change in its consequences.

4. The recognition that objects exist independently of an individual's action or awareness; an important cognitive acquisition of infancy.

6. Seeks to clarify the typical communication patterns of the partners and then to improve the quality of their interaction.

8. Processes of knowing, including attending, remembering, and reasoning.

9. One of the branched fibers of neurons that receive incoming signals.

10. A procedure by which participants have an equal likelihood of being assigned to any condition within an experiment.

DOWN

1. Study of the structure of mind and behavior; the view that all human mental experience can be understood as a combination of simple elements or events.

2. Learning in which the probability of a response is changed by a change in its consequences.

4. The recognition that objects exist independently of an individual's action or awareness; an important cognitive acquisition of infancy.

6. Seeks to clarify the typical communication patterns of the partners and then to improve the quality of their interaction.

8. Processes of knowing, including attending, remembering, and reasoning.

9. One of the branched fibers of neurons that receive incoming signals.

10. A procedure by which participants have an equal likelihood of being assigned to any condition within an experiment.

A. Couple therapy   B. Amnesia   C. Dendrite
D. Operant conditioning E. Phonology   F. Teratogen
G. Structuralism   H. Cognition   I. Object permanence
J. Opiate   K. Random assignment L. Synapse

17. *Using the Across and Down clues, write the correct words in the numbered grid below.*

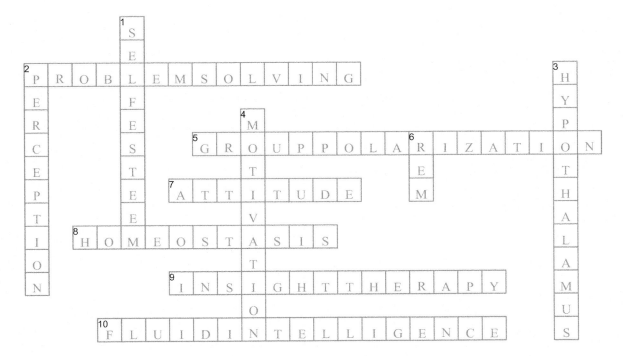

ACROSS

2. Thinking that is directed toward solving specific problems and that moves from an initial state to a goal state by means of a set of mental operations.

5. The tendency for groups to make decisions that are more extreme than the decisions that would be made by the members acting alone.

7. The learned, relatively stable tendency to respond to people, concepts, and events in an evaluative way.

8. Constancy or equilibrium of the internal conditions of the body.

9. A technique by which the therapist guides a patient toward discovering insights between present symptoms and past origins.

10. The aspect of intelligence that involves the ability to see complex relationships and solve problems; measured by tests of block designs and spatial visualization.

DOWN

2. Thinking that is directed toward solving specific problems and that moves from an initial state to a goal state by means of a set of mental operations.

5. The tendency for groups to make decisions that are more extreme than the decisions that would be made by the members acting alone.

7. The learned, relatively stable tendency to respond to people, concepts, and events in an evaluative way.

8. Constancy or equilibrium of the internal conditions of the body.

9. A technique by which the therapist guides a patient toward discovering insights between present symptoms and past origins.

10. The aspect of intelligence that involves the ability to see complex relationships and solve problems; measured by tests of block designs and spatial visualization.

A. Self esteem
E. Group polarization
I. Insight therapy

B. Attitude
F. REM
J. Motivation

C. Homeostasis
G. Perception
K. Hypothalamus

D. Problem solving
H. Fluid intelligence

18. Using the Across and Down clues, write the correct words in the numbered grid below.

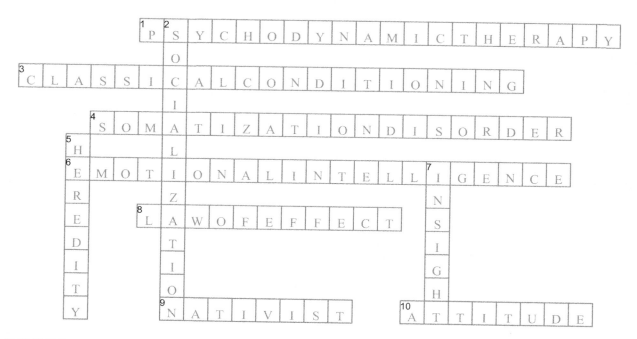

ACROSS

1. Type of therapy that assumes that a patient's problems have been caused by the psychological tension between unconscious impulses and the constraints of his or her life situation.

3. A type of learning in which a behavior (conditioned response) comes to be elicited by a stimulus (conditioned stimulus).

4. A disorder characterized by unexplained physical complaints in several categories over many years.

6. Type of intelligence defined as the abilities to perceive, appraise, and express emotions accurately and appropriately.

8. A basic law of learning that states that the power of a stimulus to evoke a response is strengthened when the response is followed by a reward and weakened when it is not followed by a reward.

9. People begin life with mental structures that provide constraints on how they experience the world.

10. The learned, relatively stable tendency to respond to people, concepts, and events in an evaluative way.

DOWN

1. Type of therapy that assumes that a patient's problems have been caused by the psychological tension between unconscious impulses and the constraints of his or her life situation.

3. A type of learning in which a behavior (conditioned response) comes to be elicited by a stimulus (conditioned stimulus).

4. A disorder characterized by unexplained physical complaints in several categories over many years.

6. Type of intelligence defined as the abilities to perceive, appraise, and express emotions accurately and appropriately.

8. A basic law of learning that states that the power of a stimulus to evoke a response is strengthened when the response is followed by a reward and weakened when it is not followed by a reward.

9. People begin life with mental structures that provide constraints on how they experience the world.

10. The learned, relatively stable tendency to respond to people, concepts, and events in an evaluative way.

A. Classical conditioning
D. Emotional intelligence
G. Law of effect
J. Socialization

B. Psychodynamic therapy
E. Heredity
H. Attitude

C. Nativist
F. Insight
I. Somatization disorder

19. *Using the Across and Down clues, write the correct words in the numbered grid below.*

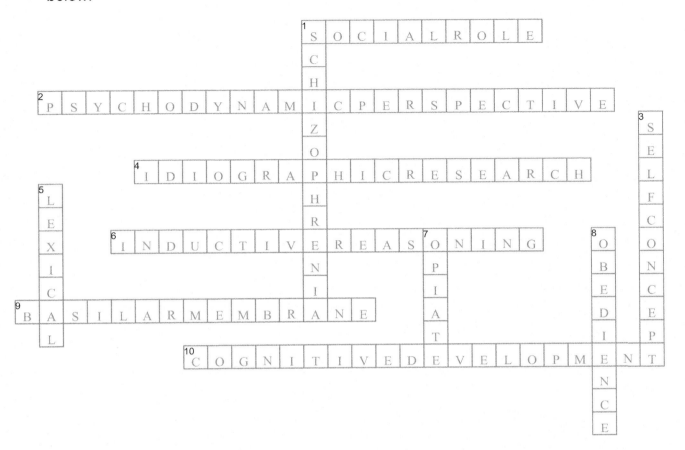

ACROSS

1. A socially defined pattern of behavior that is expected of a person who is functioning in a given setting or group.
2. A psychological model in which behavior is explained in terms of past experiences and motivational forces.
4. Focuses on the individual. Suggests that because everyone is unique and should be studied in an individual way, no general laws are possible.
6. A form of reasoning in which a conclusion is made about the probability of something happening based on the available evidence and experience.
9. A membrane running along the length of the cochlea.
10. The development of processes of knowing, including imagining, perceiving, reasoning, and problem solving.

DOWN

1. A socially defined pattern of behavior that is expected of a person who is functioning in a given setting or group.
2. A psychological model in which behavior is explained in terms of past experiences and motivational forces.
4. Focuses on the individual. Suggests that because everyone is unique and should be studied in an individual way, no general laws are possible.
6. A form of reasoning in which a conclusion is made about the probability of something happening based on the available evidence and experience.
9. A membrane running along the length of the cochlea.
10. The development of processes of knowing, including imagining, perceiving, reasoning, and problem solving.

A. Cognitive development
D. Social role
G. Schizophrenia
J. Opiate

B. Obedience
E. Psychodynamic perspective
H. Lexical
K. Inductive reasoning

C. Self concept
F. Basilar membrane
I. Idiographic research

20. *Using the Across and Down clues, write the correct words in the numbered grid below.*

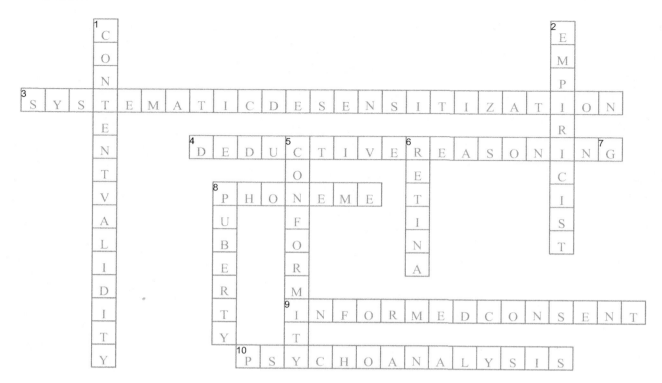

ACROSS

3. A behavioral therapy technique in which a client is taught to prevent the arousal of anxiety by confronting the feared stimulus while relaxed.

4. A form of thinking in which one draws a conclusion that is intended to follow logically from two or more statements or premises.

8. Minimal unit of speech in any given language that makes a meaningful difference in speech and production and reception.

9. The process through which individuals are informed about experimental procedures, risks, and benefits before they provide formal consent to become research participants.

10. The form of psychodynamic therapy developed by Freud; and intensive prolonged technique for exploring unconscious motivations and conflicts in neurotic, anxiety-ridden individuals.

DOWN

3. A behavioral therapy technique in which a client is taught to prevent the arousal of anxiety by confronting the feared stimulus while relaxed.

4. A form of thinking in which one draws a conclusion that is intended to follow logically from two or more statements or premises.

8. Minimal unit of speech in any given language that makes a meaningful difference in speech and production and reception.

9. The process through which individuals are informed about experimental procedures, risks, and benefits before they provide formal consent to become research participants.

10. The form of psychodynamic therapy developed by Freud; and intensive prolonged technique for exploring unconscious motivations and conflicts in neurotic, anxiety-ridden individuals.

A. Psychoanalysis
D. Retina
G. Deductive reasoning
J. Empiricist

B. G
E. Puberty
H. Content validity
K. Systematic desensitization

C. Informed consent
F. Phoneme
I. Conformity

21. *Using the Across and Down clues, write the correct words in the numbered grid below.*

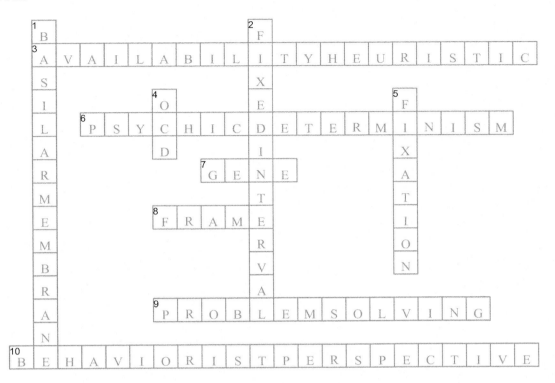

ACROSS

3. A judgment based on the information readily available in memory.

6. The assumption that mental and behavioral reactions are determined by previous experiences.

7. The biological unit of heredity; discrete section of a chromosome responsible for transmission of traits.

8. A particular description of a choice; the perspective from which a choice is described or framed affects how a decision is made and which option is ultimately exercised.

9. Thinking that is directed toward solving specific problems and that moves from an initial state to a goal state by means of a set of mental operations.

10. The psychological perspective primarily concerned with observable behavior that can be objectively recorded.

DOWN

3. A judgment based on the information readily available in memory.

6. The assumption that mental and behavioral reactions are determined by previous experiences.

7. The biological unit of heredity; discrete section of a chromosome responsible for transmission of traits.

8. A particular description of a choice; the perspective from which a choice is described or framed affects how a decision is made and which option is ultimately exercised.

9. Thinking that is directed toward solving specific problems and that moves from an initial state to a goal state by means of a set of mental operations.

10. The psychological perspective primarily concerned with observable behavior that can be objectively recorded.

A. Fixation
D. Frame
G. Behaviorist perspective
J. Gene

B. Psychic determinism
E. Availability heuristic
H. OCD

C. Problem solving
F. Basilar membrane
I. Fixed interval

22. *Using the Across and Down clues, write the correct words in the numbered grid below.*

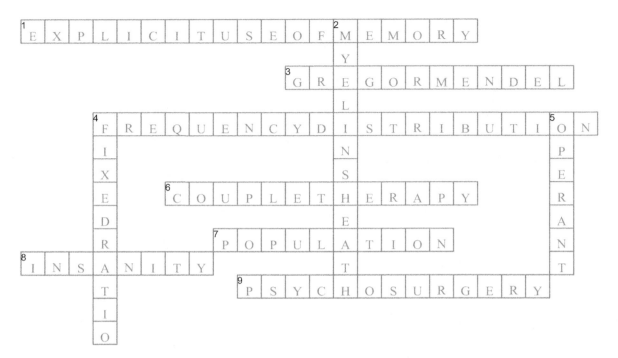

ACROSS

1. Conscious effort to encode or recover information through memory processes.

3. Researched the relationship between parents and their offspring by carrying out experiments on pea plants.

4. A summary of how frequently each score appears in a set of observations.

6. Seeks to clarify the typical communication patterns of the partners and then to improve the quality of their interaction.

7. The entire set of individuals to which generalizations will be made based on an experimental sample.

8. The legal (not clinical) designation for the state of an individual judged to be legally irresponsible or incompetent.

9. A surgical procedure performed on brain tissue to alleviate a psychological disorder.

DOWN

1. Conscious effort to encode or recover information through memory processes.

3. Researched the relationship between parents and their offspring by carrying out experiments on pea plants.

4. A summary of how frequently each score appears in a set of observations.

6. Seeks to clarify the typical communication patterns of the partners and then to improve the quality of their interaction.

7. The entire set of individuals to which generalizations will be made based on an experimental sample.

8. The legal (not clinical) designation for the state of an individual judged to be legally irresponsible or incompetent.

9. A surgical procedure performed on brain tissue to alleviate a psychological disorder.

A. Operant
D. Explicit use of memory
G. Population
J. Gregor Mendel

B. Fixed ratio
E. Frequency distribution
H. Couple therapy

C. Psychosurgery
F. Myelin sheath
I. Insanity

23. *Using the Across and Down clues, write the correct words in the numbered grid below.*

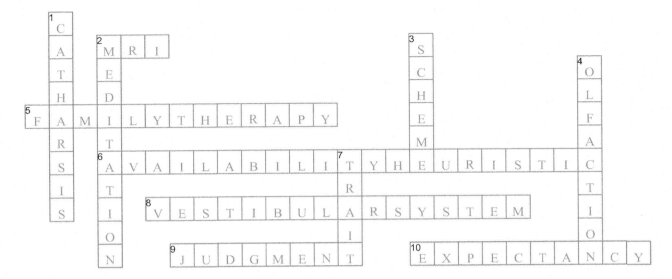

ACROSS

2. Magnetic resonance imaging. A technique for brain imaging that scans the brain using magnetic fields and radio waves.

5. The client is a whole nuclear family and each family member is treated as a member of a system of relationships.

6. A judgment based on the information readily available in memory.

8. The receptors for this information are tiny hairs in fluid-filled sacs and canals in the inner ear.

9. The process by which people form opinions, reach conclusions, and make critical evaluations of events and people based on available material; also, the product of the mental activity.

10. The extent to which people believe that their behaviors situations will bring about rewards.

DOWN

2. Magnetic resonance imaging. A technique for brain imaging that scans the brain using magnetic fields and radio waves.

5. The client is a whole nuclear family and each family member is treated as a member of a system of relationships.

6. A judgment based on the information readily available in memory.

8. The receptors for this information are tiny hairs in fluid-filled sacs and canals in the inner ear.

9. The process by which people form opinions, reach conclusions, and make critical evaluations of events and people based on available material; also, the product of the mental activity.

10. The extent to which people believe that their behaviors situations will bring about rewards.

A. Expectancy
E. Olfaction
I. MRI

B. Judgment
F. Family therapy
J. Meditation

C. Vestibular system
G. Scheme
K. Catharsis

D. Availability heuristic
H. Trait

24. *Using the Across and Down clues, write the correct words in the numbered grid below.*

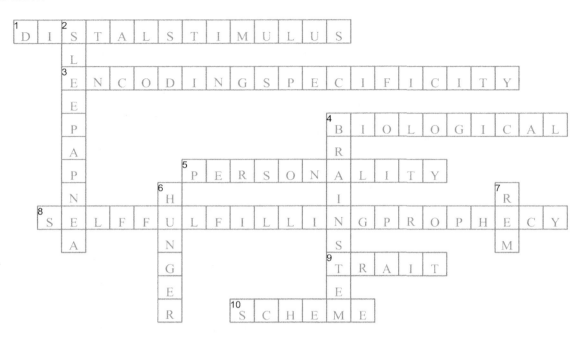

ACROSS

1. In the processes of perception, the physical object in the world.

3. The principle that subsequent retrieval of information is enhanced if cues received at the time of recall are consistent with those present at the time of encoding.

4. The approach to identifying causes of behavior that focuses on the functioning of the genes, the brain, the nervous system, and the endocrine system.

5. The psychological qualities of an individual that influence a variety of characteristic behavior patterns across different situations and over time.

8. A prediction made about some future behavior or event that modifies interactions to produce what is expected.

9. Enduring personal quality or attribute that influences behavior across situations.

10. Piaget's term for a cognitive structure that develops as infants and young children learn to interpret the world and adapt to their environment.

DOWN

1. In the processes of perception, the physical object in the world.

3. The principle that subsequent retrieval of information is enhanced if cues received at the time of recall are consistent with those present at the time of encoding.

4. The approach to identifying causes of behavior that focuses on the functioning of the genes, the brain, the nervous system, and the endocrine system.

5. The psychological qualities of an individual that influence a variety of characteristic behavior patterns across different situations and over time.

8. A prediction made about some future behavior or event that modifies interactions to produce what is expected.

9. Enduring personal quality or attribute that influences behavior across situations.

10. Piaget's term for a cognitive structure that develops as infants and young children learn to interpret the world and adapt to their environment.

A. Scheme
D. Hunger
G. Trait
J. Brain stem

B. REM
E. Biological
H. Sleep apnea
K. Self fulfilling prophecy

C. Personality
F. Distal stimulus
I. Encoding specificity

25. *Using the Across and Down clues, write the correct words in the numbered grid below.*

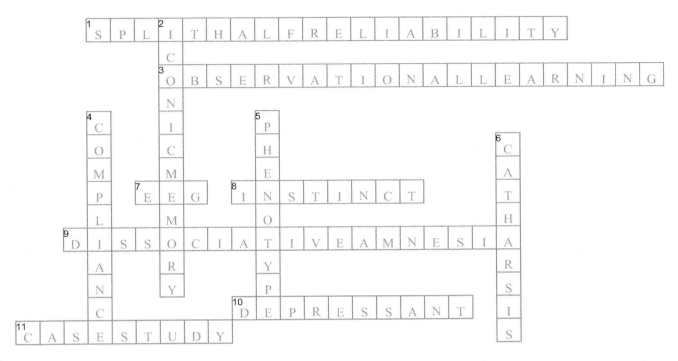

ACROSS

1. A measure of the correlation between test takers' performance on different halves (such as odd- and even-numbered items) of a test.

3. The process of learning new responses by watching the behavior of another.

7. A recording of the electrical activity of the brain.

8. Preprogrammed tendency that is essential to a species' survival.

9. The inability to remember important personal experiences, caused by psychological factors in the absence of any organic dysfunction.

10. Drug that depresses or slows down the activity of the central nervous system.

11. Intensive observation of an individual or small group of individuals.

DOWN

1. A measure of the correlation between test takers' performance on different halves (such as odd- and even-numbered items) of a test.

3. The process of learning new responses by watching the behavior of another.

7. A recording of the electrical activity of the brain.

8. Preprogrammed tendency that is essential to a species' survival.

9. The inability to remember important personal experiences, caused by psychological factors in the absence of any organic dysfunction.

10. Drug that depresses or slows down the activity of the central nervous system.

11. Intensive observation of an individual or small group of individuals.

A. Dissociative amnesia
D. Iconic memory
G. Instinct
J. Split half reliability

B. Depressant
E. Case study
H. EEG
K. Compliance

C. Observational learning
F. Phenotype
I. Catharsis

26. *Using the Across and Down clues, write the correct words in the numbered grid below.*

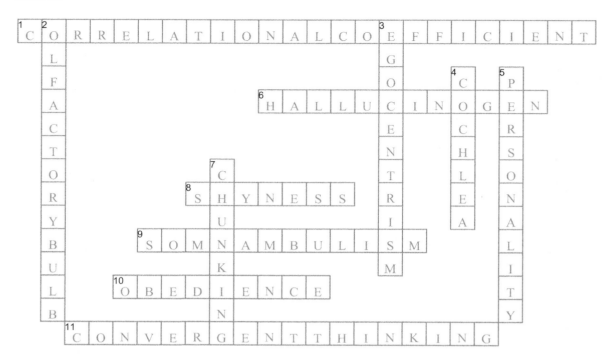

ACROSS

1. A statistic that indicates the degree of relationship between to variables. +1.0 is a perfect positive correlation, -1.0 is perfect negative correlation.

6. A drug that alters cognitions and perceptions and causes hallucinations.

8. An individual's discomfort and

9. A disorder that causes sleep walking.

10. Blind obedience is less a product of dispositional characteristics than the outcome of situational forces that could engulf anyone. (Milgram studies)

11. An aspect of creativity characterized by the ability to gather together different sources of information to solve a problem.

DOWN

1. A statistic that indicates the degree of relationship between to variables. +1.0 is a perfect positive correlation, -1.0 is perfect negative correlation.

6. A drug that alters cognitions and perceptions and causes hallucinations.

8. An individual's discomfort and

9. A disorder that causes sleep walking.

10. Blind obedience is less a product of dispositional characteristics than the outcome of situational forces that could engulf anyone. (Milgram studies)

11. An aspect of creativity characterized by the ability to gather together different sources of information to solve a problem.

A. Hallucinogen
D. Obedience
G. Personality
J. Chunking

B. Cochlea
E. Convergent thinking
H. Somnambulism
K. Egocentrism

C. Correlational coefficient
F. Shyness
I. Olfactory bulb

27. *Using the Across and Down clues, write the correct words in the numbered grid below.*

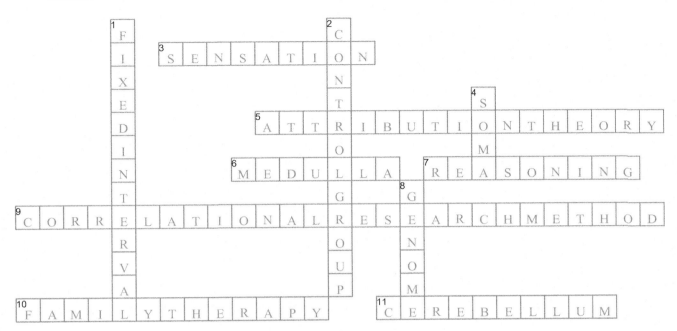

ACROSS

3. The process by which stimulation of a sensory receptor gives rise to neutral impulses that result in an experience, or awareness, of conditions inside or outside the body.

5. A social-cognitive approach to describing the ways the social perceiver uses information to generate causal explanations.

6. The region of the brain stem that regulates breathing, waking, and heartbeat.

7. The process of thinking in which conclusions are drawn from a set of facts; thinking directed toward a given goal or objective.

9. Research methodology that determines to what extent two variables, traits, or attributes are related.

10. The client is a whole nuclear family and each family member is treated as a member of a system of relationships.

11. The region of the brain attached to the brain stem that controls motor coordination, posture, and balance as well as the ability to learn control of body movements.

DOWN

3. The process by which stimulation of a sensory receptor gives rise to neutral impulses that result in an experience, or awareness, of conditions inside or outside the body.

5. A social-cognitive approach to describing the ways the social perceiver uses information to generate causal explanations.

6. The region of the brain stem that regulates breathing, waking, and heartbeat.

7. The process of thinking in which conclusions are drawn from a set of facts; thinking directed toward a given goal or objective.

9. Research methodology that determines to what extent two variables, traits, or attributes are related.

10. The client is a whole nuclear family and each family member is treated as a member of a system of relationships.

11. The region of the brain attached to the brain stem that controls motor coordination, posture, and balance as well as the ability to learn control of body movements.

A. Control group
D. Fixed interval
G. Cerebellum
J. Genome

B. Family therapy
E. Medulla
H. Reasoning
K. Sensation

C. Correlational research method
F. Attribution theory
I. Soma

28. *Using the Across and Down clues, write the correct words in the numbered grid below.*

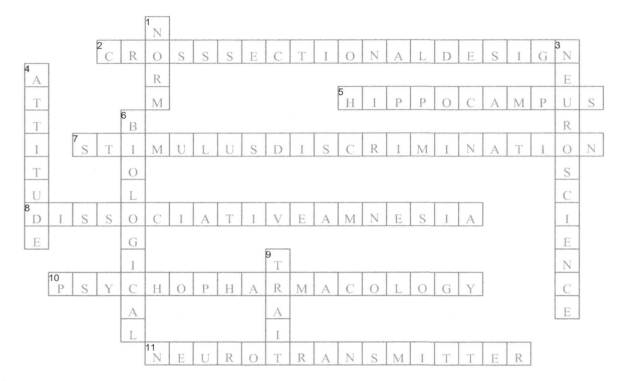

ACROSS

2. A research method in which groups of participants of different chronological ages are observed and compared at a given time.

5. The part of the limbic system that is involved in the acquisition of explicit memory.

7. A conditioning process in which an organism learns to respond differently to stimuli that differ from the conditioned stimulus on some dimension.

8. The inability to remember important personal experiences, caused by psychological factors in the absence of any organic dysfunction.

10. The branch of psychology that investigates the effects of drugs on behavior.

11. Chemical messenger released from a neuron that crosses the synapse from one neuron to another, stimulating the postsynaptic neuron.

DOWN

2. A research method in which groups of participants of different chronological ages are observed and compared at a given time.

5. The part of the limbic system that is involved in the acquisition of explicit memory.

7. A conditioning process in which an organism learns to respond differently to stimuli that differ from the conditioned stimulus on some dimension.

8. The inability to remember important personal experiences, caused by psychological factors in the absence of any organic dysfunction.

10. The branch of psychology that investigates the effects of drugs on behavior.

11. Chemical messenger released from a neuron that crosses the synapse from one neuron to another, stimulating the postsynaptic neuron.

A. Neurotransmitter
D. Dissociative amnesia
G. Trait
J. Hippocampus

B. Attitude
E. Stimulus discrimination
H. Psychopharmacology
K. Cross sectional design

C. Biological
F. Neuroscience
I. Norm

29. *Using the Across and Down clues, write the correct words in the numbered grid below.*

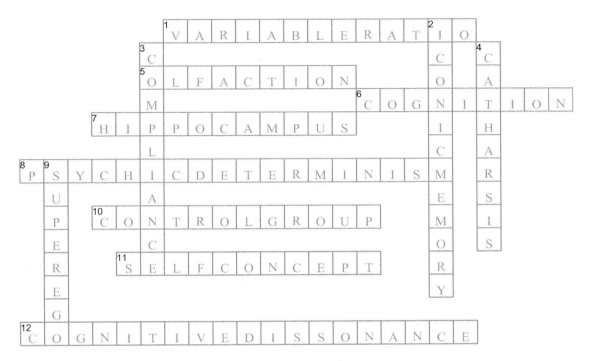

ACROSS

1. A schedule of reinforcement in which a reinforcer is delivered for the first response made after a variable number of responses whose average is predetermined.

5. The sense of smell.

6. Processes of knowing, including attending, remembering, and reasoning.

7. The part of the limbic system that is involved in the acquisition of explicit memory.

8. The assumption that mental and behavioral reactions are determined by previous experiences.

10. A group in an experiment that is not exposed to a treatment or does not experience a manipulation of the independent variable.

11. A person's mental model of his or her abilities and attributes.

12. The state of conflict someone experiences after deciding, taking an action, or being exposed to information that is contrary to prior beliefs, feelings, or values. Impels you to act to reduce the unpleasant feeling.

DOWN

1. A schedule of reinforcement in which a reinforcer is delivered for the first response made after a variable number of responses whose average is predetermined.

5. The sense of smell.

6. Processes of knowing, including attending, remembering, and reasoning.

7. The part of the limbic system that is involved in the acquisition of explicit memory.

8. The assumption that mental and behavioral reactions are determined by previous experiences.

10. A group in an experiment that is not exposed to a treatment or does not experience a manipulation of the independent variable.

11. A person's mental model of his or her abilities and attributes.

12. The state of conflict someone experiences after deciding, taking an action, or being exposed to information that is contrary to prior beliefs, feelings, or values. Impels you to act to reduce the unpleasant feeling.

A. Variable ratio
D. Cognitive dissonance
G. Superego
J. Cognition

B. Control group
E. Catharsis
H. Self concept
K. Psychic determinism

C. Compliance
F. Hippocampus
I. Iconic memory
L. Olfaction

30. *Using the Across and Down clues, write the correct words in the numbered grid below.*

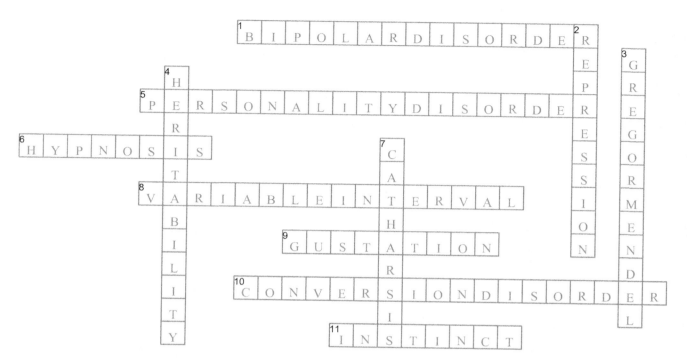

ACROSS

1. A mood disorder characterized by alternating periods of depression and mania.

5. A chronic, inflexible, maladaptive pattern of perceiving, thinking, and behaving that seriously impairs an individual's ability to function in social or other settings.

6. An altered state of awareness characterized by deep relaxation, susceptibility to suggestions, and changes in perception, memory, motivation, and self-control.

8. A schedule of reinforcement in which a reinforcer is delivered for the first response made after a variable period whose average is predetermined.

9. The sense of taste.

10. A disorder in which psychological conflict or stress brings about loss of motor or sensory function.

11. Preprogrammed tendency that is essential to a species' survival.

DOWN

1. A mood disorder characterized by alternating periods of depression and mania.

5. A chronic, inflexible, maladaptive pattern of perceiving, thinking, and behaving that seriously impairs an individual's ability to function in social or other settings.

6. An altered state of awareness characterized by deep relaxation, susceptibility to suggestions, and changes in perception, memory, motivation, and self-control.

8. A schedule of reinforcement in which a reinforcer is delivered for the first response made after a variable period whose average is predetermined.

9. The sense of taste.

10. A disorder in which psychological conflict or stress brings about loss of motor or sensory function.

11. Preprogrammed tendency that is essential to a species' survival.

A. Conversion disorder
E. Catharsis
I. Gregor Mendel

B. Bipolar disorder
F. Heritability
J. Variable interval

C. Hypnosis
G. Repression
K. Gustation

D. Instinct
H. Personality disorder

31. *Using the Across and Down clues, write the correct words in the numbered grid below.*

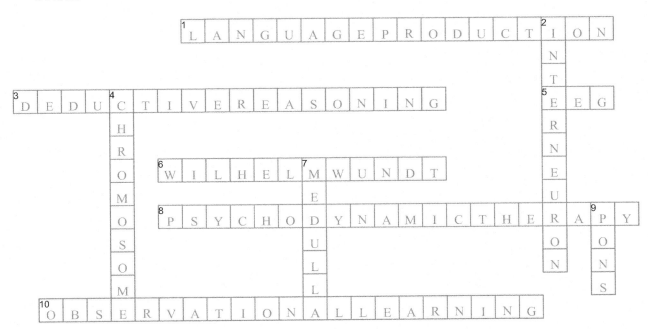

ACROSS

1. What people say, sign, and write, as well as the processes the go through to produce these messages.

3. A form of thinking in which one draws a conclusion that is intended to follow logically from two or more statements or premises.

5. A recording of the electrical activity of the brain.

6. Founded the first formal experimental psychology laboratory in 1879 in Leipzig, Germany.

8. Type of therapy that assumes that a patient's problems have been caused by the psychological tension between unconscious impulses and the constraints of his or her life situation.

10. The process of learning new responses by watching the behavior of another.

DOWN

1. What people say, sign, and write, as well as the processes the go through to produce these messages.

3. A form of thinking in which one draws a conclusion that is intended to follow logically from two or more statements or premises.

5. A recording of the electrical activity of the brain.

6. Founded the first formal experimental psychology laboratory in 1879 in Leipzig, Germany.

8. Type of therapy that assumes that a patient's problems have been caused by the psychological tension between unconscious impulses and the constraints of his or her life situation.

10. The process of learning new responses by watching the behavior of another.

A. Chromosome
D. Psychodynamic therapy
G. Deductive reasoning
J. Wilhelm Wundt

B. Language production
E. Observational learning
H. EEG

C. Interneuron
F. Medulla
I. Pons

32. *Using the Across and Down clues, write the correct words in the numbered grid below.*

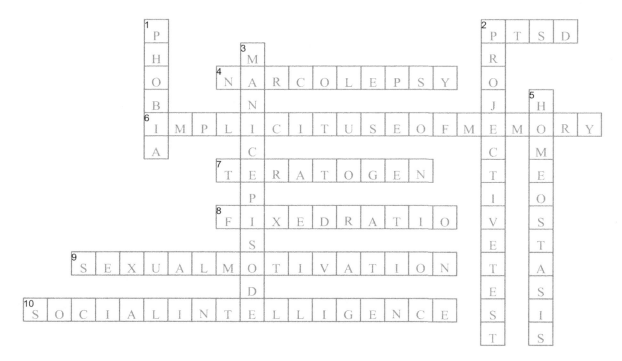

ACROSS

2. Posttraumatic stress disorder. An anxiety disorder characterized by the persistent re-experience of those traumatic events through distressing recollections, dreams, hallucinations, or flashbacks.

4. A sleep disorder characterized by an irresistible compulsion to sleep during the daytime.

6. Availability of information through memory processes without conscious effort to encode or recover information.

7. Environmental factors such as diseases and drugs that cause structural abnormalities in a developing fetus.

8. A schedule of reinforcement in which a reinforcer is delivered for the first response made after a fixed number of responses.

9. Sexual arousal is the motivational state of excitement and tension brought about by physiological and cognitive reactions to erotic stimuli.

10. A theory of personality that refers to the expertise people bring to their experience of life tasks.

DOWN

2. Posttraumatic stress disorder. An anxiety disorder characterized by the persistent re-experience of those traumatic events through distressing recollections, dreams, hallucinations, or flashbacks.

4. A sleep disorder characterized by an irresistible compulsion to sleep during the daytime.

6. Availability of information through memory processes without conscious effort to encode or recover information.

7. Environmental factors such as diseases and drugs that cause structural abnormalities in a developing fetus.

8. A schedule of reinforcement in which a reinforcer is delivered for the first response made after a fixed number of responses.

9. Sexual arousal is the motivational state of excitement and tension brought about by physiological and cognitive reactions to erotic stimuli.

10. A theory of personality that refers to the expertise people bring to their experience of life tasks.

A. Sexual motivation
D. PTSD
G. Narcolepsy
J. Manic episode

B. Homeostasis
E. Projective test
H. Phobia
K. Social intelligence

C. Fixed ratio
F. Implicit use of memory
I. Teratogen

33. *Using the Across and Down clues, write the correct words in the numbered grid below.*

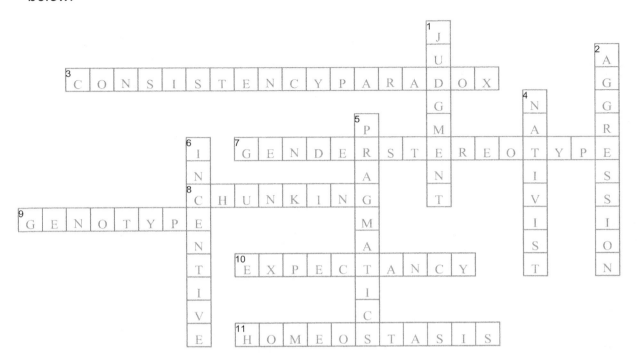

ACROSS

3. The observation that personality ratings across time and among different observers are consistent while behavior ratings across situations are not consistent.

7. Belief about attributes and behaviors regarded as appropriate for males and females in a particular culture.

8. The process of reconfiguring items by grouping based on similarity or some other organizing principle.

9. The genetic structure an organism inherits from its parents.

10. The extent to which people believe that their behaviors situations will bring about rewards.

11. Constancy or equilibrium of the internal conditions of the body.

DOWN

3. The observation that personality ratings across time and among different observers are consistent while behavior ratings across situations are not consistent.

7. Belief about attributes and behaviors regarded as appropriate for males and females in a particular culture.

8. The process of reconfiguring items by grouping based on similarity or some other organizing principle.

9. The genetic structure an organism inherits from its parents.

10. The extent to which people believe that their behaviors situations will bring about rewards.

11. Constancy or equilibrium of the internal conditions of the body.

A. Genotype
E. Pragmatics
I. Gender stereotype

B. Consistency paradox
F. Expectancy
J. Aggression

C. Chunking
G. Nativist
K. Incentive

D. Judgment
H. Homeostasis

34. *Using the Across and Down clues, write the correct words in the numbered grid below.*

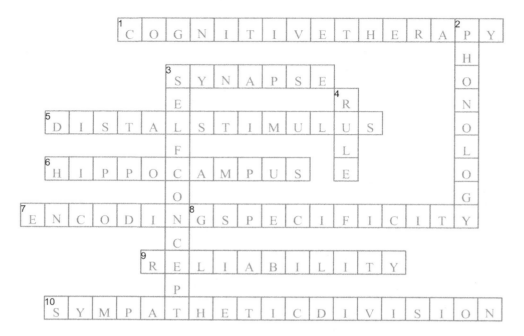

ACROSS

1. A type of psychotherapeutic treatment that attempts to change feelings and behaviors by changing the way a client thinks about or perceives significant life experience.

3. The gap between one neuron and another.

5. In the processes of perception, the physical object in the world.

6. The part of the limbic system that is involved in the acquisition of explicit memory.

7. The principle that subsequent retrieval of information is enhanced if cues received at the time of recall are consistent with those present at the time of encoding.

9. The degree to which a test produces similar scores each time it is used; stability or consistency of the scores produced by an instrument.

10. The subdivision of the ANS that deals with emergency response and the mobilization of energy.

DOWN

1. A type of psychotherapeutic treatment that attempts to change feelings and behaviors by changing the way a client thinks about or perceives significant life experience.

3. The gap between one neuron and another.

5. In the processes of perception, the physical object in the world.

6. The part of the limbic system that is involved in the acquisition of explicit memory.

7. The principle that subsequent retrieval of information is enhanced if cues received at the time of recall are consistent with those present at the time of encoding.

9. The degree to which a test produces similar scores each time it is used; stability or consistency of the scores produced by an instrument.

10. The subdivision of the ANS that deals with emergency response and the mobilization of energy.

A. Self concept
B. Cognitive therapy
C. Synapse
D. Encoding specificity
E. G
F. Rule
G. Reliability
H. Phonology
I. Sympathetic division
J. Hippocampus
K. Distal stimulus

35. *Using the Across and Down clues, write the correct words in the numbered grid below.*

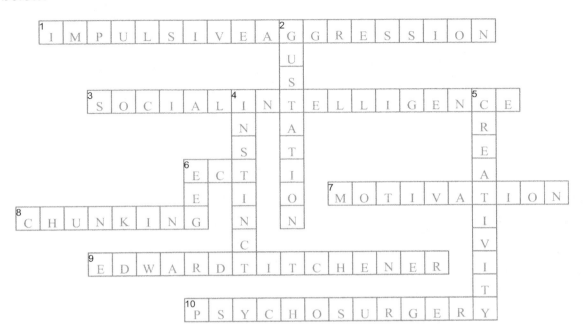

ACROSS

1. Produced in reaction to situations and is emotion driven.

3. A theory of personality that refers to the expertise people bring to their experience of life tasks.

6. Electroconvulsive therapy. The use of electroconvulsive shock as an effective treatment for severe depression.

7. The process of starting, directing, and maintaining physical and psychological activities; includes mechanisms involved in preferences for one activity over another and the vigor and persistence of responses.

8. The process of reconfiguring items by grouping based on similarity or some other organizing principle.

9. Founded a psychology laboratory at Cornell University in 1892, student of Wilhelm Wundt.

10. A surgical procedure performed on brain tissue to alleviate a psychological disorder.

DOWN

1. Produced in reaction to situations and is emotion driven.

3. A theory of personality that refers to the expertise people bring to their experience of life tasks.

6. Electroconvulsive therapy. The use of electroconvulsive shock as an effective treatment for severe depression.

7. The process of starting, directing, and maintaining physical and psychological activities; includes mechanisms involved in preferences for one activity over another and the vigor and persistence of responses.

8. The process of reconfiguring items by grouping based on similarity or some other organizing principle.

9. Founded a psychology laboratory at Cornell University in 1892, student of Wilhelm Wundt.

10. A surgical procedure performed on brain tissue to alleviate a psychological disorder.

A. Instinct
B. Motivation
C. Creativity
D. Chunking
E. Impulsive aggression
F. Gustation
G. EEG
H. Psychosurgery
I. ECT
J. Social intelligence
K. Edward Titchener

36. *Using the Across and Down clues, write the correct words in the numbered grid below.*

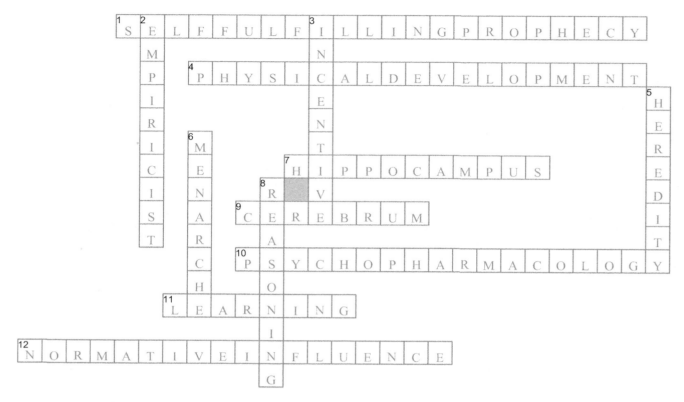

ACROSS

1. A prediction made about some future behavior or event that modifies interactions to produce what is expected.

4. The bodily changes, maturation, and growth that occur in an organism starting with conception and continuing across the life span.

7. The part of the limbic system that is involved in the acquisition of explicit memory.

9. The region of the brain that regulates higher cognitive and emotional functions.

10. The branch of psychology that investigates the effects of drugs on behavior.

11. A process based on experience that results in a relatively permanent change in behavior or behavioral potential.

12. Group effects that arise from individuals' desire to be like, accepted, and approved of by others.

DOWN

1. A prediction made about some future behavior or event that modifies interactions to produce what is expected.

4. The bodily changes, maturation, and growth that occur in an organism starting with conception and continuing across the life span.

7. The part of the limbic system that is involved in the acquisition of explicit memory.

9. The region of the brain that regulates higher cognitive and emotional functions.

10. The branch of psychology that investigates the effects of drugs on behavior.

11. A process based on experience that results in a relatively permanent change in behavior or behavioral potential.

12. Group effects that arise from individuals' desire to be like, accepted, and approved of by others.

A. Heredity
D. Psychopharmacology
G. Menarche
J. Physical development

B. Self fulfilling prophecy
E. Learning
H. Incentive
K. Reasoning

C. Empiricist
F. Normative influence
I. Cerebrum
L. Hippocampus

37. *Using the Across and Down clues, write the correct words in the numbered grid below.*

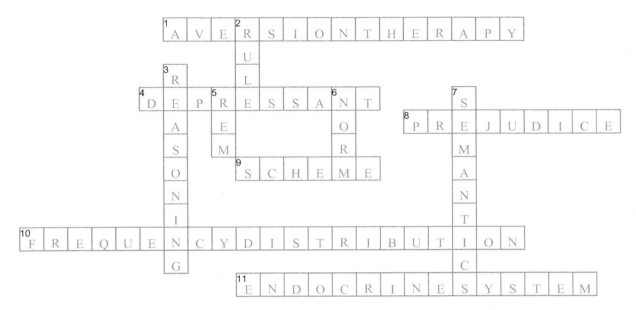

ACROSS

1. A type of behavioral therapy used to treat individuals attracted to harmful stimuli.

4. Drug that depresses or slows down the activity of the central nervous system.

8. A learned attitude toward a target object, involving negative affect (dislike or fear), negative beliefs (stereotypes), that justify the attitude, and a behavioral intention to avoid, control, dominate, or eliminate the target object.

9. Piaget's term for a cognitive structure that develops as infants and young children learn to interpret the world and adapt to their environment.

10. A summary of how frequently each score appears in a set of observations.

11. The network of glands that manufacture and secrete hormones into the bloodstream.

DOWN

1. A type of behavioral therapy used to treat individuals attracted to harmful stimuli.

4. Drug that depresses or slows down the activity of the central nervous system.

8. A learned attitude toward a target object, involving negative affect (dislike or fear), negative beliefs (stereotypes), that justify the attitude, and a behavioral intention to avoid, control, dominate, or eliminate the target object.

9. Piaget's term for a cognitive structure that develops as infants and young children learn to interpret the world and adapt to their environment.

10. A summary of how frequently each score appears in a set of observations.

11. The network of glands that manufacture and secrete hormones into the bloodstream.

A. Semantics
D. Reasoning
G. REM
J. Endocrine system

B. Frequency distribution
E. Depressant
H. Rule
K. Scheme

C. Norm
F. Prejudice
I. Aversion therapy

38. *Using the Across and Down clues, write the correct words in the numbered grid below.*

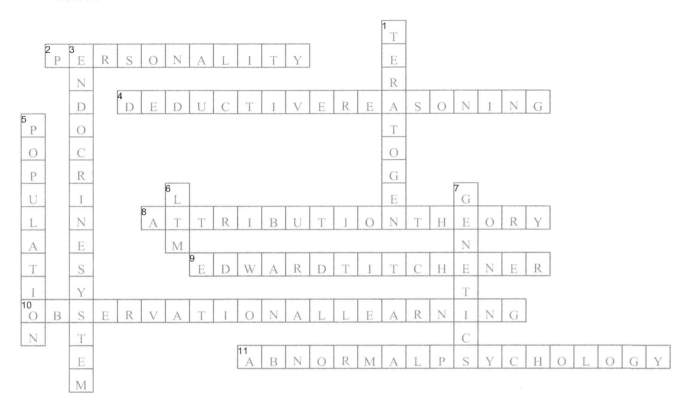

ACROSS

2. The psychological qualities of an individual that influence a variety of characteristic behavior patterns across different situations and over time.

4. A form of thinking in which one draws a conclusion that is intended to follow logically from two or more statements or premises.

8. A social-cognitive approach to describing the ways the social perceiver uses information to generate causal explanations.

9. Founded a psychology laboratory at Cornell University in 1892, student of Wilhelm Wundt.

10. The process of learning new responses by watching the behavior of another.

11. The area of psychological investigation concerned with understanding the nature of individual pathologies of mind, mood, and behavior.

DOWN

2. The psychological qualities of an individual that influence a variety of characteristic behavior patterns across different situations and over time.

4. A form of thinking in which one draws a conclusion that is intended to follow logically from two or more statements or premises.

8. A social-cognitive approach to describing the ways the social perceiver uses information to generate causal explanations.

9. Founded a psychology laboratory at Cornell University in 1892, student of Wilhelm Wundt.

10. The process of learning new responses by watching the behavior of another.

11. The area of psychological investigation concerned with understanding the nature of individual pathologies of mind, mood, and behavior.

A. Abnormal psychology
D. Population
G. Teratogen
J. LTM

B. Attribution theory
E. Observational learning
H. Endocrine system
K. Personality

C. Deductive reasoning
F. Edward Titchener
I. Genetics

39. *Using the Across and Down clues, write the correct words in the numbered grid below.*

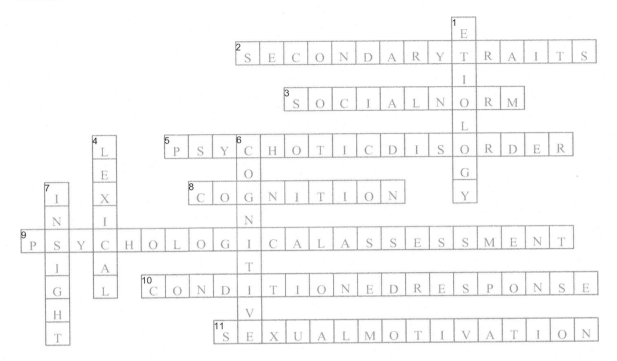

ACROSS

2. Specific personal features that help predict an individual's behavior but are less useful for understanding an individual's personality, such as food or dress preferences.

3. The expectation a group has for its members regarding acceptable and appropriate attitudes and behaviors.

5. Severe mental disorder in which a person experiences impairment manifested through thought, emotional, or perceptual difficulties.

8. Processes of knowing, including attending, remembering, and reasoning.

9. The use of specified procedures to evaluate the abilities, behaviors, and personal qualities of people.

10. Is a response elicited by some previously neutral stimulus that occurs as a result of pairing the neutral stimulus with an unconditioned stimulus.

11. Sexual arousal is the motivational state of excitement and tension brought about by physiological and cognitive reactions to erotic stimuli.

DOWN

2. Specific personal features that help predict an individual's behavior but are less useful for understanding an individual's personality, such as food or dress preferences.

3. The expectation a group has for its members regarding acceptable and appropriate attitudes and behaviors.

5. Severe mental disorder in which a person experiences impairment manifested through thought, emotional, or perceptual difficulties.

8. Processes of knowing, including attending, remembering, and reasoning.

9. The use of specified procedures to evaluate the abilities, behaviors, and personal qualities of people.

10. Is a response elicited by some previously neutral stimulus that occurs as a result of pairing the neutral stimulus with an unconditioned stimulus.

11. Sexual arousal is the motivational state of excitement and tension brought about by physiological and cognitive reactions to erotic stimuli.

A. Conditioned response   B. Psychological assessment   C. Secondary traits
D. Etiology   E. Cognition   F. Social norm
G. Lexical   H. Sexual motivation   I. Psychotic disorder
J. Insight   K. Cognitive

40. *Using the Across and Down clues, write the correct words in the numbered grid below.*

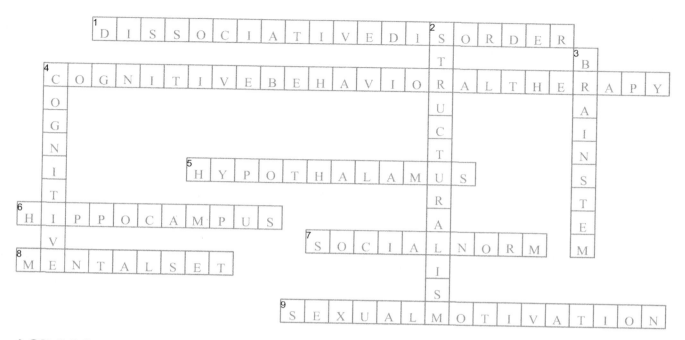

ACROSS

1. A personality disorder marked by a disturbance in the integration of identity, memory, or consciousness.
4. A therapeutic approach that combines the cognitive emphasis on thoughts and attitudes with the behavioral emphasis on changing performance.
5. The brain structure that regulates motivated behavior and homeostasis.
6. The part of the limbic system that is involved in the acquisition of explicit memory.
7. The expectation a group has for its members regarding acceptable and appropriate attitudes and behaviors.
8. The tendency to respond to a new problem in the manner used to respond to a previous problem.
9. Sexual arousal is the motivational state of excitement and tension brought about by physiological and cognitive reactions to erotic stimuli.

DOWN

1. A personality disorder marked by a disturbance in the integration of identity, memory, or consciousness.
4. A therapeutic approach that combines the cognitive emphasis on thoughts and attitudes with the behavioral emphasis on changing performance.
5. The brain structure that regulates motivated behavior and homeostasis.
6. The part of the limbic system that is involved in the acquisition of explicit memory.
7. The expectation a group has for its members regarding acceptable and appropriate attitudes and behaviors.
8. The tendency to respond to a new problem in the manner used to respond to a previous problem.
9. Sexual arousal is the motivational state of excitement and tension brought about by physiological and cognitive reactions to erotic stimuli.

A. Mental set
D. Cognitive behavioral therapy
G. Hippocampus
J. Structuralism

B. Dissociative disorder
E. Hypothalamus
H. Brain stem

C. Social norm
F. Cognitive
I. Sexual motivation

41. *Using the Across and Down clues, write the correct words in the numbered grid below.*

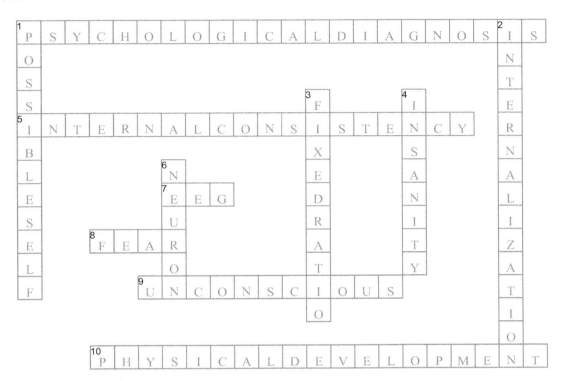

ACROSS

1. The label given to psychological abnormality by classifying and categorizing the observed behavior pattern into an approved diagnostic system.

5. A measure of reliability; the degree to which a test yields similar scores across its different parts, such as odd versus even items.

7. A recording of the electrical activity of the brain.

8. A rational reaction to an objectively identified external danger that may induce a person to flee or attack in self-defense.

9. The domain of the psyche that stores repressed urges and primitive impulses.

10. The bodily changes, maturation, and growth that occur in an organism starting with conception and continuing across the life span.

DOWN

1. The label given to psychological abnormality by classifying and categorizing the observed behavior pattern into an approved diagnostic system.

5. A measure of reliability; the degree to which a test yields similar scores across its different parts, such as odd versus even items.

7. A recording of the electrical activity of the brain.

8. A rational reaction to an objectively identified external danger that may induce a person to flee or attack in self-defense.

9. The domain of the psyche that stores repressed urges and primitive impulses.

10. The bodily changes, maturation, and growth that occur in an organism starting with conception and continuing across the life span.

A. Insanity
D. Internal consistency
G. Fixed ratio
J. EEG

B. Psychological diagnosis
E. Possible self
H. Neuron
K. Fear

C. Internalization
F. Unconscious
I. Physical development

42. *Using the Across and Down clues, write the correct words in the numbered grid below.*

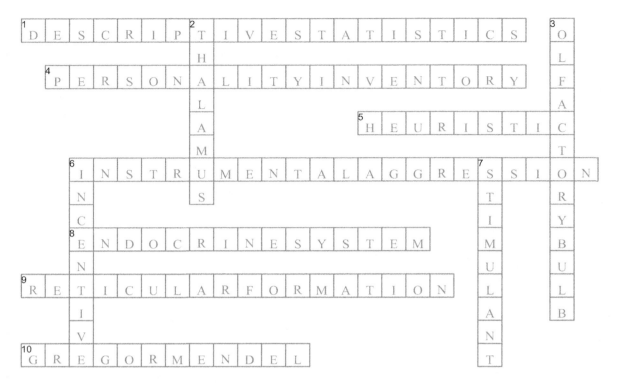

ACROSS

1. Statistical procedures that are used to summarize sets of scores with respect to central tendencies, variability, and correlations.

4. A self-report questionnaire used for personality assessment that includes a series of items about personal thoughts, feelings, and behaviors.

5. Cognitive strategies, or "rules of thumb," often used as shortcuts in solving a complex inferential task.

6. Is goal directed, and cognition based carried out with premeditated thought to achieve specific aims.

8. The network of glands that manufacture and secrete hormones into the bloodstream.

9. The region of the brain stem that alerts the cerebral cortex to incoming sensory signals and is responsible for maintaining consciousness and awakening from sleep.

10. Researched the relationship between parents and their offspring by carrying out experiments on pea plants.

DOWN

1. Statistical procedures that are used to summarize sets of scores with respect to central tendencies, variability, and correlations.

4. A self-report questionnaire used for personality assessment that includes a series of items about personal thoughts, feelings, and behaviors.

5. Cognitive strategies, or "rules of thumb," often used as shortcuts in solving a complex inferential task.

6. Is goal directed, and cognition based carried out with premeditated thought to achieve specific aims.

8. The network of glands that manufacture and secrete hormones into the bloodstream.

9. The region of the brain stem that alerts the cerebral cortex to incoming sensory signals and is responsible for maintaining consciousness and awakening from sleep.

10. Researched the relationship between parents and their offspring by carrying out experiments on pea plants.

A. Olfactory bulb
D. Instrumental aggression
G. Reticular formation
J. Gregor Mendel
B. Incentive
E. Heuristic
H. Descriptive statistics
K. Endocrine system
C. Thalamus
F. Personality inventory
I. Stimulant

43. *Using the Across and Down clues, write the correct words in the numbered grid below.*

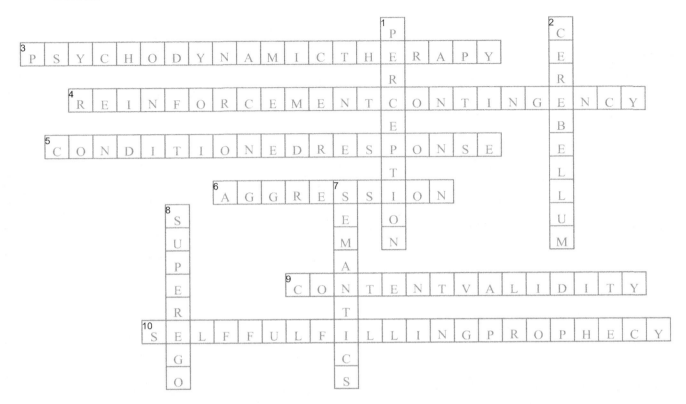

ACROSS

3. Type of therapy that assumes that a patient's problems have been caused by the psychological tension between unconscious impulses and the constraints of his or her life situation.

4. A consistent relationship between a response and the changes in the environment that it produces.

5. Is a response elicited by some previously neutral stimulus that occurs as a result of pairing the neutral stimulus with an unconditioned stimulus.

6. Behaviors that cause psychological or physical harm to another individual.

9. The extent to which a test adequately measures the full range of the domain of interest.

10. A prediction made about some future behavior or event that modifies interactions to produce what is expected.

DOWN

3. Type of therapy that assumes that a patient's problems have been caused by the psychological tension between unconscious impulses and the constraints of his or her life situation.

4. A consistent relationship between a response and the changes in the environment that it produces.

5. Is a response elicited by some previously neutral stimulus that occurs as a result of pairing the neutral stimulus with an unconditioned stimulus.

6. Behaviors that cause psychological or physical harm to another individual.

9. The extent to which a test adequately measures the full range of the domain of interest.

10. A prediction made about some future behavior or event that modifies interactions to produce what is expected.

A. Reinforcement contingency
D. Cerebellum
G. Psychodynamic therapy
J. Superego

B. Self fulfilling prophecy
E. Aggression
H. Conditioned response

C. Content validity
F. Perception
I. Semantics

44. *Using the Across and Down clues, write the correct words in the numbered grid below.*

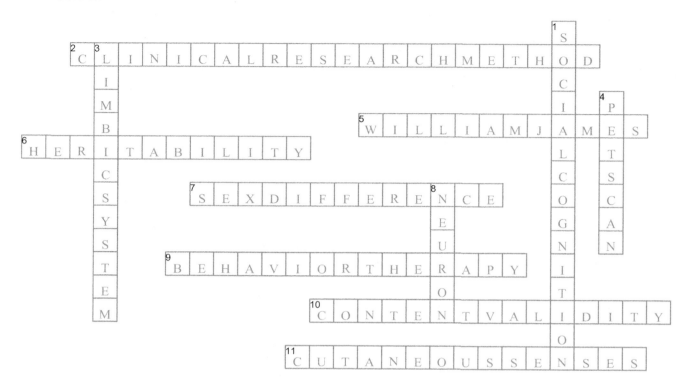

ACROSS

2. Research conducted with human subjects in which the investigator interacts directly with the subjects.

5. Author of "The Principles of Psychology."

6. The relative influence of genetics versus environment in determining patterns of behavior.

7. One of the biologically based characteristics that distinguish males from females.

9. The systematic use of principles of learning to increase the frequency of desired behaviors and

10. The extent to which a test adequately measures the full range of the domain of interest.

11. The skin senses that register sensations or pressure, warmth, and cold.

DOWN

2. Research conducted with human subjects in which the investigator interacts directly with the subjects.

5. Author of "The Principles of Psychology."

6. The relative influence of genetics versus environment in determining patterns of behavior.

7. One of the biologically based characteristics that distinguish males from females.

9. The systematic use of principles of learning to increase the frequency of desired behaviors and

10. The extent to which a test adequately measures the full range of the domain of interest.

11. The skin senses that register sensations or pressure, warmth, and cold.

A. Sex difference
D. Heritability
G. Limbic system
J. Clinical research method

B. William James
E. Neuron
H. PET scan
K. Social cognition

C. Cutaneous senses
F. Content validity
I. Behavior therapy

45. *Using the Across and Down clues, write the correct words in the numbered grid below.*

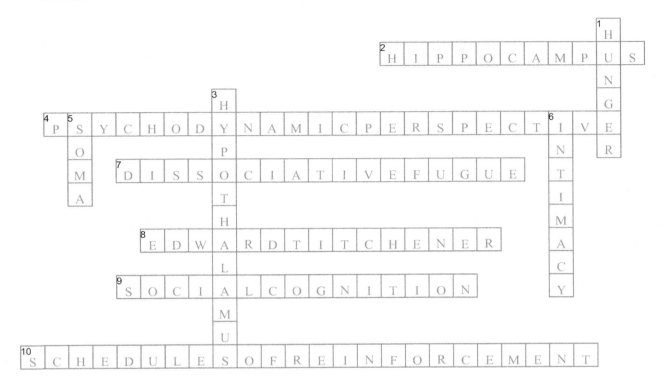

ACROSS

2. The part of the limbic system that is involved in the acquisition of explicit memory.

4. A psychological model in which behavior is explained in terms of past experiences and motivational forces.

7. A disorder characterized by a flight from home or work accompanied by a loss of ability to recall the personal past.

8. Founded a psychology laboratory at Cornell University in 1892, student of Wilhelm Wundt.

9. The process by which people select, interpret, and remember social information.

10. In operant conditioning, a pattern of delivering and withholding reinforcement.

DOWN

2. The part of the limbic system that is involved in the acquisition of explicit memory.

4. A psychological model in which behavior is explained in terms of past experiences and motivational forces.

7. A disorder characterized by a flight from home or work accompanied by a loss of ability to recall the personal past.

8. Founded a psychology laboratory at Cornell University in 1892, student of Wilhelm Wundt.

9. The process by which people select, interpret, and remember social information.

10. In operant conditioning, a pattern of delivering and withholding reinforcement.

A. Schedules of reinforcement
B. Hippocampus
C. Social cognition
D. Psychodynamic perspective
E. Hunger
F. Intimacy
G. Edward Titchener
H. Hypothalamus
I. Dissociative fugue
J. Soma

46. *Using the Across and Down clues, write the correct words in the numbered grid below.*

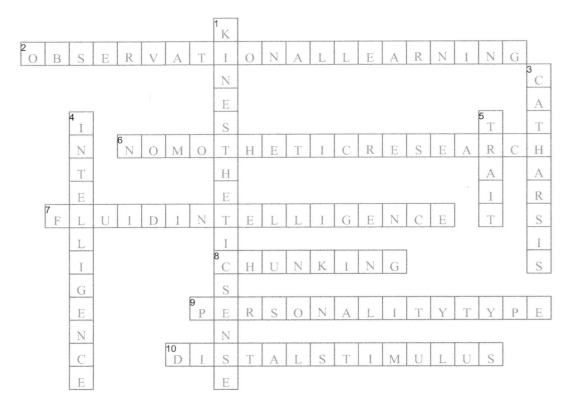

ACROSS

2. The process of learning new responses by watching the behavior of another.

6. Attempts to establish general laws and generalizations, and seeks to obtain objective knowledge through scientific methods.

7. The aspect of intelligence that involves the ability to see complex relationships and solve problems; measured by tests of block designs and spatial visualization.

8. The process of reconfiguring items by grouping based on similarity or some other organizing principle.

9. Distinct patter of personality characteristics used to assign people to categories; qualitative differences, rather than differences in degree, used to discriminate among people.

10. In the processes of perception, the physical object in the world.

DOWN

2. The process of learning new responses by watching the behavior of another.

6. Attempts to establish general laws and generalizations, and seeks to obtain objective knowledge through scientific methods.

7. The aspect of intelligence that involves the ability to see complex relationships and solve problems; measured by tests of block designs and spatial visualization.

8. The process of reconfiguring items by grouping based on similarity or some other organizing principle.

9. Distinct patter of personality characteristics used to assign people to categories; qualitative differences, rather than differences in degree, used to discriminate among people.

10. In the processes of perception, the physical object in the world.

A. Fluid intelligence
D. Catharsis
G. Trait
J. Distal stimulus

B. Observational learning
E. Personality type
H. Intelligence

C. Nomothetic research
F. Kinesthetic sense
I. Chunking

47. *Using the Across and Down clues, write the correct words in the numbered grid below.*

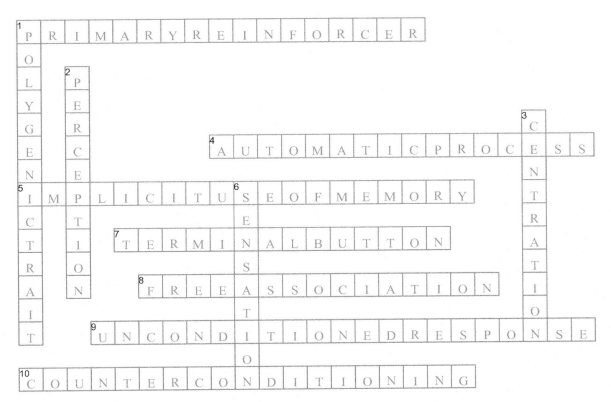

ACROSS

1. A biologically determined reinforcer, such as food and water.

4. Process that does not require attention; it can often be performed along with other tasks without interference.

5. Availability of information through memory processes without conscious effort to encode or recover information.

7. A bulblike structure at the branched ending of an axon that contains vesicles filled with neurotransmitters.

8. The therapeutic method in which a patient gives a running account of thoughts, wishes, physical sensations, and mental images as the occur.

9. Is the response elicited by an unconditioned stimulus without prior training or learning.

10. A technique used in therapy to substitute a new response for a maladaptive one by means of conditioning process.

DOWN

1. A biologically determined reinforcer, such as food and water.

4. Process that does not require attention; it can often be performed along with other tasks without interference.

5. Availability of information through memory processes without conscious effort to encode or recover information.

7. A bulblike structure at the branched ending of an axon that contains vesicles filled with neurotransmitters.

8. The therapeutic method in which a patient gives a running account of thoughts, wishes, physical sensations, and mental images as the occur.

9. Is the response elicited by an unconditioned stimulus without prior training or learning.

10. A technique used in therapy to substitute a new response for a maladaptive one by means of conditioning process.

A. Automatic process
D. Free association
G. Implicit use of memory
J. Unconditioned response

B. Centration
E. Counterconditioning
H. Terminal button
K. Perception

C. Polygenic trait
F. Primary reinforcer
I. Sensation

48. *Using the Across and Down clues, write the correct words in the numbered grid below.*

ACROSS

3. A cognitive theory of work motivation that proposes that workers are motivated to maintain fair and equitable relationships with other relevant persons.

6. The gap between one neuron and another.

9. The sense of taste.

10. Specific personal features that help predict an individual's behavior but are less useful for understanding an individual's personality, such as food or dress preferences.

11. One of the biologically based characteristics that distinguish males from females.

12. The facet of intelligence involving the knowledge a person has already acquired and the ability to access that knowledge; measures by vocabulary, arithmetic, and general information tests.

DOWN

3. A cognitive theory of work motivation that proposes that workers are motivated to maintain fair and equitable relationships with other relevant persons.

6. The gap between one neuron and another.

9. The sense of taste.

10. Specific personal features that help predict an individual's behavior but are less useful for understanding an individual's personality, such as food or dress preferences.

11. One of the biologically based characteristics that distinguish males from females.

12. The facet of intelligence involving the knowledge a person has already acquired and the ability to access that knowledge; measures by vocabulary, arithmetic, and general information tests.

A. Panic disorder
D. Control group
G. Self handicapping
J. Gustation

B. Sex difference
E. Teratogen
H. Synapse
K. Crystallized intelligence

C. Equity theory
F. Vestibular sense
I. ECT
L. Secondary traits

49. *Using the Across and Down clues, write the correct words in the numbered grid below.*

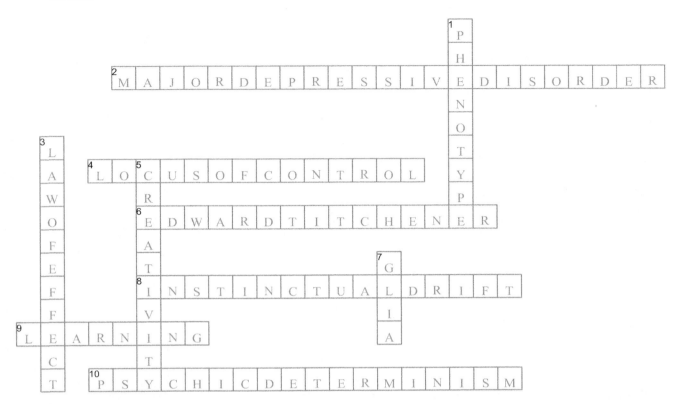

ACROSS

2. A mood disorder characterized by intense feelings of depression over an extended time, without the manic high phase of bipolar depression

4. An aspect of Rotter's expectancy theory; people's general expectancy about the extent to which the rewards they obtain are contingent on their own actions or on environmental factors.

6. Founded a psychology laboratory at Cornell University in 1892, student of Wilhelm Wundt.

8. The tendency for learned behavior to drift toward instinctual behavior over time.

9. A process based on experience that results in a relatively permanent change in behavior or behavioral potential.

10. The assumption that mental and behavioral reactions are determined by previous experiences.

DOWN

2. A mood disorder characterized by intense feelings of depression over an extended time, without the manic high phase of bipolar depression

4. An aspect of Rotter's expectancy theory; people's general expectancy about the extent to which the rewards they obtain are contingent on their own actions or on environmental factors.

6. Founded a psychology laboratory at Cornell University in 1892, student of Wilhelm Wundt.

8. The tendency for learned behavior to drift toward instinctual behavior over time.

9. A process based on experience that results in a relatively permanent change in behavior or behavioral potential.

10. The assumption that mental and behavioral reactions are determined by previous experiences.

A. Psychic determinism
D. Creativity
G. Phenotype
J. Locus of control

B. Law of effect
E. Major depressive disorder
H. Edward Titchener

C. Glia
F. Learning
I. Instinctual drift

50. *Using the Across and Down clues, write the correct words in the numbered grid below.*

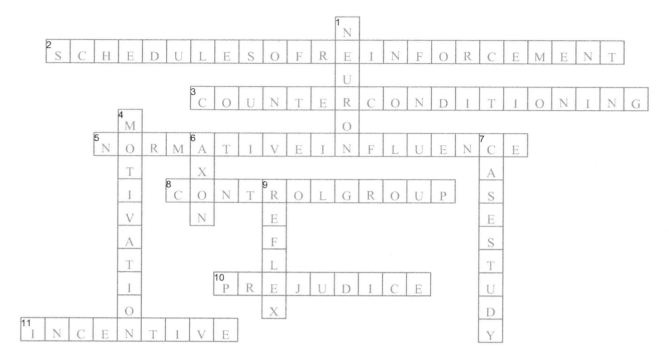

ACROSS

2. In operant conditioning, a pattern of delivering and withholding reinforcement.

3. A technique used in therapy to substitute a new response for a maladaptive one by means of conditioning process.

5. Group effects that arise from individuals' desire to be like, accepted, and approved of by others.

8. A group in an experiment that is not exposed to a treatment or does not experience a manipulation of the independent variable.

10. A learned attitude toward a target object, involving negative affect (dislike or fear), negative beliefs (stereotypes), that justify the attitude, and a behavioral intention to avoid, control, dominate, or eliminate the target object.

11. External stimulus or reward that motivates behavior although it does not related directly to biological needs.

DOWN

2. In operant conditioning, a pattern of delivering and withholding reinforcement.

3. A technique used in therapy to substitute a new response for a maladaptive one by means of conditioning process.

5. Group effects that arise from individuals' desire to be like, accepted, and approved of by others.

8. A group in an experiment that is not exposed to a treatment or does not experience a manipulation of the independent variable.

10. A learned attitude toward a target object, involving negative affect (dislike or fear), negative beliefs (stereotypes), that justify the attitude, and a behavioral intention to avoid, control, dominate, or eliminate the target object.

11. External stimulus or reward that motivates behavior although it does not related directly to biological needs.

A. Counterconditioning
D. Control group
G. Normative influence
J. Reflex

B. Case study
E. Motivation
H. Neuron
K. Schedules of reinforcement

C. Prejudice
F. Incentive
I. Axon

51. *Using the Across and Down clues, write the correct words in the numbered grid below.*

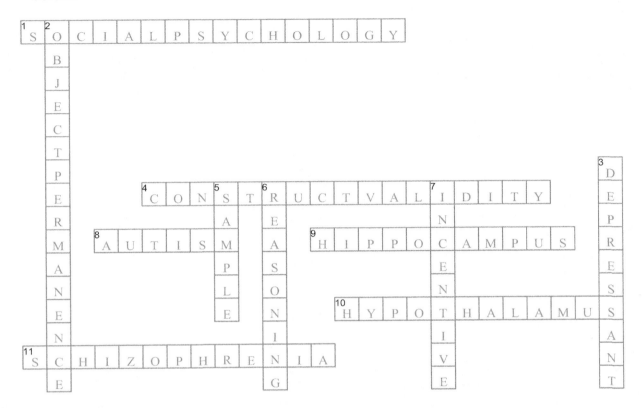

ACROSS

1.   The branch of psychology that studies the effect of social variables on individual behavior, attitudes, perceptions, and motives.

4.   The degree to which a test adequately measures an underlying construct.

8.   A developmental disorder characterized by severe disruption of children's ability to form social bonds and use language.

9.   The part of the limbic system that is involved in the acquisition of explicit memory.

10.   The brain structure that serves as a relay station between the endocrine system and the CNS.

11.   A severe form of psychopathology characterized by the breakdown of integrated personality functioning, withdrawal from reality, emotional distortions, and disturbed thoughts.

DOWN

1.   The branch of psychology that studies the effect of social variables on individual behavior, attitudes, perceptions, and motives.

4.   The degree to which a test adequately measures an underlying construct.

8.   A developmental disorder characterized by severe disruption of children's ability to form social bonds and use language.

9.   The part of the limbic system that is involved in the acquisition of explicit memory.

10.   The brain structure that serves as a relay station between the endocrine system and the CNS.

11.   A severe form of psychopathology characterized by the breakdown of integrated personality functioning, withdrawal from reality, emotional distortions, and disturbed thoughts.

A. Construct validity   B. Depressant   C. Sample   D. Incentive
E. Social psychology   F. Schizophrenia G. Reasoning H. Object permanence
I. Autism   J. Hippocampus   K. Hypothalamus

52. *Using the Across and Down clues, write the correct words in the numbered grid below.*

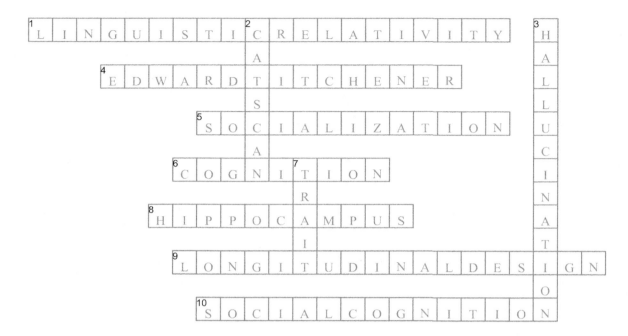

ACROSS

1. The hypothesis that the structure of the language and individual speaks has an impact on the way in which that individual thinks about the world.

4. Founded a psychology laboratory at Cornell University in 1892, student of Wilhelm Wundt.

5. The lifelong process whereby an individual's behavioral patterns, values, standards, skills, attitudes, and motives are shaped to conform to those regarded as desirable in a particular society.

6. Processes of knowing, including attending, remembering, and reasoning.

8. The part of the limbic system that is involved in the acquisition of explicit memory.

9. A research design in which the same participants are observed repeatedly, sometimes over many years.

10. The process by which people select, interpret, and remember social information.

DOWN

1. The hypothesis that the structure of the language and individual speaks has an impact on the way in which that individual thinks about the world.

4. Founded a psychology laboratory at Cornell University in 1892, student of Wilhelm Wundt.

5. The lifelong process whereby an individual's behavioral patterns, values, standards, skills, attitudes, and motives are shaped to conform to those regarded as desirable in a particular society.

6. Processes of knowing, including attending, remembering, and reasoning.

8. The part of the limbic system that is involved in the acquisition of explicit memory.

9. A research design in which the same participants are observed repeatedly, sometimes over many years.

10. The process by which people select, interpret, and remember social information.

A. Trait
B. Cognition
C. Hippocampus
D. Socialization
E. Hallucination
F. Linguistic relativity
G. Longitudinal design
H. Social cognition
I. CAT Scan
J. Edward Titchener

53. *Using the Across and Down clues, write the correct words in the numbered grid below.*

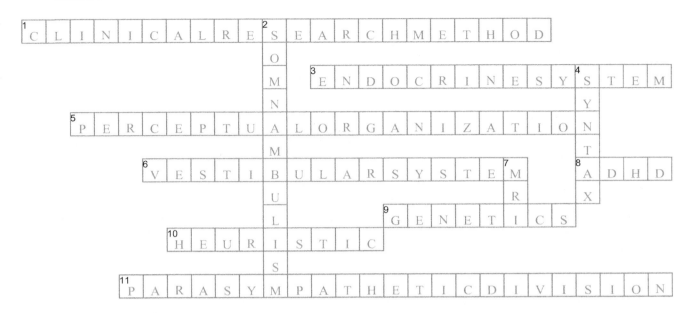

ACROSS

1. Research conducted with human subjects in which the investigator interacts directly with the subjects.

3. The network of glands that manufacture and secrete hormones into the bloodstream.

5. The processes that put sensory information together to give the perception of a coherent scene over the whole visual field.

6. The receptors for this information are tiny hairs in fluid-filled sacs and canals in the inner ear.

8. A disorder of childhood characterized by inattention and hyperactivity-impulsivity.

9. The study of the inheritance of physical and psychological traits from ancestors.

10. Cognitive strategies, or "rules of thumb," often used as shortcuts in solving a complex inferential task.

11. The subdivision of the ANS that monitors the routine operation of the body's internal functions and conserves and restores body energy.

DOWN

1. Research conducted with human subjects in which the investigator interacts directly with the subjects.

3. The network of glands that manufacture and secrete hormones into the bloodstream.

5. The processes that put sensory information together to give the perception of a coherent scene over the whole visual field.

6. The receptors for this information are tiny hairs in fluid-filled sacs and canals in the inner ear.

8. A disorder of childhood characterized by inattention and hyperactivity-impulsivity.

9. The study of the inheritance of physical and psychological traits from ancestors.

10. Cognitive strategies, or "rules of thumb," often used as shortcuts in solving a complex inferential task.

11. The subdivision of the ANS that monitors the routine operation of the body's internal functions and conserves and restores body energy.

A. Somnambulism
D. Syntax
G. Perceptual organization
J. Clinical research method

B. Genetics
E. Endocrine system
H. ADHD
K. Heuristic

C. Vestibular system
F. Parasympathetic division
I. MRI

54. *Using the Across and Down clues, write the correct words in the numbered grid below.*

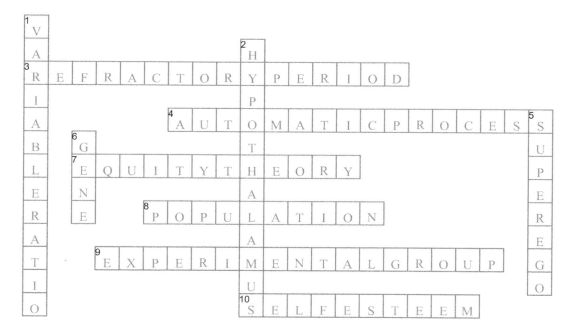

ACROSS

3. The period of rest during which a new nerve impulse cannot be activated in a segment of an axon.

4. Process that does not require attention; it can often be performed along with other tasks without interference.

7. A cognitive theory of work motivation that proposes that workers are motivated to maintain fair and equitable relationships with other relevant persons.

8. The entire set of individuals to which generalizations will be made based on an experimental sample.

9. A group in an experiment that is exposed to a treatment or experiences a manipulation of the independent variable.

10. A generalized evaluative attitude toward the self that influences both moods and behavior and that exerts a powerful effect on a range of personal and social behaviors.

DOWN

3. The period of rest during which a new nerve impulse cannot be activated in a segment of an axon.

4. Process that does not require attention; it can often be performed along with other tasks without interference.

7. A cognitive theory of work motivation that proposes that workers are motivated to maintain fair and equitable relationships with other relevant persons.

8. The entire set of individuals to which generalizations will be made based on an experimental sample.

9. A group in an experiment that is exposed to a treatment or experiences a manipulation of the independent variable.

10. A generalized evaluative attitude toward the self that influences both moods and behavior and that exerts a powerful effect on a range of personal and social behaviors.

A. Experimental group
E. Superego
I. Automatic process
B. Equity theory
F. Gene
J. Hypothalamus
C. Refractory period
G. Population
D. Self esteem
H. Variable ratio

55. *Using the Across and Down clues, write the correct words in the numbered grid below.*

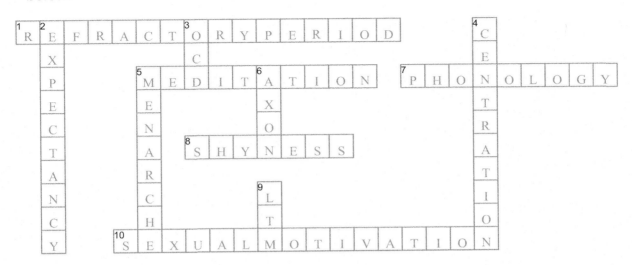

ACROSS

1. The period of rest during which a new nerve impulse cannot be activated in a segment of an axon.

5. A form of consciousness alteration designed to enhance self-knowledge and well-being by achieving a deep state of tranquility.

7. The study of the sounds that are put together to form words.

8. An individual's discomfort and

10. Sexual arousal is the motivational state of excitement and tension brought about by physiological and cognitive reactions to erotic stimuli.

DOWN

1. The period of rest during which a new nerve impulse cannot be activated in a segment of an axon.

5. A form of consciousness alteration designed to enhance self-knowledge and well-being by achieving a deep state of tranquility.

7. The study of the sounds that are put together to form words.

8. An individual's discomfort and

10. Sexual arousal is the motivational state of excitement and tension brought about by physiological and cognitive reactions to erotic stimuli.

A. LTM   B. Centration   C. Shyness   D. Refractory period
E. OCD   F. Axon   G. Expectancy   H. Meditation
I. Phonology   J. Sexual motivation   K. Menarche

56. *Using the Across and Down clues, write the correct words in the numbered grid below.*

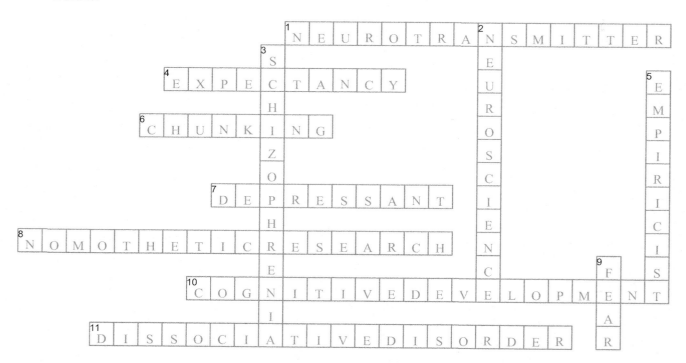

ACROSS

1. Chemical messenger released from a neuron that crosses the synapse from one neuron to another, stimulating the postsynaptic neuron.

4. The extent to which people believe that their behaviors situations will bring about rewards.

6. The process of reconfiguring items by grouping based on similarity or some other organizing principle.

7. Drug that depresses or slows down the activity of the central nervous system.

8. Attempts to establish general laws and generalizations, and seeks to obtain objective knowledge through scientific methods.

10. The development of processes of knowing, including imagining, perceiving, reasoning, and problem solving.

11. A personality disorder marked by a disturbance in the integration of identity, memory, or consciousness.

DOWN

1. Chemical messenger released from a neuron that crosses the synapse from one neuron to another, stimulating the postsynaptic neuron.

4. The extent to which people believe that their behaviors situations will bring about rewards.

6. The process of reconfiguring items by grouping based on similarity or some other organizing principle.

7. Drug that depresses or slows down the activity of the central nervous system.

8. Attempts to establish general laws and generalizations, and seeks to obtain objective knowledge through scientific methods.

10. The development of processes of knowing, including imagining, perceiving, reasoning, and problem solving.

11. A personality disorder marked by a disturbance in the integration of identity, memory, or consciousness.

A. Nomothetic research
D. Neurotransmitter
G. Neuroscience
J. Cognitive development

B. Chunking
E. Dissociative disorder
H. Depressant
K. Expectancy

C. Empiricist
F. Fear
I. Schizophrenia

57. *Using the Across and Down clues, write the correct words in the numbered grid below.*

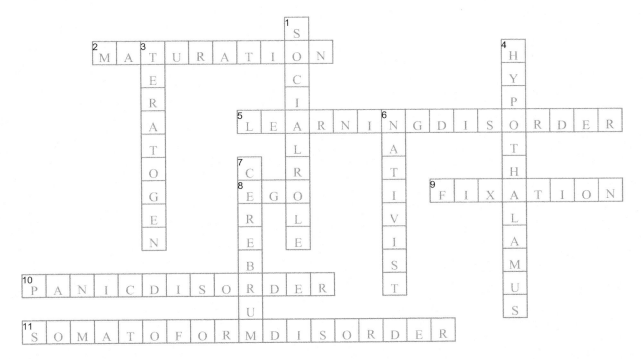

ACROSS

2. The age-related physical and behavioral changes characteristic of a species; the process of growth typical of all members of a species who are reared in the specie's usual habitat.

5. A disorder defined by a large discrepancy between individuals' measured IQ and their actual performance.

8. The reality-based aspect of the self that arbitrates the conflict between id impulses and superego demands.

9. According to Freud, a state in which a person remains attached to objects or activities more appropriate for an earlier stage of psychosexual development.

10. An anxiety disorder in which sufferers experience unexpected, severe panic attacks that begin with a feeling of intense apprehension, fear, or terror.

11. A disorder in which people have physical illnesses or complaints that cannot be fully explained by actual medical conditions.

DOWN

2. The age-related physical and behavioral changes characteristic of a species; the process of growth typical of all members of a species who are reared in the specie's usual habitat.

5. A disorder defined by a large discrepancy between individuals' measured IQ and their actual performance.

8. The reality-based aspect of the self that arbitrates the conflict between id impulses and superego demands.

9. According to Freud, a state in which a person remains attached to objects or activities more appropriate for an earlier stage of psychosexual development.

10. An anxiety disorder in which sufferers experience unexpected, severe panic attacks that begin with a feeling of intense apprehension, fear, or terror.

11. A disorder in which people have physical illnesses or complaints that cannot be fully explained by actual medical conditions.

A. Nativist
E. Panic disorder
I. Social role
B. Learning disorder
F. Somatoform disorder
J. Cerebrum
C. Teratogen
G. Ego
K. Maturation
D. Fixation
H. Hypothalamus

58. *Using the Across and Down clues, write the correct words in the numbered grid below.*

ACROSS

2. A type of learning in which a behavior (conditioned response) comes to be elicited by a stimulus (conditioned stimulus).

3. A general treatment strategy involving changing behavior by modifying its consequences.

4. The approach to identifying causes of behavior that focuses on the functioning of the genes, the brain, the nervous system, and the endocrine system.

6. A generalized evaluative attitude toward the self that influences both moods and behavior and that exerts a powerful effect on a range of personal and social behaviors.

8. The negative reaction of people to an individual or group because of some assumed inferiority or source of difference that is degraded.

9. A disorder in which psychological conflict or stress brings about loss of motor or sensory function.

DOWN

2. A type of learning in which a behavior (conditioned response) comes to be elicited by a stimulus (conditioned stimulus).

3. A general treatment strategy involving changing behavior by modifying its consequences.

4. The approach to identifying causes of behavior that focuses on the functioning of the genes, the brain, the nervous system, and the endocrine system.

6. A generalized evaluative attitude toward the self that influences both moods and behavior and that exerts a powerful effect on a range of personal and social behaviors.

8. The negative reaction of people to an individual or group because of some assumed inferiority or source of difference that is degraded.

9. A disorder in which psychological conflict or stress brings about loss of motor or sensory function.

A. Contingency management
D. Synapse
G. Biological
J. Conversion disorder

B. Classical conditioning
E. Self esteem
H. Edward Titchener

C. Sample
F. Groupthink
I. Stigma

59. *Using the Across and Down clues, write the correct words in the numbered grid below.*

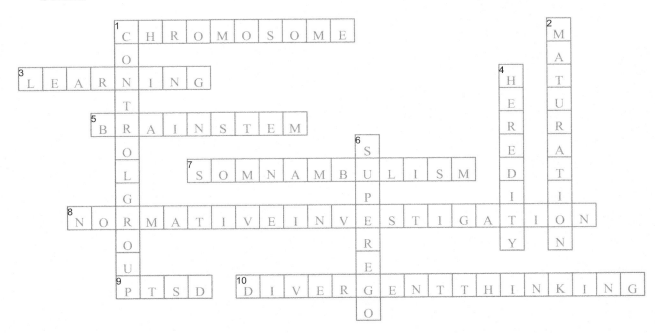

ACROSS

1. A thread-like structure found in the nucleus of cells and made of protein and DNA

3. A process based on experience that results in a relatively permanent change in behavior or behavioral potential.

5. The brain structure that regulates the body's basic life processes.

7. A disorder that causes sleep walking.

8. Research effort designed to describe what is characteristic of a specific age or developmental stage.

9. Posttraumatic stress disorder. An anxiety disorder characterized by the persistent re-experience of those traumatic events through distressing recollections, dreams, hallucinations, or flashbacks.

10. An aspect of creativity characterized by an ability to produce unusual but appropriate response to problems.

DOWN

1. A thread-like structure found in the nucleus of cells and made of protein and DNA

3. A process based on experience that results in a relatively permanent change in behavior or behavioral potential.

5. The brain structure that regulates the body's basic life processes.

7. A disorder that causes sleep walking.

8. Research effort designed to describe what is characteristic of a specific age or developmental stage.

9. Posttraumatic stress disorder. An anxiety disorder characterized by the persistent re-experience of those traumatic events through distressing recollections, dreams, hallucinations, or flashbacks.

10. An aspect of creativity characterized by an ability to produce unusual but appropriate response to problems.

A. PTSD
D. Superego
G. Learning
J. Maturation

B. Normative investigation
E. Control group
H. Divergent thinking
K. Brain stem

C. Somnambulism
F. Chromosome
I. Heredity

60. *Using the Across and Down clues, write the correct words in the numbered grid below.*

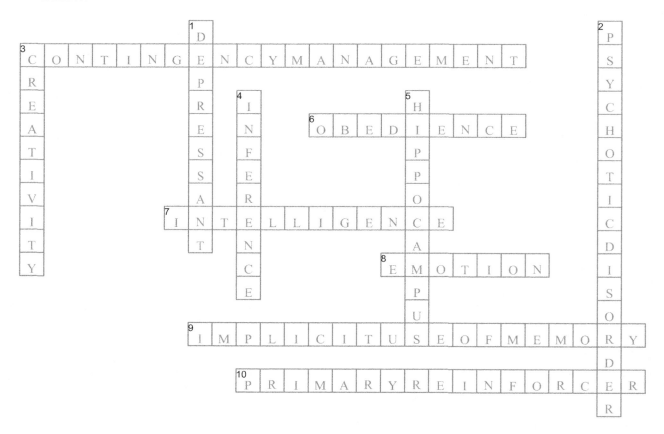

ACROSS

3. A general treatment strategy involving changing behavior by modifying its consequences.

6. Blind obedience is less a product of dispositional characteristics than the outcome of situational forces that could engulf anyone. (Milgram studies)

7. The global capacity to profit from experience and to go beyond given information about the environment.

8. A complex pattern of changes, including physiological arousal, feelings, cognitive processes, and behavioral reactions, made in response to a situation perceived to be personally significant.

9. Availability of information through memory processes without conscious effort to encode or recover information.

10. A biologically determined reinforcer, such as food and water.

DOWN

3. A general treatment strategy involving changing behavior by modifying its consequences.

6. Blind obedience is less a product of dispositional characteristics than the outcome of situational forces that could engulf anyone. (Milgram studies)

7. The global capacity to profit from experience and to go beyond given information about the environment.

8. A complex pattern of changes, including physiological arousal, feelings, cognitive processes, and behavioral reactions, made in response to a situation perceived to be personally significant.

9. Availability of information through memory processes without conscious effort to encode or recover information.

10. A biologically determined reinforcer, such as food and water.

A. Hippocampus
D. Depressant
G. Implicit use of memory
J. Contingency management

B. Obedience
E. Inference
H. Emotion
K. Primary reinforcer

C. Creativity
F. Intelligence
I. Psychotic disorder

61. *Using the Across and Down clues, write the correct words in the numbered grid below.*

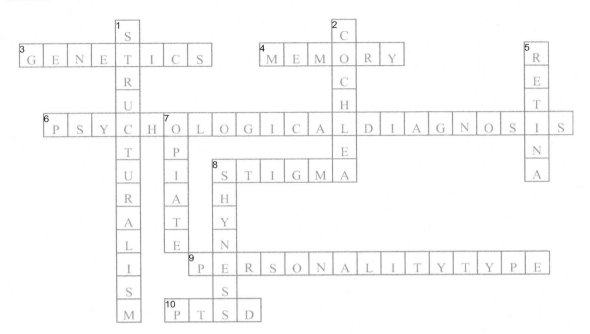

ACROSS

3. The study of the inheritance of physical and psychological traits from ancestors.

4. The mental capacity to encode, store, and retrieve information.

6. The label given to psychological abnormality by classifying and categorizing the observed behavior pattern into an approved diagnostic system.

8. The negative reaction of people to an individual or group because of some assumed inferiority or source of difference that is degraded.

9. Distinct patter of personality characteristics used to assign people to categories; qualitative differences, rather than differences in degree, used to discriminate among people.

10. Posttraumatic stress disorder. An anxiety disorder characterized by the persistent re-experience of those traumatic events through distressing recollections, dreams, hallucinations, or flashbacks.

DOWN

3. The study of the inheritance of physical and psychological traits from ancestors.

4. The mental capacity to encode, store, and retrieve information.

6. The label given to psychological abnormality by classifying and categorizing the observed behavior pattern into an approved diagnostic system.

8. The negative reaction of people to an individual or group because of some assumed inferiority or source of difference that is degraded.

9. Distinct patter of personality characteristics used to assign people to categories; qualitative differences, rather than differences in degree, used to discriminate among people.

10. Posttraumatic stress disorder. An anxiety disorder characterized by the persistent re-experience of those traumatic events through distressing recollections, dreams, hallucinations, or flashbacks.

A. Stigma
D. Cochlea
G. Psychological diagnosis
J. Genetics

B. Retina
E. Opiate
H. PTSD
K. Personality type

C. Shyness
F. Structuralism
I. Memory

62. *Using the Across and Down clues, write the correct words in the numbered grid below.*

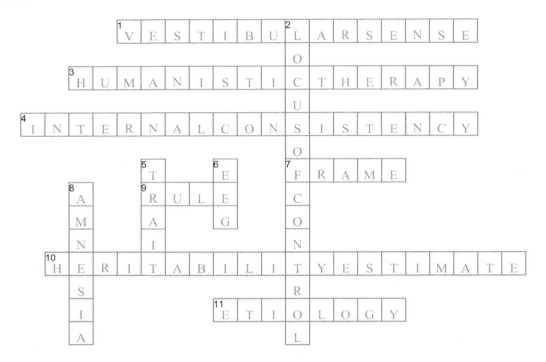

ACROSS

1. The sense that tells how one's own body is oriented in the world with respect to gravity.

3. Centers around the concept of a whole person in the continual process of changing and of becoming.

4. A measure of reliability; the degree to which a test yields similar scores across its different parts, such as odd versus even items.

7. A particular description of a choice; the perspective from which a choice is described or framed affects how a decision is made and which option is ultimately exercised.

9. Behavioral guideline for acting in a certain way in a certain instance.

10. A statistical estimate of the degree of inheritance of a given trait or behavior, asses by the degree of similarity between individuals who vary in their extent of genetic similarity.

11. The study of the causes and factors leading to the development of a disorder.

DOWN

1. The sense that tells how one's own body is oriented in the world with respect to gravity.

3. Centers around the concept of a whole person in the continual process of changing and of becoming.

4. A measure of reliability; the degree to which a test yields similar scores across its different parts, such as odd versus even items.

7. A particular description of a choice; the perspective from which a choice is described or framed affects how a decision is made and which option is ultimately exercised.

9. Behavioral guideline for acting in a certain way in a certain instance.

10. A statistical estimate of the degree of inheritance of a given trait or behavior, asses by the degree of similarity between individuals who vary in their extent of genetic similarity.

11. The study of the causes and factors leading to the development of a disorder.

A. Humanistic therapy	B. Amnesia
E. Internal consistency	F. Heritability estimate
I. Rule	J. EEG

C. Etiology	D. Vestibular sense
G. Locus of control	H. Frame
K. Trait	

63. *Using the Across and Down clues, write the correct words in the numbered grid below.*

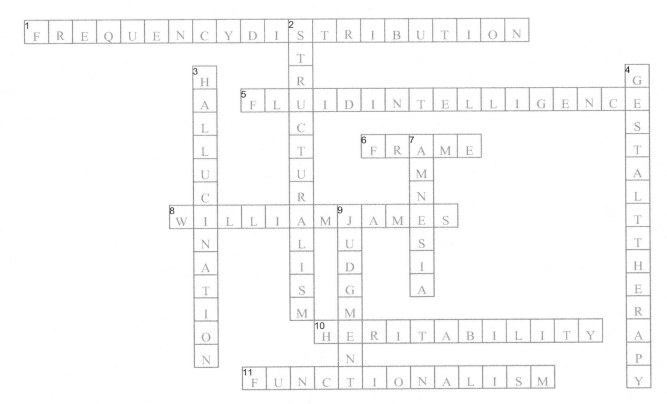

ACROSS

1. A summary of how frequently each score appears in a set of observations.

5. The aspect of intelligence that involves the ability to see complex relationships and solve problems; measured by tests of block designs and spatial visualization.

6. A particular description of a choice; the perspective from which a choice is described or framed affects how a decision is made and which option is ultimately exercised.

8. Author of "The Principles of Psychology."

10. The relative influence of genetics versus environment in determining patterns of behavior.

11. The perspective on mind and behavior that focuses on the examination of their functions in an organism's interactions with the environment.

DOWN

1. A summary of how frequently each score appears in a set of observations.

5. The aspect of intelligence that involves the ability to see complex relationships and solve problems; measured by tests of block designs and spatial visualization.

6. A particular description of a choice; the perspective from which a choice is described or framed affects how a decision is made and which option is ultimately exercised.

8. Author of "The Principles of Psychology."

10. The relative influence of genetics versus environment in determining patterns of behavior.

11. The perspective on mind and behavior that focuses on the examination of their functions in an organism's interactions with the environment.

A. Judgment
D. Hallucination
G. Amnesia
J. Fluid intelligence

B. Functionalism
E. Frame
H. Structuralism
K. Heritability

C. Frequency distribution
F. William James
I. Gestalt therapy

64. *Using the Across and Down clues, write the correct words in the numbered grid below.*

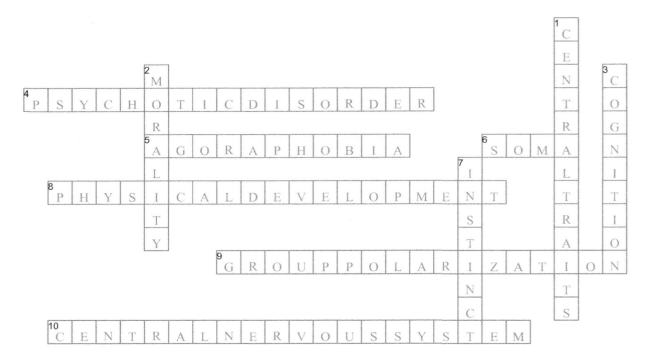

ACROSS

4. Severe mental disorder in which a person experiences impairment manifested through thought, emotional, or perceptual difficulties.

5. An extreme fear of being in public places or open spaces from which escape may be difficult or embarrassing.

6. The cell body of a neuron, containing the nucleus and cytoplasm.

8. The bodily changes, maturation, and growth that occur in an organism starting with conception and continuing across the life span.

9. The tendency for groups to make decisions that are more extreme than the decisions that would be made by the members acting alone.

10. The part of the nervous system consisting of the brain and spinal cord.

DOWN

4. Severe mental disorder in which a person experiences impairment manifested through thought, emotional, or perceptual difficulties.

5. An extreme fear of being in public places or open spaces from which escape may be difficult or embarrassing.

6. The cell body of a neuron, containing the nucleus and cytoplasm.

8. The bodily changes, maturation, and growth that occur in an organism starting with conception and continuing across the life span.

9. The tendency for groups to make decisions that are more extreme than the decisions that would be made by the members acting alone.

10. The part of the nervous system consisting of the brain and spinal cord.

A. Soma
D. Group polarization
G. Instinct
J. Morality

B. Central traits
E. Central nervous system
H. Psychotic disorder

C. Agoraphobia
F. Cognition
I. Physical development

65. *Using the Across and Down clues, write the correct words in the numbered grid below.*

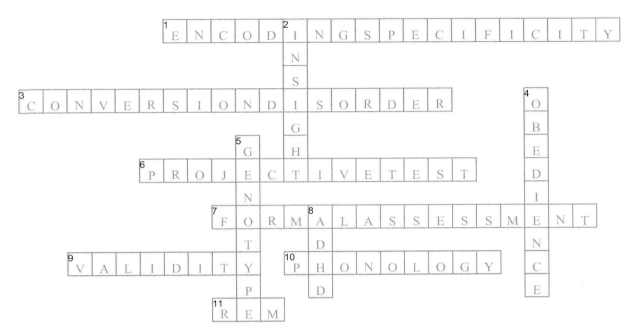

ACROSS

1. The principle that subsequent retrieval of information is enhanced if cues received at the time of recall are consistent with those present at the time of encoding.

3. A disorder in which psychological conflict or stress brings about loss of motor or sensory function.

6. A method of personality assessment in which an individual is presented with a standardized set of ambiguous, abstract stimuli and asked to interpret their meanings.

7. The systematic procedures and measurement instruments used by trained professionals to assess and individual's functioning, aptitudes, abilities, or mental states.

9. The extent to which a test measures what it was intended to measure.

10. The study of the sounds that are put together to form words.

11. Rapid eye movements. A behavioral sign of the phase of sleep during which the sleeper is likely to be experiencing dreamlike mental activity.

DOWN

1. The principle that subsequent retrieval of information is enhanced if cues received at the time of recall are consistent with those present at the time of encoding.

3. A disorder in which psychological conflict or stress brings about loss of motor or sensory function.

6. A method of personality assessment in which an individual is presented with a standardized set of ambiguous, abstract stimuli and asked to interpret their meanings.

7. The systematic procedures and measurement instruments used by trained professionals to assess and individual's functioning, aptitudes, abilities, or mental states.

9. The extent to which a test measures what it was intended to measure.

10. The study of the sounds that are put together to form words.

11. Rapid eye movements. A behavioral sign of the phase of sleep during which the sleeper is likely to be experiencing dreamlike mental activity.

A. Encoding specificity   B. Phonology   C. Obedience   D. Formal assessment
E. Insight   F. Validity   G. Projective test   H. Conversion disorder
I. REM   J. ADHD   K. Genotype

66. *Using the Across and Down clues, write the correct words in the numbered grid below.*

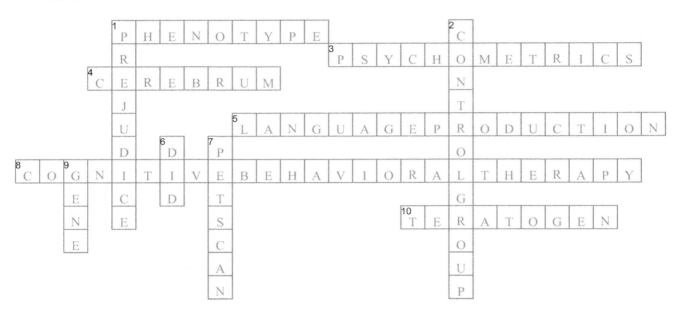

ACROSS

1. The observable characteristics of an organism, resulting from the interaction between the organism's genotype and its environment.

3. The field of psychology that specializes in mental testing.

4. The region of the brain that regulates higher cognitive and emotional functions.

5. What people say, sign, and write, as well as the processes the go through to produce these messages.

8. A therapeutic approach that combines the cognitive emphasis on thoughts and attitudes with the behavioral emphasis on changing performance.

10. Environmental factors such as diseases and drugs that cause structural abnormalities in a developing fetus.

DOWN

1. The observable characteristics of an organism, resulting from the interaction between the organism's genotype and its environment.

3. The field of psychology that specializes in mental testing.

4. The region of the brain that regulates higher cognitive and emotional functions.

5. What people say, sign, and write, as well as the processes the go through to produce these messages.

8. A therapeutic approach that combines the cognitive emphasis on thoughts and attitudes with the behavioral emphasis on changing performance.

10. Environmental factors such as diseases and drugs that cause structural abnormalities in a developing fetus.

A. Phenotype
D. DID
G. Psychometrics
J. Gene

B. Prejudice
E. Cerebrum
H. Teratogen
K. Control group

C. Language production
F. PET scan
I. Cognitive behavioral therapy

67. *Using the Across and Down clues, write the correct words in the numbered grid below.*

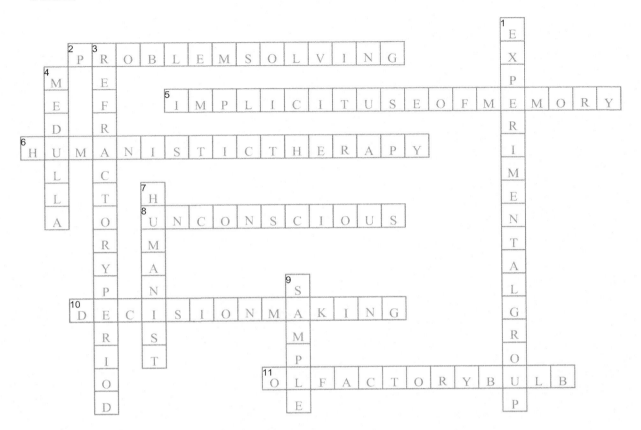

ACROSS

2. Thinking that is directed toward solving specific problems and that moves from an initial state to a goal state by means of a set of mental operations.

5. Availability of information through memory processes without conscious effort to encode or recover information.

6. Centers around the concept of a whole person in the continual process of changing and of becoming.

8. The domain of the psyche that stores repressed urges and primitive impulses.

10. The process of choosing between alternatives; selecting or rejecting available options.

11. The center where odor-sensitive receptors send their signals, located just below the frontal lobes of the cortex.

DOWN

2. Thinking that is directed toward solving specific problems and that moves from an initial state to a goal state by means of a set of mental operations.

5. Availability of information through memory processes without conscious effort to encode or recover information.

6. Centers around the concept of a whole person in the continual process of changing and of becoming.

8. The domain of the psyche that stores repressed urges and primitive impulses.

10. The process of choosing between alternatives; selecting or rejecting available options.

11. The center where odor-sensitive receptors send their signals, located just below the frontal lobes of the cortex.

A. Medulla
D. Implicit use of memory
G. Humanistic therapy
J. Problem solving

B. Humanist
E. Unconscious
H. Decision making
K. Olfactory bulb

C. Sample
F. Refractory period
I. Experimental group

68. *Using the Across and Down clues, write the correct words in the numbered grid below.*

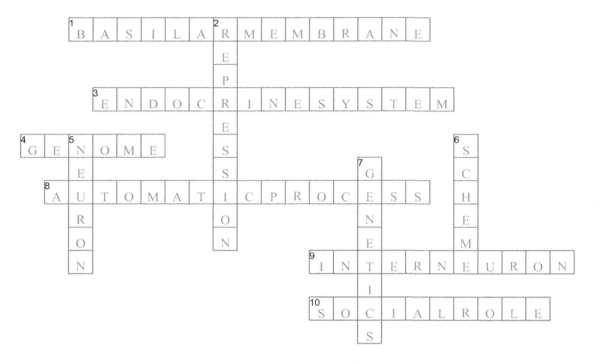

ACROSS

1. A membrane running along the length of the cochlea.
3. The network of glands that manufacture and secrete hormones into the bloodstream.
4. The genetic information for an organism, stored in the DNA of its chromosomes.
8. Process that does not require attention; it can often be performed along with other tasks without interference.
9. Brain neuron that relays massages from sensory neurons to other interneurons or to motor neurons.
10. A socially defined pattern of behavior that is expected of a person who is functioning in a given setting or group.

DOWN

1. A membrane running along the length of the cochlea.
3. The network of glands that manufacture and secrete hormones into the bloodstream.
4. The genetic information for an organism, stored in the DNA of its chromosomes.
8. Process that does not require attention; it can often be performed along with other tasks without interference.
9. Brain neuron that relays massages from sensory neurons to other interneurons or to motor neurons.
10. A socially defined pattern of behavior that is expected of a person who is functioning in a given setting or group.

A. Neuron
E. Genetics
I. Basilar membrane
B. Scheme
F. Interneuron
J. Endocrine system
C. Social role
G. Genome
D. Automatic process
H. Repression

69. *Using the Across and Down clues, write the correct words in the numbered grid below.*

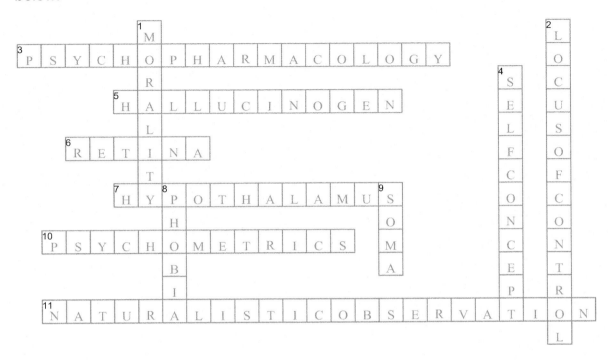

ACROSS

3. The branch of psychology that investigates the effects of drugs on behavior.

5. A drug that alters cognitions and perceptions and causes hallucinations.

6. The layer at the back of the eye that contains photoreceptors and converts light energy to neural responses.

7. The brain structure that regulates motivated behavior and homeostasis.

10. The field of psychology that specializes in mental testing.

11. A research technique in which unobtrusive observations are made of behaviors that occur in natural environments.

DOWN

3. The branch of psychology that investigates the effects of drugs on behavior.

5. A drug that alters cognitions and perceptions and causes hallucinations.

6. The layer at the back of the eye that contains photoreceptors and converts light energy to neural responses.

7. The brain structure that regulates motivated behavior and homeostasis.

10. The field of psychology that specializes in mental testing.

11. A research technique in which unobtrusive observations are made of behaviors that occur in natural environments.

A. Psychopharmacology
D. Self concept
G. Hypothalamus
J. Morality

B. Naturalistic observation
E. Hallucinogen
H. Soma
K. Psychometrics

C. Locus of control
F. Phobia
I. Retina

70. *Using the Across and Down clues, write the correct words in the numbered grid below.*

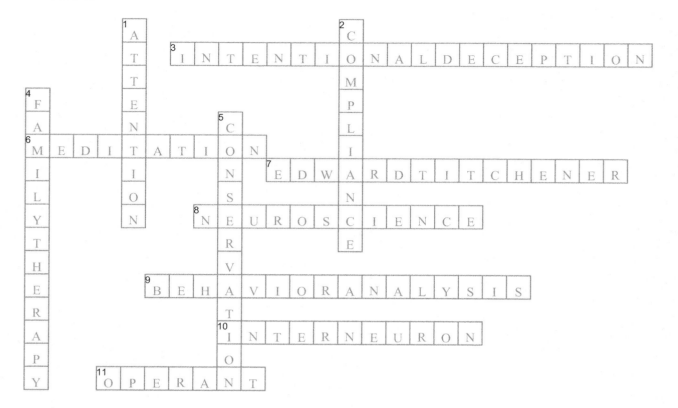

ACROSS

3. Sometimes necessary when revealing certain information to the patient would bias the results.
6. A form of consciousness alteration designed to enhance self-knowledge and well-being by achieving a deep state of tranquility.
7. Founded a psychology laboratory at Cornell University in 1892, student of Wilhelm Wundt.
8. The scientific study of the brain and of the links between brain activity and behavior.
9. The area of psychology that focuses on the environmental determinants of learning and behavior.
10. Brain neuron that relays massages from sensory neurons to other interneurons or to motor neurons.
11. A behavior emitted by an organism that can be characterized in terms of the observable effects it has on the environment.

DOWN

3. Sometimes necessary when revealing certain information to the patient would bias the results.
6. A form of consciousness alteration designed to enhance self-knowledge and well-being by achieving a deep state of tranquility.
7. Founded a psychology laboratory at Cornell University in 1892, student of Wilhelm Wundt.
8. The scientific study of the brain and of the links between brain activity and behavior.
9. The area of psychology that focuses on the environmental determinants of learning and behavior.
10. Brain neuron that relays massages from sensory neurons to other interneurons or to motor neurons.
11. A behavior emitted by an organism that can be characterized in terms of the observable effects it has on the environment.

A. Operant
E. Neuroscience
I. Edward Titchener
B. Behavior analysis
F. Compliance
J. Intentional deception
C. Attention
G. Conservation
K. Meditation
D. Family therapy
H. Interneuron

71. *Using the Across and Down clues, write the correct words in the numbered grid below.*

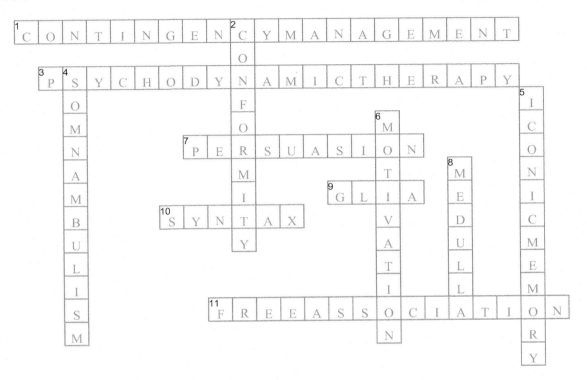

ACROSS

1. A general treatment strategy involving changing behavior by modifying its consequences.

3. Type of therapy that assumes that a patient's problems have been caused by the psychological tension between unconscious impulses and the constraints of his or her life situation.

7. Deliberate efforts to change attitudes.

9. The cells that hold neurons together and facilitate neural transmission, remove damaged and dead neurons, and prevent poisonous substances in the blood from reaching the brain.

10. The way in which words are strung together to form sentences.

11. The therapeutic method in which a patient gives a running account of thoughts, wishes, physical sensations, and mental images as the occur.

DOWN

1. A general treatment strategy involving changing behavior by modifying its consequences.

3. Type of therapy that assumes that a patient's problems have been caused by the psychological tension between unconscious impulses and the constraints of his or her life situation.

7. Deliberate efforts to change attitudes.

9. The cells that hold neurons together and facilitate neural transmission, remove damaged and dead neurons, and prevent poisonous substances in the blood from reaching the brain.

10. The way in which words are strung together to form sentences.

11. The therapeutic method in which a patient gives a running account of thoughts, wishes, physical sensations, and mental images as the occur.

A. Conformity
D. Glia
G. Syntax
J. Iconic memory

B. Motivation
E. Free association
H. Persuasion
K. Psychodynamic therapy

C. Medulla
F. Somnambulism
I. Contingency management

72. *Using the Across and Down clues, write the correct words in the numbered grid below.*

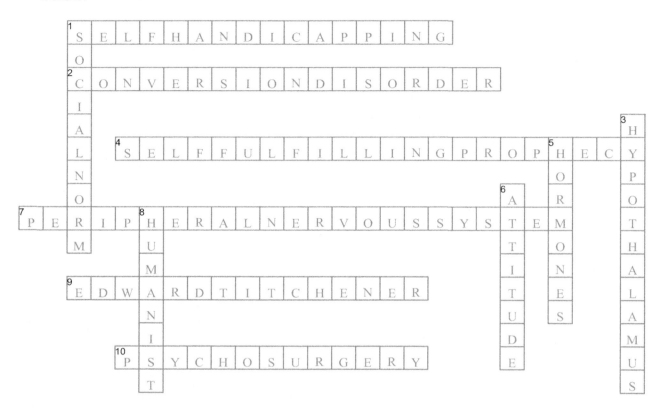

ACROSS

1. The process of developing, in anticipation of failure, behavioral reactions and explanations that minimize ability deficits as possible attributions for the failure

2. A disorder in which psychological conflict or stress brings about loss of motor or sensory function.

4. A prediction made about some future behavior or event that modifies interactions to produce what is expected.

7. The part of the nervous system composed of the spinal and cranial nerves that connect the body's sensory receptors to the CNS and the CNS to the muscles and glands.

9. Founded a psychology laboratory at Cornell University in 1892, student of Wilhelm Wundt.

10. A surgical procedure performed on brain tissue to alleviate a psychological disorder.

DOWN

1. The process of developing, in anticipation of failure, behavioral reactions and explanations that minimize ability deficits as possible attributions for the failure

2. A disorder in which psychological conflict or stress brings about loss of motor or sensory function.

4. A prediction made about some future behavior or event that modifies interactions to produce what is expected.

7. The part of the nervous system composed of the spinal and cranial nerves that connect the body's sensory receptors to the CNS and the CNS to the muscles and glands.

9. Founded a psychology laboratory at Cornell University in 1892, student of Wilhelm Wundt.

10. A surgical procedure performed on brain tissue to alleviate a psychological disorder.

A. Self fulfilling prophecy
D. Hormones
G. Humanist
J. Peripheral nervous system

B. Psychosurgery
E. Hypothalamus
H. Attitude
K. Edward Titchener

C. Social norm
F. Conversion disorder
I. Self handicapping

73. *Using the Across and Down clues, write the correct words in the numbered grid below.*

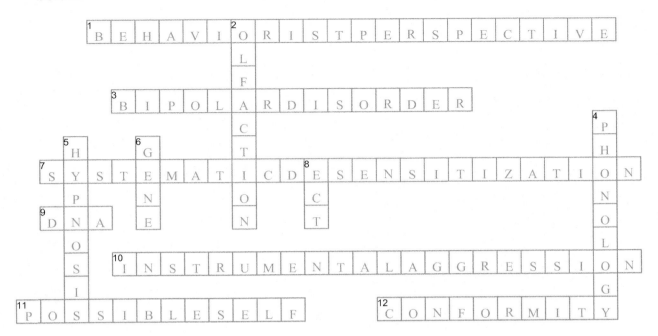

ACROSS

1. The psychological perspective primarily concerned with observable behavior that can be objectively recorded.

3. A mood disorder characterized by alternating periods of depression and mania.

7. A behavioral therapy technique in which a client is taught to prevent the arousal of anxiety by confronting the feared stimulus while relaxed.

9. The physical basis for the transmission of genetic information.

10. Is goal directed, and cognition based carried out with premeditated thought to achieve specific aims.

11. One of the ideal selves that a person would like to become, the selves a person could become, and the selves a person is afraid of becoming; components of the cognitive sense of self.

12. The tendency for people to adopt the behaviors, attitudes, and values of the members of a reference group.

DOWN

1. The psychological perspective primarily concerned with observable behavior that can be objectively recorded.

3. A mood disorder characterized by alternating periods of depression and mania.

7. A behavioral therapy technique in which a client is taught to prevent the arousal of anxiety by confronting the feared stimulus while relaxed.

9. The physical basis for the transmission of genetic information.

10. Is goal directed, and cognition based carried out with premeditated thought to achieve specific aims.

11. One of the ideal selves that a person would like to become, the selves a person could become, and the selves a person is afraid of becoming; components of the cognitive sense of self.

12. The tendency for people to adopt the behaviors, attitudes, and values of the members of a reference group.

A. ECT
D. Olfaction
G. Behaviorist perspective
J. Phonology

B. DNA
E. Systematic desensitization
H. Bipolar disorder
K. Hypnosis

C. Instrumental aggression
F. Possible self
I. Gene
L. Conformity

74. *Using the Across and Down clues, write the correct words in the numbered grid below.*

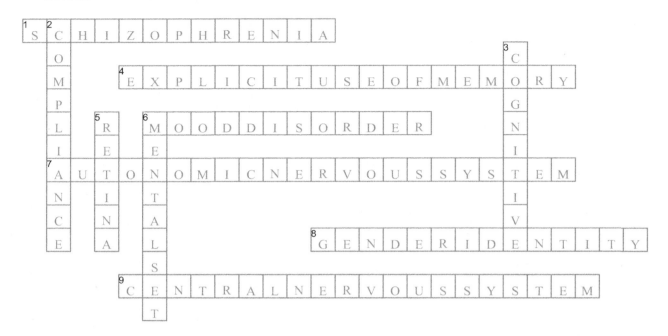

ACROSS

1. A severe form of psychopathology characterized by the breakdown of integrated personality functioning, withdrawal from reality, emotional distortions, and disturbed thoughts.

4. Conscious effort to encode or recover information through memory processes.

6. A mood disturbance such as severe depression or depression alternating with mania.

7. The subdivision of the PNS that controls the body's involuntary motor responses.

8. One's sense of maleness or femaleness; usually includes awareness and acceptance of one's biological sex.

9. The part of the nervous system consisting of the brain and spinal cord.

DOWN

1. A severe form of psychopathology characterized by the breakdown of integrated personality functioning, withdrawal from reality, emotional distortions, and disturbed thoughts.

4. Conscious effort to encode or recover information through memory processes.

6. A mood disturbance such as severe depression or depression alternating with mania.

7. The subdivision of the PNS that controls the body's involuntary motor responses.

8. One's sense of maleness or femaleness; usually includes awareness and acceptance of one's biological sex.

9. The part of the nervous system consisting of the brain and spinal cord.

A. Mental set
D. Gender identity
G. Mood disorder
J. Cognitive

B. Explicit use of memory
E. Retina
H. Autonomic nervous system

C. Compliance
F. Schizophrenia
I. Central nervous system

75. *Using the Across and Down clues, write the correct words in the numbered grid below.*

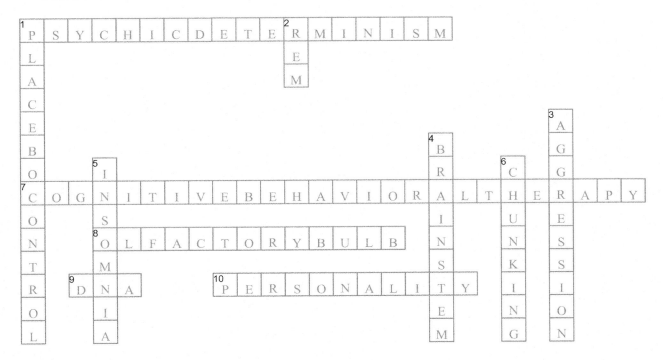

ACROSS

1. The assumption that mental and behavioral reactions are determined by previous experiences.

7. A therapeutic approach that combines the cognitive emphasis on thoughts and attitudes with the behavioral emphasis on changing performance.

8. The center where odor-sensitive receptors send their signals, located just below the frontal lobes of the cortex.

9. The physical basis for the transmission of genetic information.

10. The psychological qualities of an individual that influence a variety of characteristic behavior patterns across different situations and over time.

DOWN

1. The assumption that mental and behavioral reactions are determined by previous experiences.

7. A therapeutic approach that combines the cognitive emphasis on thoughts and attitudes with the behavioral emphasis on changing performance.

8. The center where odor-sensitive receptors send their signals, located just below the frontal lobes of the cortex.

9. The physical basis for the transmission of genetic information.

10. The psychological qualities of an individual that influence a variety of characteristic behavior patterns across different situations and over time.

A. Brain stem
D. Personality
G. Aggression
J. Chunking

B. DNA
E. REM
H. Olfactory bulb
K. Cognitive behavioral therapy

C. Placebo control
F. Insomnia
I. Psychic determinism

76. *Using the Across and Down clues, write the correct words in the numbered grid below.*

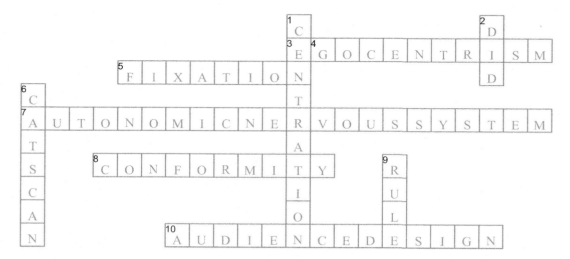

ACROSS

3. In cognitive development, the inability of a young child at the preoperational stage to take the perceptive of another person.

5. According to Freud, a state in which a person remains attached to objects or activities more appropriate for an earlier stage of psychosexual development.

7. The subdivision of the PNS that controls the body's involuntary motor responses.

8. The tendency for people to adopt the behaviors, attitudes, and values of the members of a reference group.

10. The process of shaping a message depending on the audience for which it is intended.

DOWN

3. In cognitive development, the inability of a young child at the preoperational stage to take the perceptive of another person.

5. According to Freud, a state in which a person remains attached to objects or activities more appropriate for an earlier stage of psychosexual development.

7. The subdivision of the PNS that controls the body's involuntary motor responses.

8. The tendency for people to adopt the behaviors, attitudes, and values of the members of a reference group.

10. The process of shaping a message depending on the audience for which it is intended.

A. DID
D. Centration
G. Conformity
J. Audience design

B. Egocentrism
E. Rule
H. Autonomic nervous system

C. CAT Scan
F. Fixation
I. G

77. *Using the Across and Down clues, write the correct words in the numbered grid below.*

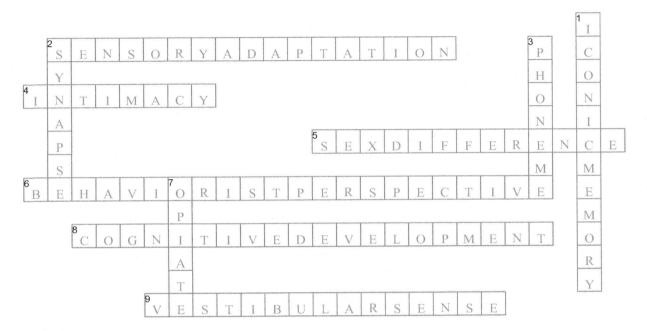

ACROSS

2. The diminishing responsiveness of sensory systems to prolonged stimulus input; allows a more rapid reaction to new (different) sources of information.

4. The capacity to make a full commitment - sexual, emotional, and moral - to another person.

5. One of the biologically based characteristics that distinguish males from females.

6. The psychological perspective primarily concerned with observable behavior that can be objectively recorded.

8. The development of processes of knowing, including imagining, perceiving, reasoning, and problem solving.

9. The sense that tells how one's own body is oriented in the world with respect to gravity.

DOWN

2. The diminishing responsiveness of sensory systems to prolonged stimulus input; allows a more rapid reaction to new (different) sources of information.

4. The capacity to make a full commitment - sexual, emotional, and moral - to another person.

5. One of the biologically based characteristics that distinguish males from females.

6. The psychological perspective primarily concerned with observable behavior that can be objectively recorded.

8. The development of processes of knowing, including imagining, perceiving, reasoning, and problem solving.

9. The sense that tells how one's own body is oriented in the world with respect to gravity.

A. Behaviorist perspective
D. Intimacy
G. Synapse
J. Iconic memory

B. Cognitive development
E. Opiate
H. Vestibular sense

C. Phoneme
F. Sex difference
I. Sensory adaptation

78. *Using the Across and Down clues, write the correct words in the numbered grid below.*

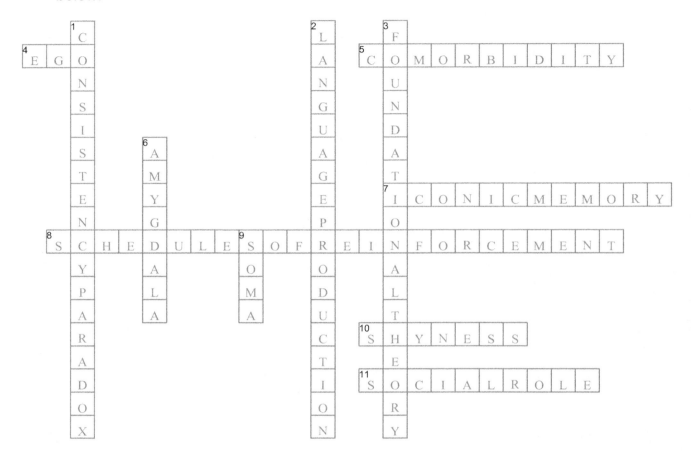

ACROSS

4. The reality-based aspect of the self that arbitrates the conflict between id impulses and superego demands.

5. The experience of more than one disorder at the same time.

7. Memory system in the visual domain that allows large amounts of information to be stored for very brief durations.

8. In operant conditioning, a pattern of delivering and withholding reinforcement.

10. An individual's discomfort and

11. A socially defined pattern of behavior that is expected of a person who is functioning in a given setting or group.

DOWN

4. The reality-based aspect of the self that arbitrates the conflict between id impulses and superego demands.

5. The experience of more than one disorder at the same time.

7. Memory system in the visual domain that allows large amounts of information to be stored for very brief durations.

8. In operant conditioning, a pattern of delivering and withholding reinforcement.

10. An individual's discomfort and

11. A socially defined pattern of behavior that is expected of a person who is functioning in a given setting or group.

A. Soma
D. Foundational theory
G. Amygdala
J. Social role

B. Schedules of reinforcement
E. Ego
H. Iconic memory
K. Language production

C. Comorbidity
F. Consistency paradox
I. Shyness

79. *Using the Across and Down clues, write the correct words in the numbered grid below.*

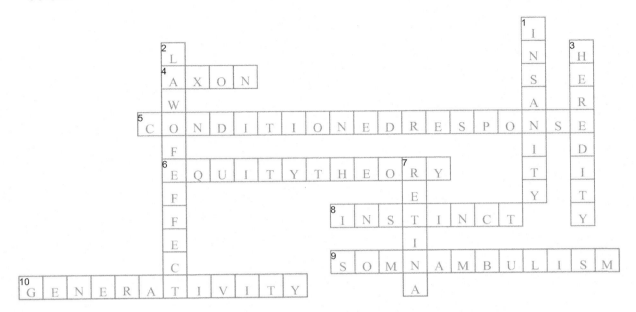

ACROSS

4. The extended fiber of a neuron through which nerve impulses travel from the soma to the terminal buttons.

5. Is a response elicited by some previously neutral stimulus that occurs as a result of pairing the neutral stimulus with an unconditioned stimulus.

6. A cognitive theory of work motivation that proposes that workers are motivated to maintain fair and equitable relationships with other relevant persons.

8. Preprogrammed tendency that is essential to a species' survival.

9. A disorder that causes sleep walking.

10. A commitment beyond one's self and one's partner to family, work, society, and future generations; typically, a crucial state in development in one's 30's and 40's.

DOWN

4. The extended fiber of a neuron through which nerve impulses travel from the soma to the terminal buttons.

5. Is a response elicited by some previously neutral stimulus that occurs as a result of pairing the neutral stimulus with an unconditioned stimulus.

6. A cognitive theory of work motivation that proposes that workers are motivated to maintain fair and equitable relationships with other relevant persons.

8. Preprogrammed tendency that is essential to a species' survival.

9. A disorder that causes sleep walking.

10. A commitment beyond one's self and one's partner to family, work, society, and future generations; typically, a crucial state in development in one's 30's and 40's.

A. Retina
B. Equity theory
C. Insanity
D. Somnambulism
E. Law of effect
F. Instinct
G. Generativity
H. Heredity
I. Conditioned response
J. Axon

80. *Using the Across and Down clues, write the correct words in the numbered grid below.*

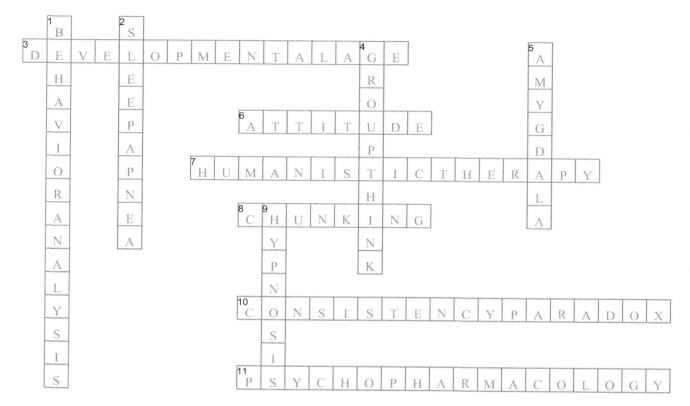

ACROSS

3. The chronological age at which most children show a level of physical or mental development.

6. The learned, relatively stable tendency to respond to people, concepts, and events in an evaluative way.

7. Centers around the concept of a whole person in the continual process of changing and of becoming.

8. The process of reconfiguring items by grouping based on similarity or some other organizing principle.

10. The observation that personality ratings across time and among different observers are consistent while behavior ratings across situations are not consistent.

11. The branch of psychology that investigates the effects of drugs on behavior.

DOWN

3. The chronological age at which most children show a level of physical or mental development.

6. The learned, relatively stable tendency to respond to people, concepts, and events in an evaluative way.

7. Centers around the concept of a whole person in the continual process of changing and of becoming.

8. The process of reconfiguring items by grouping based on similarity or some other organizing principle.

10. The observation that personality ratings across time and among different observers are consistent while behavior ratings across situations are not consistent.

11. The branch of psychology that investigates the effects of drugs on behavior.

A. Humanistic therapy   B. Behavior analysis   C. Groupthink   D. Consistency paradox
E. Attitude   F. Psychopharmacology   G. Hypnosis   H. Developmental age
I. Sleep apnea   J. Chunking   K. Amygdala

81. *Using the Across and Down clues, write the correct words in the numbered grid below.*

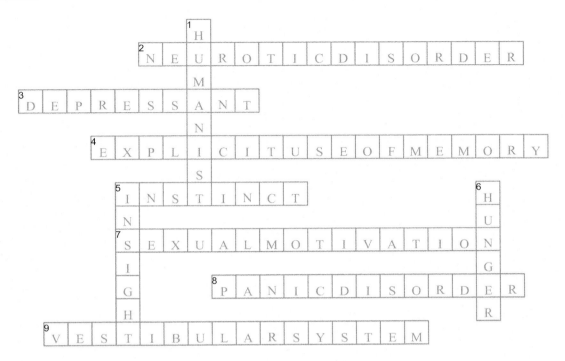

ACROSS

2. Mental disorder in which a person does not have signs of brain abnormalities and does not display grossly irrational thinking or violate basic norms

3. Drug that depresses or slows down the activity of the central nervous system.

4. Conscious effort to encode or recover information through memory processes.

5. Preprogrammed tendency that is essential to a species' survival.

7. Sexual arousal is the motivational state of excitement and tension brought about by physiological and cognitive reactions to erotic stimuli.

8. An anxiety disorder in which sufferers experience unexpected, severe panic attacks that begin with a feeling of intense apprehension, fear, or terror.

9. The receptors for this information are tiny hairs in fluid-filled sacs and canals in the inner ear.

DOWN

2. Mental disorder in which a person does not have signs of brain abnormalities and does not display grossly irrational thinking or violate basic norms

3. Drug that depresses or slows down the activity of the central nervous system.

4. Conscious effort to encode or recover information through memory processes.

5. Preprogrammed tendency that is essential to a species' survival.

7. Sexual arousal is the motivational state of excitement and tension brought about by physiological and cognitive reactions to erotic stimuli.

8. An anxiety disorder in which sufferers experience unexpected, severe panic attacks that begin with a feeling of intense apprehension, fear, or terror.

9. The receptors for this information are tiny hairs in fluid-filled sacs and canals in the inner ear.

A. Neurotic disorder
D. Vestibular system
G. Panic disorder
J. Depressant

B. Insight
E. Humanist
H. Hunger

C. Explicit use of memory
F. Sexual motivation
I. Instinct

82. *Using the Across and Down clues, write the correct words in the numbered grid below.*

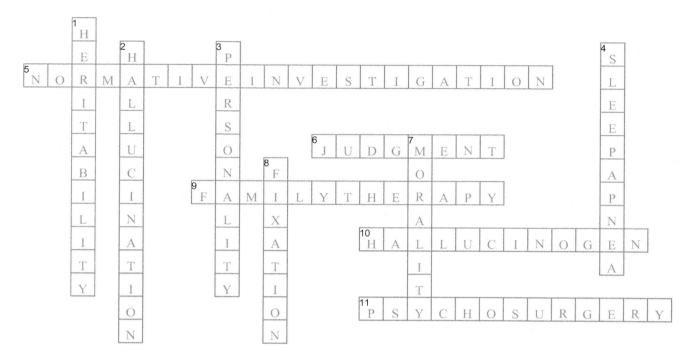

ACROSS

5. Research effort designed to describe what is characteristic of a specific age or developmental stage.

6. The process by which people form opinions, reach conclusions, and make critical evaluations of events and people based on available material; also, the product of the mental activity.

9. The client is a whole nuclear family and each family member is treated as a member of a system of relationships.

10. A drug that alters cognitions and perceptions and causes hallucinations.

11. A surgical procedure performed on brain tissue to alleviate a psychological disorder.

DOWN

5. Research effort designed to describe what is characteristic of a specific age or developmental stage.

6. The process by which people form opinions, reach conclusions, and make critical evaluations of events and people based on available material; also, the product of the mental activity.

9. The client is a whole nuclear family and each family member is treated as a member of a system of relationships.

10. A drug that alters cognitions and perceptions and causes hallucinations.

11. A surgical procedure performed on brain tissue to alleviate a psychological disorder.

A. Judgment
D. Hallucinogen
G. Normative investigation
J. Family therapy

B. Morality
E. Sleep apnea
H. Heritability
K. Fixation

C. Hallucination
F. Psychosurgery
I. Personality

83. *Using the Across and Down clues, write the correct words in the numbered grid below.*

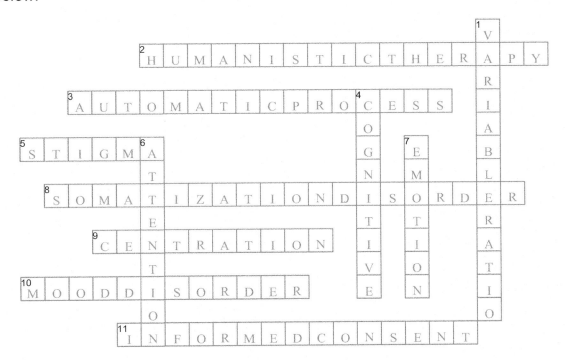

ACROSS

2. Centers around the concept of a whole person in the continual process of changing and of becoming.

3. Process that does not require attention; it can often be performed along with other tasks without interference.

5. The negative reaction of people to an individual or group because of some assumed inferiority or source of difference that is degraded.

8. A disorder characterized by unexplained physical complaints in several categories over many years.

9. Preoperational children's tendency to focus their attention on only one aspect of a situation and disregard other relevant aspects.

10. A mood disturbance such as severe depression or depression alternating with mania.

11. The process through which individuals are informed about experimental procedures, risks, and benefits before they provide formal consent to become research participants.

DOWN

2. Centers around the concept of a whole person in the continual process of changing and of becoming.

3. Process that does not require attention; it can often be performed along with other tasks without interference.

5. The negative reaction of people to an individual or group because of some assumed inferiority or source of difference that is degraded.

8. A disorder characterized by unexplained physical complaints in several categories over many years.

9. Preoperational children's tendency to focus their attention on only one aspect of a situation and disregard other relevant aspects.

10. A mood disturbance such as severe depression or depression alternating with mania.

11. The process through which individuals are informed about experimental procedures, risks, and benefits before they provide formal consent to become research participants.

A. Variable ratio
D. Informed consent
G. Mood disorder
J. Attention

B. Centration
E. Cognitive
H. Somatization disorder
K. Automatic process

C. Humanistic therapy
F. Emotion
I. Stigma

84. *Using the Across and Down clues, write the correct words in the numbered grid below.*

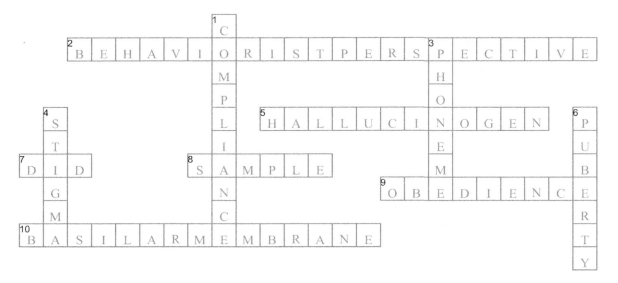

ACROSS

2. The psychological perspective primarily concerned with observable behavior that can be objectively recorded.

5. A drug that alters cognitions and perceptions and causes hallucinations.

7. Dissociative identity disorder. A dissociative mental disorder in which two or more distinct personalities exist within the same individual; formerly known as multiple personality disorder.

8. A subset of a population selected as participants in an experiment.

9. Blind obedience is less a product of dispositional characteristics than the outcome of situational forces that could engulf anyone. (Milgram studies)

10. A membrane running along the length of the cochlea.

DOWN

2. The psychological perspective primarily concerned with observable behavior that can be objectively recorded.

5. A drug that alters cognitions and perceptions and causes hallucinations.

7. Dissociative identity disorder. A dissociative mental disorder in which two or more distinct personalities exist within the same individual; formerly known as multiple personality disorder.

8. A subset of a population selected as participants in an experiment.

9. Blind obedience is less a product of dispositional characteristics than the outcome of situational forces that could engulf anyone. (Milgram studies)

10. A membrane running along the length of the cochlea.

A. Obedience	B. Sample
D. Behaviorist perspective	E. Compliance
G. Basilar membrane	H. Stigma
J. Hallucinogen	

C. Phoneme
F. DID
I. Puberty

85. *Using the Across and Down clues, write the correct words in the numbered grid below.*

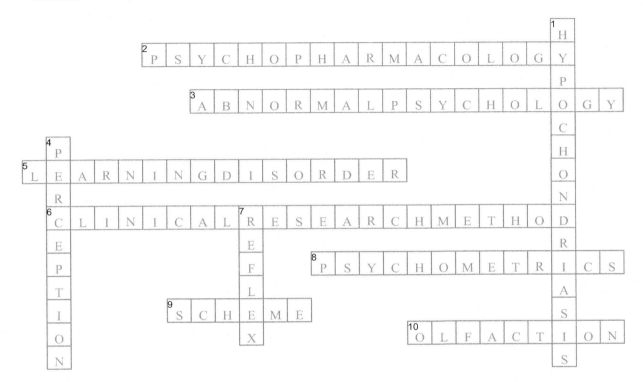

ACROSS

2. The branch of psychology that investigates the effects of drugs on behavior.

3. The area of psychological investigation concerned with understanding the nature of individual pathologies of mind, mood, and behavior.

5. A disorder defined by a large discrepancy between individuals' measured IQ and their actual performance.

6. Research conducted with human subjects in which the investigator interacts directly with the subjects.

8. The field of psychology that specializes in mental testing.

9. Piaget's term for a cognitive structure that develops as infants and young children learn to interpret the world and adapt to their environment.

10. The sense of smell.

DOWN

2. The branch of psychology that investigates the effects of drugs on behavior.

3. The area of psychological investigation concerned with understanding the nature of individual pathologies of mind, mood, and behavior.

5. A disorder defined by a large discrepancy between individuals' measured IQ and their actual performance.

6. Research conducted with human subjects in which the investigator interacts directly with the subjects.

8. The field of psychology that specializes in mental testing.

9. Piaget's term for a cognitive structure that develops as infants and young children learn to interpret the world and adapt to their environment.

10. The sense of smell.

A. Reflex
D. Scheme
G. Abnormal psychology
J. Psychopharmacology

B. Psychometrics
E. Olfaction
H. Hypochondriasis

C. Perception
F. Clinical research method
I. Learning disorder

86. *Using the Across and Down clues, write the correct words in the numbered grid below.*

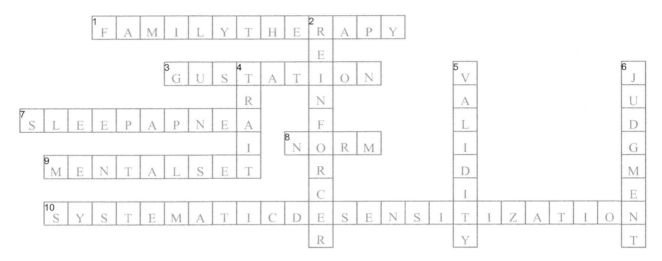

ACROSS

1. The client is a whole nuclear family and each family member is treated as a member of a system of relationships.

3. The sense of taste.

7. A sleep disorder of the upper respiratory system that causes the person to stop breathing while asleep.

8. Standard based on measurement of a large group of people; used for comparing the scores of an individual with those of others within a well-defined group.

9. The tendency to respond to a new problem in the manner used to respond to a previous problem.

10. A behavioral therapy technique in which a client is taught to prevent the arousal of anxiety by confronting the feared stimulus while relaxed.

DOWN

1. The client is a whole nuclear family and each family member is treated as a member of a system of relationships.

3. The sense of taste.

7. A sleep disorder of the upper respiratory system that causes the person to stop breathing while asleep.

8. Standard based on measurement of a large group of people; used for comparing the scores of an individual with those of others within a well-defined group.

9. The tendency to respond to a new problem in the manner used to respond to a previous problem.

10. A behavioral therapy technique in which a client is taught to prevent the arousal of anxiety by confronting the feared stimulus while relaxed.

A. Judgment
D. Reinforcer
G. Trait
J. Sleep apnea

B. Family therapy
E. Validity
H. Mental set

C. Gustation
F. Systematic desensitization
I. Norm

87. *Using the Across and Down clues, write the correct words in the numbered grid below.*

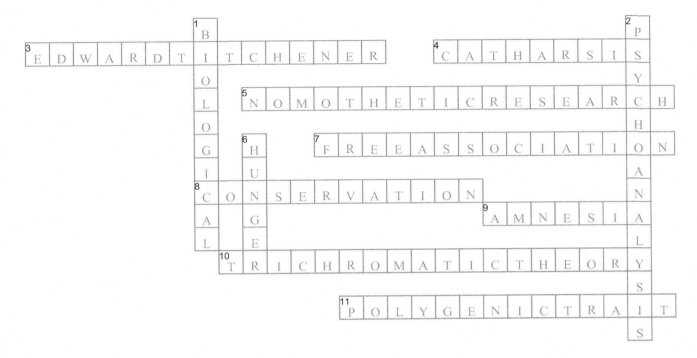

ACROSS

3. Founded a psychology laboratory at Cornell University in 1892, student of Wilhelm Wundt.

4. The process of expressing strongly felt but usually repressed emotions.

5. Attempts to establish general laws and generalizations, and seeks to obtain objective knowledge through scientific methods.

7. The therapeutic method in which a patient gives a running account of thoughts, wishes, physical sensations, and mental images as the occur.

8. According to Piaget, the understanding that physical properties do not change when nothing is added or taken away, even though appearances may change.

9. A failure of memory caused by physical injury, disease, drug use, or psychological trauma.

10. The theory that there are three types of color receptors that produce the primary color sensations of red, green, and blue.

11. Characteristic that is influenced by more than one gene.

DOWN

3. Founded a psychology laboratory at Cornell University in 1892, student of Wilhelm Wundt.

4. The process of expressing strongly felt but usually repressed emotions.

5. Attempts to establish general laws and generalizations, and seeks to obtain objective knowledge through scientific methods.

7. The therapeutic method in which a patient gives a running account of thoughts, wishes, physical sensations, and mental images as the occur.

8. According to Piaget, the understanding that physical properties do not change when nothing is added or taken away, even though appearances may change.

9. A failure of memory caused by physical injury, disease, drug use, or psychological trauma.

10. The theory that there are three types of color receptors that produce the primary color sensations of red, green, and blue.

11. Characteristic that is influenced by more than one gene.

A. Psychoanalysis   B. Hunger   C. Nomothetic research   D. Biological
E. Polygenic trait   F. Conservation   G. Catharsis   H. Trichromatic theory
I. Free association   J. Edward Titchener   K. Amnesia

88. *Using the Across and Down clues, write the correct words in the numbered grid below.*

ACROSS

3. Any stimulus that, when made contingent on a response, respectively increases or decreases the probability of that response.

4. An aspect of creativity characterized by the ability to gather together different sources of information to solve a problem.

5. The biological transmission of traits from parents to offspring.

6. According to Lev Vygotsky, the process through which children absorb knowledge from the social environment.

8. Sometimes necessary when revealing certain information to the patient would bias the results.

9. Rules for participation in conversations; social conventions for communicating, sequencing sentences, and responding appropriately to others.

DOWN

3. Any stimulus that, when made contingent on a response, respectively increases or decreases the probability of that response.

4. An aspect of creativity characterized by the ability to gather together different sources of information to solve a problem.

5. The biological transmission of traits from parents to offspring.

6. According to Lev Vygotsky, the process through which children absorb knowledge from the social environment.

8. Sometimes necessary when revealing certain information to the patient would bias the results.

9. Rules for participation in conversations; social conventions for communicating, sequencing sentences, and responding appropriately to others.

A. Intentional deception   B. Insight   C. Exposure therapy   D. Pragmatics
E. Reinforcer   F. Internalization   G. Judgment   H. Convergent thinking
I. Heredity   J. Retina

89. *Using the Across and Down clues, write the correct words in the numbered grid below.*

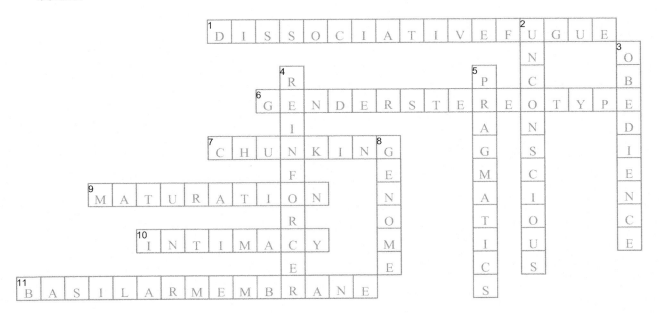

ACROSS

1. A disorder characterized by a flight from home or work accompanied by a loss of ability to recall the personal past.

6. Belief about attributes and behaviors regarded as appropriate for males and females in a particular culture.

7. The process of reconfiguring items by grouping based on similarity or some other organizing principle.

9. The age-related physical and behavioral changes characteristic of a species; the process of growth typical of all members of a species who are reared in the specie's usual habitat.

10. The capacity to make a full commitment - sexual, emotional, and moral - to another person.

11. A membrane running along the length of the cochlea.

DOWN

1. A disorder characterized by a flight from home or work accompanied by a loss of ability to recall the personal past.

6. Belief about attributes and behaviors regarded as appropriate for males and females in a particular culture.

7. The process of reconfiguring items by grouping based on similarity or some other organizing principle.

9. The age-related physical and behavioral changes characteristic of a species; the process of growth typical of all members of a species who are reared in the specie's usual habitat.

10. The capacity to make a full commitment - sexual, emotional, and moral - to another person.

11. A membrane running along the length of the cochlea.

A. Dissociative fugue   B. Basilar membrane   C. Obedience   D. Gender stereotype
E. Chunking   F. Maturation   G. Reinforcer   H. Genome
I. Pragmatics   J. Intimacy   K. Unconscious

90. *Using the Across and Down clues, write the correct words in the numbered grid below.*

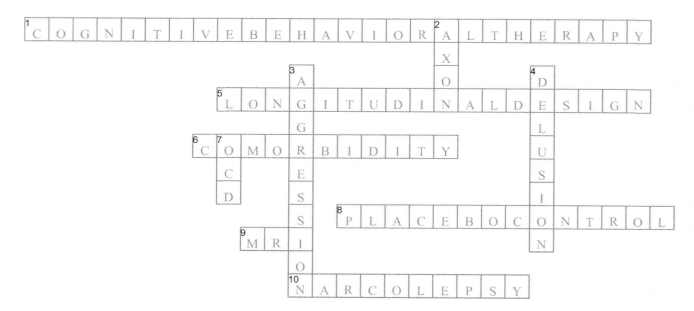

ACROSS

1. A therapeutic approach that combines the cognitive emphasis on thoughts and attitudes with the behavioral emphasis on changing performance.

5. A research design in which the same participants are observed repeatedly, sometimes over many years.

6. The experience of more than one disorder at the same time.

8. An experimental condition in which treatment is not administered; it is used in cases where a placebo effect might occur.

9. Magnetic resonance imaging. A technique for brain imaging that scans the brain using magnetic fields and radio waves.

10. A sleep disorder characterized by an irresistible compulsion to sleep during the daytime.

DOWN

1. A therapeutic approach that combines the cognitive emphasis on thoughts and attitudes with the behavioral emphasis on changing performance.

5. A research design in which the same participants are observed repeatedly, sometimes over many years.

6. The experience of more than one disorder at the same time.

8. An experimental condition in which treatment is not administered; it is used in cases where a placebo effect might occur.

9. Magnetic resonance imaging. A technique for brain imaging that scans the brain using magnetic fields and radio waves.

10. A sleep disorder characterized by an irresistible compulsion to sleep during the daytime.

A. Narcolepsy
D. MRI
G. Placebo control
J. Delusion

B. Cognitive behavioral therapy
E. Longitudinal design
H. OCD

C. Aggression
F. Comorbidity
I. Axon

91. *Using the Across and Down clues, write the correct words in the numbered grid below.*

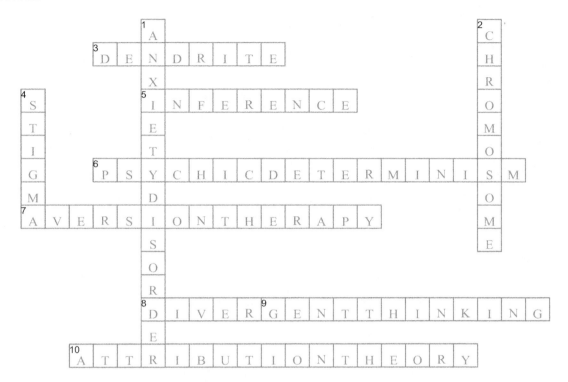

ACROSS

3. One of the branched fibers of neurons that receive incoming signals.

5. Missing information filled in on the basis of a sample of evidence or on the basis of prior beliefs and theories.

6. The assumption that mental and behavioral reactions are determined by previous experiences.

7. A type of behavioral therapy used to treat individuals attracted to harmful stimuli.

8. An aspect of creativity characterized by an ability to produce unusual but appropriate response to problems.

10. A social-cognitive approach to describing the ways the social perceiver uses information to generate causal explanations.

DOWN

1. Mental disorder marked by psychological arousal, feeling of tension, and intense apprehension without apparent reason.

2. A thread-like structure found in the nucleus of cells and made of protein and DNA

4. The negative reaction of people to an individual or group because of some assumed inferiority or source of difference that is degraded.

9. According to Charles Spearman, the factor of general intelligence underlying all intelligent performance.

A. Aversion therapy   B. Divergent thinking   C. Anxiety disorder   D. Psychic determinism
E. Stigma   F. Dendrite   G. Attribution theory   H. G
I. Inference   J. Chromosome

92. *Using the Across and Down clues, write the correct words in the numbered grid below.*

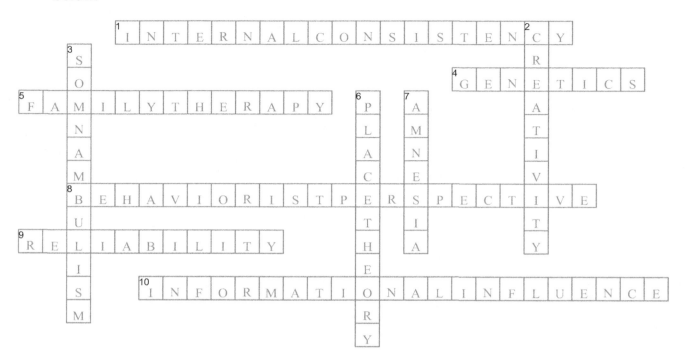

ACROSS

1. A measure of reliability; the degree to which a test yields similar scores across its different parts, such as odd versus even items.

4. The study of the inheritance of physical and psychological traits from ancestors.

5. The client is a whole nuclear family and each family member is treated as a member of a system of relationships.

8. The psychological perspective primarily concerned with observable behavior that can be objectively recorded.

9. The degree to which a test produces similar scores each time it is used; stability or consistency of the scores produced by an instrument.

10. Group effects that arise from individuals' desire to be correct and right and to understand how best to act in a given situation.

DOWN

2. The ability to generate ideas or products that are both novel and appropriate to the circumstances.

3. A disorder that causes sleep walking.

6. The theory that different frequency tones produce maximum activation at different locations along the basilar membrane.

7. A failure of memory caused by physical injury, disease, drug use, or psychological trauma.

A. Place theory
D. Creativity
G. Family therapy
J. Genetics

B. Amnesia
E. Somnambulism
H. Internal consistency

C. Behaviorist perspective
F. Reliability
I. Informational influence

93. *Using the Across and Down clues, write the correct words in the numbered grid below.*

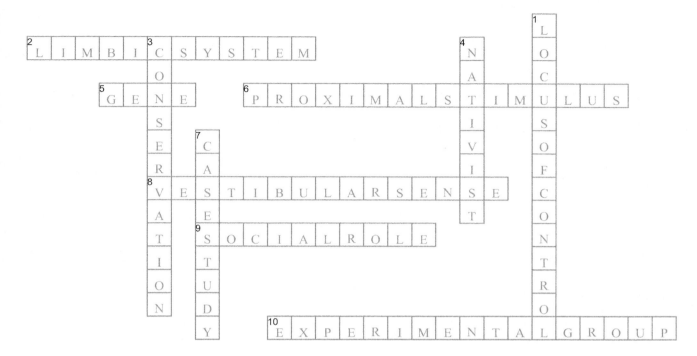

ACROSS

2. The region of the brain that regulates emotional behavior, basic motivational urges, and memory, as well as major physiological functions.

5. The biological unit of heredity; discrete section of a chromosome responsible for transmission of traits.

6. The optical image on the retina.

8. The sense that tells how one's own body is oriented in the world with respect to gravity.

9. A socially defined pattern of behavior that is expected of a person who is functioning in a given setting or group.

10. A group in an experiment that is exposed to a treatment or experiences a manipulation of the independent variable.

DOWN

1. An aspect of Rotter's expectancy theory; people's general expectancy about the extent to which the rewards they obtain are contingent on their own actions or on environmental factors.

3. According to Piaget, the understanding that physical properties do not change when nothing is added or taken away, even though appearances may change.

4. People begin life with mental structures that provide constraints on how they experience the world.

7. Intensive observation of an individual or small group of individuals.

A. Proximal stimulus
B. Social role
C. Case study
D. Experimental group
E. Vestibular sense
F. Conservation
G. Locus of control
H. Limbic system
I. Gene
J. Nativist

94. *Using the Across and Down clues, write the correct words in the numbered grid below.*

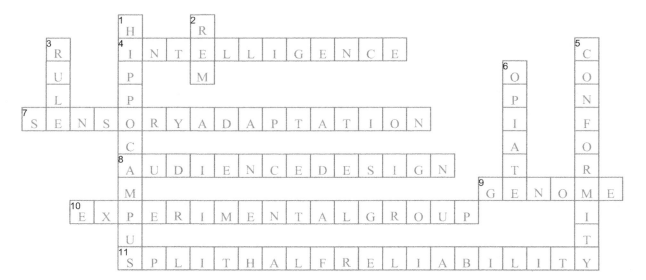

ACROSS

4. The global capacity to profit from experience and to go beyond given information about the environment.

7. The diminishing responsiveness of sensory systems to prolonged stimulus input; allows a more rapid reaction to new (different) sources of information.

8. The process of shaping a message depending on the audience for which it is intended.

9. The genetic information for an organism, stored in the DNA of its chromosomes.

10. A group in an experiment that is exposed to a treatment or experiences a manipulation of the independent variable.

11. A measure of the correlation between test takers' performance on different halves (such as odd- and even-numbered items) of a test.

DOWN

1. The part of the limbic system that is involved in the acquisition of explicit memory.

2. Rapid eye movements. A behavioral sign of the phase of sleep during which the sleeper is likely to be experiencing dreamlike mental activity.

3. Behavioral guideline for acting in a certain way in a certain instance.

5. The tendency for people to adopt the behaviors, attitudes, and values of the members of a reference group.

6. Drug that suppresses physical sensation and response to stimulation.

A. Hippocampus
E. Rule
I. Intelligence

B. Split half reliability
F. Audience design
J. Sensory adaptation

C. Conformity
G. Opiate
K. REM

D. Experimental group
H. Genome

95. *Using the Across and Down clues, write the correct words in the numbered grid below.*

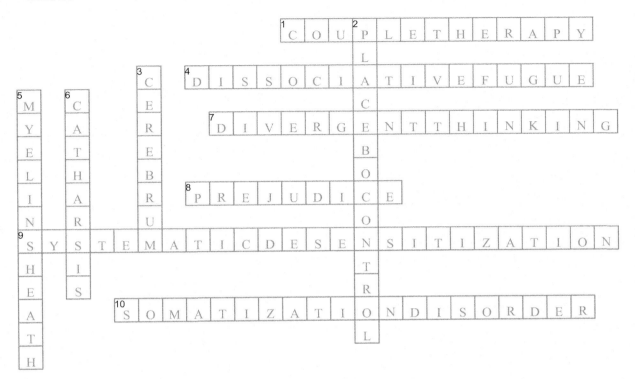

ACROSS

1. Seeks to clarify the typical communication patterns of the partners and then to improve the quality of their interaction.

4. A disorder characterized by a flight from home or work accompanied by a loss of ability to recall the personal past.

7. An aspect of creativity characterized by an ability to produce unusual but appropriate response to problems.

8. A learned attitude toward a target object, involving negative affect (dislike or fear), negative beliefs (stereotypes), that justify the attitude, and a behavioral intention to avoid, control, dominate, or eliminate the target object.

9. A behavioral therapy technique in which a client is taught to prevent the arousal of anxiety by confronting the feared stimulus while relaxed.

10. A disorder characterized by unexplained physical complaints in several categories over many years.

DOWN

2. An experimental condition in which treatment is not administered; it is used in cases where a placebo effect might occur.

3. The region of the brain that regulates higher cognitive and emotional functions.

5. Insulating material that surrounds axons and increases the speed of neural transmission.

6. The process of expressing strongly felt but usually repressed emotions.

A. Somatization disorder
D. Dissociative fugue
G. Systematic desensitization
J. Couple therapy

B. Myelin sheath
E. Catharsis
H. Cerebrum

C. Placebo control
F. Prejudice
I. Divergent thinking

96. *Using the Across and Down clues, write the correct words in the numbered grid below.*

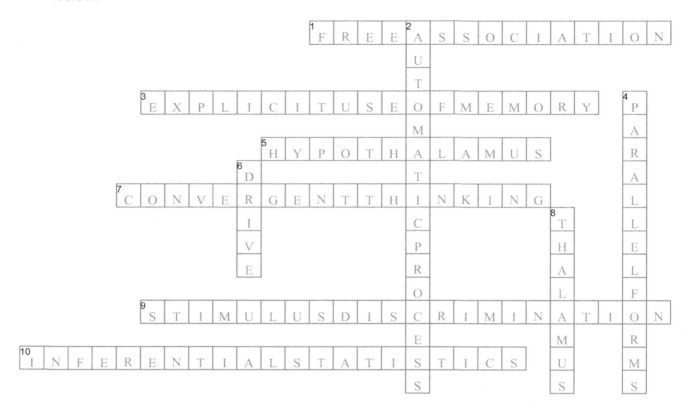

ACROSS

1. The therapeutic method in which a patient gives a running account of thoughts, wishes, physical sensations, and mental images as the occur.

3. Conscious effort to encode or recover information through memory processes.

5. The brain structure that regulates motivated behavior and homeostasis.

7. An aspect of creativity characterized by the ability to gather together different sources of information to solve a problem.

9. A conditioning process in which an organism learns to respond differently to stimuli that differ from the conditioned stimulus on some dimension.

10. Statistical procedures that allow researchers to determine whether the results they obtain support their hypotheses or can be attributed to chance variation.

DOWN

2. Process that does not require attention; it can often be performed along with other tasks without interference.

4. Different versions of a test used to assess test reliability; the change of forms reduces effects of direct practice, memory, or the desire of an individual to appear consistent on the same items.

6. Internal state that arises in response to a disequilibrium in an animal's physiological needs.

8. The brain structure that relays sensory impulses to the cerebral cortex.

A. Convergent thinking
D. Inferential statistics
G. Parallel forms
J. Stimulus discrimination

B. Explicit use of memory
E. Drive
H. Free association

C. Hypothalamus
F. Thalamus
I. Automatic process

97. *Using the Across and Down clues, write the correct words in the numbered grid below.*

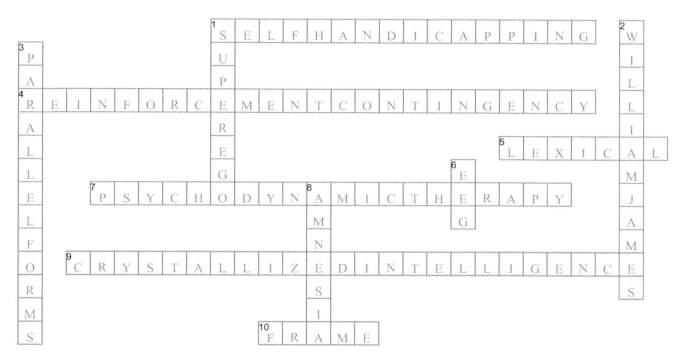

ACROSS

1. The process of developing, in anticipation of failure, behavioral reactions and explanations that minimize ability deficits as possible attributions for the failure

4. A consistent relationship between a response and the changes in the environment that it produces.

5. Meaning is the dictionary meaning of a word

7. Type of therapy that assumes that a patient's problems have been caused by the psychological tension between unconscious impulses and the constraints of his or her life situation.

9. The facet of intelligence involving the knowledge a person has already acquired and the ability to access that knowledge; measures by vocabulary, arithmetic, and general information tests.

10. A particular description of a choice; the perspective from which a choice is described or framed affects how a decision is made and which option is ultimately exercised.

DOWN

1. The part of the personality that corresponds roughly to the idea of conscience, the inner voice of should and should nots.

2. Author of "The Principles of Psychology."

3. Different versions of a test used to assess test reliability; the change of forms reduces effects of direct practice, memory, or the desire of an individual to appear consistent on the same items.

6. A recording of the electrical activity of the brain.

8. A failure of memory caused by physical injury, disease, drug use, or psychological trauma.

A. Parallel forms
D. Reinforcement contingency
G. Amnesia
J. Self handicapping

B. Psychodynamic therapy
E. William James
H. Frame
K. Superego

C. Crystallized intelligence
F. Lexical
I. EEG

98. *Using the Across and Down clues, write the correct words in the numbered grid below.*

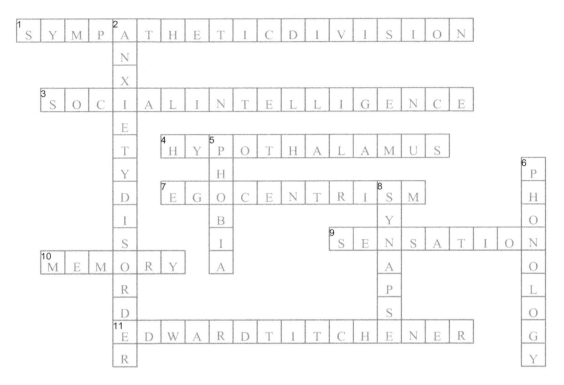

ACROSS

1. The subdivision of the ANS that deals with emergency response and the mobilization of energy.

3. A theory of personality that refers to the expertise people bring to their experience of life tasks.

4. The brain structure that serves as a relay station between the endocrine system and the CNS.

7. In cognitive development, the inability of a young child at the preoperational stage to take the perceptive of another person.

9. The process by which stimulation of a sensory receptor gives rise to neutral impulses that result in an experience, or awareness, of conditions inside or outside the body.

10. The mental capacity to encode, store, and retrieve information.

11. Founded a psychology laboratory at Cornell University in 1892, student of Wilhelm Wundt.

DOWN

2. Mental disorder marked by psychological arousal, feeling of tension, and intense apprehension without apparent reason.

5. A persistent and irrational fear of a specific object, activity, or situation that is excessive and unreasonable, given the reality of the threat.

6. The study of the sounds that are put together to form words.

8. The gap between one neuron and another.

A. Memory
E. Social intelligence
I. Sensation

B. Synapse
F. Phobia
J. Edward Titchener

C. Anxiety disorder
G. Phonology
K. Sympathetic division

D. Egocentrism
H. Hypothalamus

99. *Using the Across and Down clues, write the correct words in the numbered grid below.*

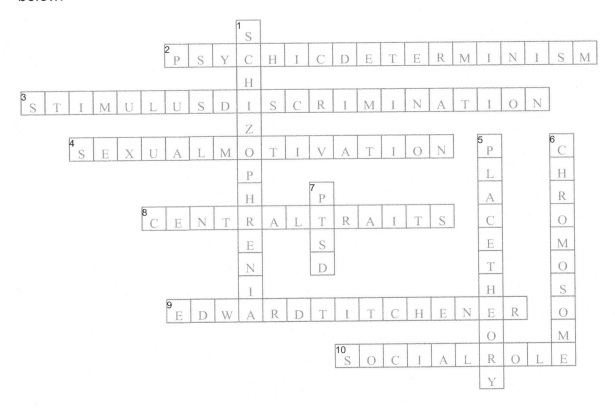

ACROSS

2. The assumption that mental and behavioral reactions are determined by previous experiences.

3. A conditioning process in which an organism learns to respond differently to stimuli that differ from the conditioned stimulus on some dimension.

4. Sexual arousal is the motivational state of excitement and tension brought about by physiological and cognitive reactions to erotic stimuli.

8. Traits that represent major characteristics of a person, such as honesty or optimism.

9. Founded a psychology laboratory at Cornell University in 1892, student of Wilhelm Wundt.

10. A socially defined pattern of behavior that is expected of a person who is functioning in a given setting or group.

DOWN

1. A severe form of psychopathology characterized by the breakdown of integrated personality functioning, withdrawal from reality, emotional distortions, and disturbed thoughts.

5. The theory that different frequency tones produce maximum activation at different locations along the basilar membrane.

6. A thread-like structure found in the nucleus of cells and made of protein and DNA

7. Posttraumatic stress disorder. An anxiety disorder characterized by the persistent re-experience of those traumatic events through distressing recollections, dreams, hallucinations, or flashbacks.

A. Schizophrenia
D. PTSD
G. Central traits
J. Chromosome

B. Psychic determinism
E. Place theory
H. Stimulus discrimination

C. Edward Titchener
F. Sexual motivation
I. Social role

100. *Using the Across and Down clues, write the correct words in the numbered grid below.*

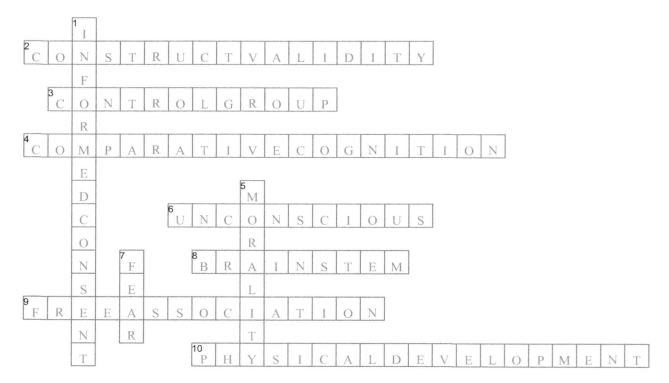

ACROSS

2. The degree to which a test adequately measures an underlying construct.

3. A group in an experiment that is not exposed to a treatment or does not experience a manipulation of the independent variable.

4. The study of the development of cognitive abilities across species and the continuity of abilities from nonhuman animals to humans.

6. The domain of the psyche that stores repressed urges and primitive impulses.

8. The brain structure that regulates the body's basic life processes.

9. The therapeutic method in which a patient gives a running account of thoughts, wishes, physical sensations, and mental images as the occur.

10. The bodily changes, maturation, and growth that occur in an organism starting with conception and continuing across the life span.

DOWN

1. The process through which individuals are informed about experimental procedures, risks, and benefits before they provide formal consent to become research participants.

5. A system of beliefs and values that ensures that individuals will keep their obligations to others in society and will behave in ways that do not interfere with the rights and interests of others.

7. A rational reaction to an objectively identified external danger that may induce a person to flee or attack in self-defense.

A. Unconscious
D. Comparative cognition
G. Informed consent
J. Construct validity

B. Brain stem
E. Physical development
H. Fear

C. Free association
F. Control group
I. Morality

Printed in Great Britain
by Amazon

32901776R00112